The
Horse Lover's
BIBLE

The
Horse Lover's
BIBLE

THE COMPLETE PRACTICAL GUIDE
TO HORSE CARE AND MANAGEMENT

TAMSIN PICKERAL

FIREFLY BOOKS

A Firefly Book

Published by Firefly Books Ltd. 2014

Text © 2008 Tamsin Pickeral
Illustrations and compilation © 2008 Carroll &
Brown Limited

First printing

Publisher Cataloging-in-Publication Data (U.S.)

A CIP record for this title is available from the
Library of Congress

Library and Archives Canada Cataloguing in Publication

A CIP record for this title is available from
Library and Archives Canada

Published in the United States by
Firefly Books (U.S.) Inc.
P.O. Box 1338, Ellicott Station
Buffalo, New York 14205

Published in Canada by
Firefly Books Ltd.
50 Staples Avenue, Unit #1
Richmond Hill, Ontario L4B 0A7

Developed by Carroll & Brown Ltd.
20 Lonsdale Road
London NW6 6RD

For Carroll & Brown:
Photography: Jules Selmes
Design: Emily Cook
Production: Mandy Mackie
Picture Research: Sandra Schnieder
Index Madeline: Weston

Cover Design: Erin R. Holmes

Printed in China

CONTENTS

INTRODUCTION

Horses and humans have been intrinsically bound throughout the history of civilization. The impact of the horse on early humans — first utilized for food, hide, bones and sinew, and then as a means of transportation — was phenomenal. The recognition of the horse as a means of transportation opened up new unexplored worlds, provided opportunities to find better food and areas for settlement, and made contact with other communities possible, leading to relationships that were both loving and warring. There is something mystical about horses that cannot be explained or defined, a spiritual element that early humans appreciated, and that we keep alive.

There are still communities, such as nomadic Eurasian tribes, who depend upon horses as a fundamental part of their lives. Horses continue to work in agriculture — making accessible areas of forestry where machinery cannot penetrate, traversing mountainous regions that defy vehicles and playing a central role in North American and Australian cattle ranches. For the majority of us, however, living in affluent Western societies, our continuing relationship with horses is primarily recreational.

There is nothing more breathtaking than witnessing the perfect symbiosis of horse and rider performing at the peak of their abilities, whether that be at dressage, jumping, racing, reining, cutting or in any other of the equestrian divisions. And every enthusiast probably dreams of a winning moment, in which he or she is rewarded for the hours of training, the cold mornings mucking out and the chunk of paycheck that disappears each month. Riding and horses for many people is less a hobby and more a way of life. Such people "live and breathe" horses, and spend hours daydreaming at work about the next show, hacking out on the weekend, or which new stable rug to buy. I've been told this is a disease and, once smitten, there is no cure.

A healthy, happy and productive horse is the result of careful and intelligent stable management. This book will guide you through all areas of equine care and management, with practical solutions to problems should they arise, but more importantly, will explain how to provide for your horse so that problems are avoided. Fundamental to every aspect of horse care and management is an understanding of the horse as an animal — how it survived and evolved in the wild and what shaped its instinctive behavior.

Throughout the course of this book I will be referencing some good ways to make your money go that little bit further, but it is worth bearing in mind some of the unseen major costs that can spring up — vets' bills from an untimely bout of colic on a long weekend, escalating hay prices due to a poor harvest, repairs and maintenance to the trailer or truck and, of course, that fabulous accessory that you simply have to buy.

Our horses depend on us to provide them with the optimum care we can. We achieve this through understanding and knowledge, improving our equine education, and furthering our skills. In return, horses help us cement those endless dreams of the winner's circle.

Tamsin Pickeral

1

HORSE BASICS

All horse behavior is shaped by a horse's basic instincts, which have been modified through conditioning. To appreciate why a horse does the things it does, it is necessary to look back to its evolution and the factors that affected the formation of its most basic instincts.

The earliest ancestors of horses were no bigger than a small dog and had four toes on their front feet and three on their back. Gradually, these mammals moved from the forests into open grasslands, where food was more plentiful, though the wide-open spaces held little protection from predators.

These early horses developed longer legs for speed, evolving into running animals with a single toe. Their leg conformation and single toe allowed them short bursts of great speed, and the quickness of their reaction ensured their survival. Their teeth and digestion altered to accommodate the tough, coarse grass and the necessity for eating on the run; horses eat small amounts for up to 18 hours a day. This digestive system, with a small stomach and effective intestinal tract, meant they were always capable of fleeing.

The early horse became extinct in North America at the end of the Ice Age, but it continued to evolve in Eurasia, where it migrated to the warmer climates of the steppes and eastern plains. Early horses lived in small herds based around a dominant stallion that provided leadership and security for the group. It ranged over great distances and was constantly mobile.

Horses are highly gregarious creatures and the herd social system is fundamental to all horse behavior. Both a horse's sociable nature and need for mobility are key issues to consider when caring for a horse today.

The Horse as a Herd Animal

There are two main patterns of socialization associated with equines: territorial behavior, which is commonly exhibited by Grevy's zebra and the African wild ass; and harem or herd behavior, seen in horses, the mountain zebra and the plains zebra.

Territorial animals will protect and defend a large area, allowing females in to mate, but fighting off the intrusion of other breeding males. They tend not to form strong, long-lasting bonds and are often solitary. In contrast, a harem is a strongly knit unit. The stallion defends the mares in his harem, and they will travel together, hunting down better areas for feeding while maintaining the reproductive viability of the group. This form of social organization is particularly effective in areas of poor grazing, because the harem can cover large distances irrespective of territorial constraints.

The harem structure developed over the millennia and remains strong in the modern domesticated horse. This herd instinct shapes behavior in horses and is still relevant even when the horse is removed from the harem.

Why the Herd?

The benefits to the horse of belonging to a herd are a result of three interrelated factors. The first is the instinct to reproduce, which is the most primal of all. By forming harems with one dominant stallion and a small group of mares, a stable reproductive unit is created, which enables the members of the harem to travel extensively in search of food without spending time looking for a suitable mate.

The second factor contributing to the success of the herd is socialization. Horses are naturally outgoing animals and form long-lasting bonds with each other. The primary bond within the group is the sexual attraction between the stallion and mares, but strong bonds of friendship between the mares also exist. Customarily, a horse will develop a special attachment to one or

Trainer's Tip
Horses have excellent memories and will remember bad experiences and poor training as clearly as positive handling.

two of its fellow herd members, and will demonstrate affection through grooming — primarily chewing and nibbling along the withers and neck, and secondly across the back, shoulders and haunches. Grooming also involves the removal of parasites from parts that the horse is unable to reach on its own and occasionally can be performed as an apologetic interaction between two herd members following an aggressive exchange.

Finally, the herd provides its members with security. During the middle of the day, when they have the best visual field, horses will often rest; several members of the herd may lay down while at least one member stays on sentry duty. At dusk, which is a particularly vulnerable time as it is then that predators start hunting and the failing light makes it difficult to see, the herd will gather together. They usually remain closely grouped through the night on the move, grazing and watchful.

Herd Structure

The herd is a small unit — a single dominant stallion and between two to six mares with their accompanying young. It is based on a strict hierarchal system: the dominant stallion rules. By having the fortitude to form a harem, he has demonstrated his beneficial genetic situation and ensures the continuation of a strong gene pool through his offspring. After the stallion, the hierarchy tends to defer to age, although this is not a hard and fast rule, and the length of residency within a given herd is also significant.

Size does not seem to be a significant factor affecting aggressiveness, though aggressiveness is significant in determining rank within the herd.

The stallion will defend and protect his entire harem. He assumes the mantle of leader, especially in dangerous situations. Occasionally the dominant mare in the harem will lead the group, though rarely in times of peril. As herd animals, horses rely on "a leader" to direct them and provide a sense of security.

The bonds between the members of the harem hold the group together. Often a horse that is at the bottom of the hierarchy will form a friendship with a more dominant member of the harem, thereby ensuring some degree of protection from other members and a greater chance of access to food and water. Once bonds have been formed and the pecking order established, there is rarely any full-blown violence within a group. Generally, pinned ears, snaking head movements, squealing or lifting a hind leg will be enough to warn off herd members; in many cases the pecking order is maintained by little more than head movements alone.

Once young stallions reach a threatening age they will be ousted from the harem by the dominant stallion. They will then exist on the fringes of the group until they are able to form their own harems. Bachelor groups typically consist of one to three young stallions. Young fillies will often leave their foundation herd during their estrous cycles for a few hours to a few days to mate before returning. As they mature, and generally at between three to five years old, they will leave their foundation herd and enter a new group. When there is no other herd around, it is not unusual for a group of immature stallions and

Trainer's Tip

Turn mares or geldings out but avoid turning adult mares and geldings out together.

fillies to form. These groups are unstable and usually won't reproduce; the members will leave as soon as a more suitable harem becomes available.

Herds are geographically nonterritorial but do tend to return to a home range, an area that has plentiful water, grazing, shelter and security. Such areas will often be shared by several different herds, which will nonetheless maintain a respectful distance from each other. Stallions will often urinate over the top of piles of droppings from mares in their harems to mark them as part of their group and to warn off other stallions.

Removal from the Herd

When we take the horse from its herd, it still has a need both to bond and to follow direction. The domesticated horse will form a strong attachment to you as its handler, which is based on confidence and trust, and will sometimes form bonds with other animals. It is imperative that you assert your leadership role and remain in the dominant position at all times. This should never be achieved through aggression, but through body language, empathy and clear commands.

The horse, especially a young one, will at times challenge your authority, and in many instances this is nothing more than a natural need to re-establish the pecking order. By maintaining the role of leader, you afford the horse the security and assurance that the dominant member of the herd would provide.

The herd instinct in horses can work in your favor when training. As foals, horses learn from the behavior of their mothers and others around them. Drawing on this ability to learn from others, the use of a lead horse when teaching youngsters to jump, for example, is an excellent method of providing confidence. Horses will shape their behavior on the example of those around them,

and a calm "nanny" horse accompanying a young horse at its first show, or when hacking out, can be a great help. It works both ways, however, and young horses will develop bad habits if exposed continually to poor behavior in others.

The solitary horse, being removed from its safety net provided by the herd, will develop a sense of "safe area." This can be the stable or barn, and it is where it will gravitate, especially when feeling stressed or threatened. Horses are creatures of habit, and a horse that is regularly turned out during the day and brought in at night will often become noticeably agitated if left out for longer than usual. The onset of dusk is instinctively the most dangerous time for a horse, and a solitary horse left out does not have the security blanket of a herd, and feels threatened. While this behavior can be irritating, if you remain calm, confident and in charge at all times, this will enable your horse to gain in confidence.

Horse Sense

The basic instinct for survival led to the development of five extremely acute senses — sight, hearing, smell, taste and touch.

The Five Senses

A horse's vision is unique and effective, providing it with a wide visual range designed to detect predators. Similarly the sense of hearing is acute; the mobility of a horse's ears allows it to track sound and pinpoint the area where danger might be lurking. As well as having highly perceptive hearing, horses can hear a much greater range of pitch than humans, and are more susceptible to sudden, loud noises. Horses react strongly to vocal commands, and are able to differentiate the smallest change in tone, pitch and volume.

Due to the length of its nose, a horse has a "blind spot" directly in front and below it. But this same long nose endows it with a highly refined sense of smell — much greater than that in humans. This helps both to detect predators and also to find suitable food to eat. Horses can smell water from a great distance — an essential asset when living in drought-ridden areas or when searching for water at night. Horses can also smell pheromones, which are vital to the social behavior of stallions and mares within a group. They can differentiate between the smell of droppings from members of their own herd and those of threatening rival bands.

It is interesting to note that the horse's sense of taste is not dissimilar to our own. Horses are able to differentiate between sweet, sour, salty and bitter tastes and can judge if something does not taste acceptable to eat. They are able to evaluate what they eat through their sense of smell and then taste, a vital process in the prevention of ingesting toxic matter.

The horse's top lip is extremely dexterous; it can be used for grooming and to manipulate objects. Here the horse uses it to scratch a hard-to-reach itch.

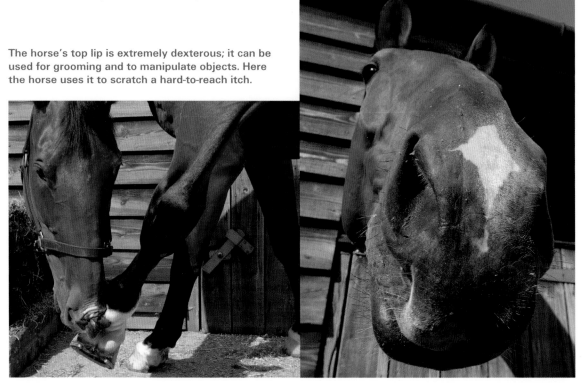

SENSORY ABILITIES

◆ HEARING
Horses have the ability to hear a greater range of pitch and to differentiate the smallest change in tone, pitch and volume.

◆ SIGHT
Horses have a wide visual field designed to detect predators.

◆ SMELL
Much greater and more refined than in humans, a horse's smelling abilities enable it to detect predators and to find suitable food.

◆ TOUCH
The top lip is highly dexterous and the whiskers vital for locating suitable forage.

◆ TASTE
This sense is similar to our own, in that horses can differentiate between sweet, sour, salty and bitter tastes.

A horse's sense of touch is often considered its weakest sense, and with regard to detecting predators this is probably the case. However, bearing in mind that the area directly in front of the horse is a visual blind spot, the sensitivity of its top lip and whiskers is vital for locating suitable forage. The horse's top lip is highly dexterous and is aided by its whiskers. Horses will use this lip to groom themselves and each other, and are able to remove small parasites and manipulate objects with it.

Horses are naturally sensitive through their bodies, a factor that we use to our advantage (and occasionally to their disadvantage) through our training.

The Sixth Sense
No mention of the natural horse is complete without a reference to the sixth sense, the most unscientific of terms. It is widely recognized that horses are perceptive to our moods and will react accordingly — especially to fear. When training, horses will often anticipate a transition before it is asked for, which can be both advantageous and disastrous when in the middle of a dressage test! They invariably will change their behavior patterns before the onset of bad weather, usually becoming agitated and nervous.

So what is the sixth sense? In many cases horses react the way they do because their senses are so much more acute than ours. This allows them to smell the subtle changes in our bodies brought about by fear. When riding we may believe we haven't asked for a transition, but just by thinking it our weight alters fractionally in preparation. This is what the horse responds to, picking up the most minute of changes. They are also highly sensitive to changes in electrical potential, which explains their reaction to the onset of poor weather. Living on the open plains, as they did thousands of years ago, storms could have dire effects on the safety of the herd. By evolving sensitivity to the change in weather patterns, the horse stood a better chance of securing shelter before a storm hit.

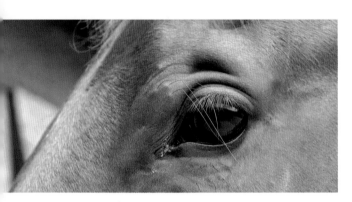

The horse's vision is very different from that of humans and understanding the way it sees and perceives the world around it can help us to understand why it reacts to things the way it does.

Memory and Intelligence

Horses developed extraordinary memories as a matter of necessity; in the past, this was vital for detecting the presence of a predator or unseen danger. How often have you seen horses in the same manège become suddenly spooked when a jump wing has been moved, or someone has left a jacket lying on the ground? Horses immediately realize when their familiar territory has undergone a change — even by the smallest margin — and to them, first and foremost, change signifies danger.

Horses have excellent homing abilities and are able to locate and return to a familiar area, whether that be a watering hole in the middle of

the plains, or the home barn. Their memory is a wonderful if fragile tool in training. The horse will remember poor experiences and bad technique as readily as it will respond to intelligent, sensitive application of the aids. It is worth noting at this point that horses are creatures of immediate response. If the horse does something well, it must be praised immediately, and vice versa for poor behavior. Waiting until the end of a session or the completion of a transition, movement or task to praise or reprimand is pointless. The horse will only associate the praise/reprimand with the immediate action.

Horses are often said to be stupid, which is clearly not the case. Were they stupid, they would not have flourished and become the adaptable and successful species that they are.

Vision

The horse's vision is very different from that found in humans. The side placing of the eyes give the horse a huge visual field,

A horse is able to see between 320 degrees to 350 degrees around it, with its only blind spots being directly in front of its nose, and a few yards behind it. This panoramic field of vision clearly aided the horse in the wild, allowing it to watch for predators. Even with its head down when grazing, the horse is still able to watch for would-be attackers.

The length of the horse's nose and the distance between its eyes and the end of its nose mean that the horse is unable to see directly beneath it without turning its head slightly. When jumping, as the horse takes off, it is actually unable to see the fence, and instead relies on the image of the fence seen several strides before takeoff. It is not unusual to see a horse cock its head slightly while jumping, allowing it to view the fence beneath it.

Horses' eyes are among the largest eyes of all mammals — bigger even than those of elephants! For years, the size of the eye was believed to imply that the horse saw objects bigger than they were. This is not the case. The large eye actually means that the horse is better able to process visual information in poor light, which dispels another myth — that horses can't see in the dark! In fact, they have seminocturnal vision and are able to see far better in the dark than humans. However, it is thought that their night vision lacks clarity, so while horses can determine large shapes and forms, they cannot make out detail.

In Focus

A horse's eyes focus very differently from our own. Described simply, the retina in a horse's eye has a single horizontal strip of densely concentrated light-sensitive cells, while above and below this strip, the concentration of these cells is greatly reduced. This means that objects that are on the same horizontal plane as the sensitive part of the retina will be seen in great detail, while objects that fall to either side of this plane will lack clarity. When a horse moves its head up and down, some images will come into sharp focus, and others will become unfocused. This sudden

Trainer's Tip

It is a bad idea to ride wearing jewelry, not only from a safety point of view but also because the sound of jangling bracelets to the acute ears of a horse can be highly distracting when riding and schooling.

focusing on images explains why horses suddenly spook at objects that they have clearly been able to see for some time.

Due to the side positioning of a horse's eyes, it will have a limited amount of binocular vision — that is the field of vision that both eyes see together. This makes a horse's depth perception less accurate than that found in humans and predators with forward-facing eyes.

It is interesting to watch a horse's reaction on seeing white painted lines on the road for the first time. I have seen horses, who are used to cattle guards, who simply will not be persuaded to cross a series of lines painted on the road. They see the lines, believe them to be a cattle guard, and are unable to ascertain that there is no depth underneath them.

Color Perception

The necessity for a horse to see color is limited, which is not to say that they do not see color — they do, just not all colors. The retina is packed with two kinds of photosensitive cells: rod cells and cone cells.

Rod cells determine brightness and darkness, while cone cells distinguish change in intensity and color. People who have full-color vision have three types of cone cells; studies on horses suggest that they have only two types of cone cells. This means they have limited color perception, somewhat similar to color blindness in humans. Studies show that horses are able to distinguish blue and red from gray, but not green.

quick reference

Vision and Hearing

- Horses can have up to a 350-degree field of vision.
- Horses have two blind spots, one directly beneath their noses, and the other directly behind them.
- Horses' eyes focus differently from our own; when they move their heads up and down, this allows them to bring objects into focus.
- Horses can see some color, but are not able to discern green from gray – they are partially color blind.
- Horses have better night vision than humans but their depth perception is less clear than our own.
- Horses have acute hearing and their ability to respond well to vocal communications is an invaluable training tool.

Hearing and Vocalization

A horse's hearing, like its vision, is very different from that of humans. Their ears are receptive to a much wider range of pitch and tone.

Horses have mobile ears that are able to track noise. The ears can move through 180 degrees, which allows the horse to pinpoint the direction that a noise is coming from, this being vital in the wild to ascertain in which direction danger lies. Their honed sense of hearing also allows herds to communicate and stay together, especially in situations where different herds might mix, such as at watering holes or good feeding areas.

A foal and its mother will keep in contact through vocalizing, and the range and pitch of that vocalization can be easily read — from fear and alarm to soothing.

Due to the range of the horse's hearing, it is able to hear sounds inaudible to the human ear, which can account for sudden spooking. A horse is also particularly sensitive to pitch and tone, which is an important consideration in training. This sensitivity means that vocal encouragement and commands can be used as vital training tools, but can just as easily be misused. A horse that is working well and listening will invariably have one ear cocked to the rider or ground trainer while the other is forward — listening both to the handler and the world at large.

Above left: The ears are turned toward a sound's direction. Left: Ears are pricked and the horse is concentrating on stimuli in front of it.

Flight, Freeze and Fight

Flee first, think later — this is a basic premise for the horse and stems from its lowly position in the food chain. In the wild, a horse's predators were numerous and unrelenting, and many of them fleet of foot as well. Horses, as single-toed animals, developed the capability of short bursts of sudden great speed, which allowed them to outrun virtually all of their would-be attackers, providing the horses saw them first. So, in order to survive, the horse developed a rapid flight response to danger, or suspected danger. This instinct is still very evident, whether observing the domesticated horse suddenly startled in a field, or when riding a young or nervous horse.

There are occasions, however, when the "freeze" reaction occurs. If a horse sees something unexpected or frightening, it will sometimes become rooted to the spot. Its head will rise, nostrils flare and muscles tense; at this point it is reading the situation and will generally wheel and flee after a matter of seconds. If a horse of yours reacts similarly, calmly reassure it and allow it a moment to assess the danger before quietly asking it to move on. In this way, a horse will gain confidence in itself and in its rider.

A horse's "fight" response to danger will be exhibited in the wild where there is no room for flight. Left with no alternative, a horse will turn and act aggressively. In domesticated horses we repress the flight instinct, and in some cases this can cause the fight instinct to become stimulated, and aggressive behavior, although unusual, can be triggered. In situations such as this, the horse's behavior is a reflection of a lack of confidence – in itself, its surroundings and its handler. By working with a horse and establishing ground rules, your hierarchy and trust, aggressive behavior borne of insecurity can be overcome.

The startled horse raises its head and is poised for flight. If it has been chewing, it will stop to aid its hearing and pinpoint the danger, while its raised head will afford it a greater visual field. A horse's sense of smell, too, will be on high alert for any signs of predators. If it considers the situation to be dangerous, it will flee, quickly removing itself from the supposed danger.

Digestion

The makeup and structure of the horse's digestive tract is highly specialized and evolved specifically to suit the needs of a prey animal, constantly on the move and foraging on rough, fibrous matter.

Trickle Feeders

Horses in their natural state will graze for up to 18 hours a day, taking a few small mouthfuls of grass before moving onto the next patch. This is known as "trickle feeding," and means that the digestive tract is constantly moving food through. Grass and feed is sought out by the dexterous and sensitive upper lip, chopped with the incisors and then chewed. The horse's jaw is extremely mobile; chewing is very important to the whole digestive process, both in stimulating salivation and in the initial breaking down of the feed matter. Horses that bolt their feed or are unable to chew properly will not be able to utilize their feed efficiently. Horses are naturally grazers, and eat with their heads down. Studies have shown that by eating in this way the integrity of their teeth remains optimal. Horses eating from a raised head position, i.e., from a haynet, will not wear their teeth as evenly (see page 82).

The feed matter, mixed with saliva, is swallowed and moves down the esophagus to the stomach. Relative to its size, the horse's stomach is small, and has a capacity of 2–5 gallons (8–19 l). The stomach itself is relatively inelastic, and its muscular makeup makes it virtually impossible for vomiting or gastric reflux. Unlike predators that eat a big meal then rest and

Trainer's Tip

Continual trickle feeding is the most natural for the horse; try and allow your horse as much time at pasture as possible or, alternatively, ensure that it has a constant supply of good-quality hay in front of it.

quick reference

Digestion

- A horse's digestive tract is designed for small quantities of food on a virtually continuous basis.
- Horses can graze for 18 hours a day.
- Horses have small stomachs compared to their size.
- Horses are not ruminants; unlike many grass eating mammals, they do not chew the cud.
- Horses are unable to vomit; in severe cases, if the stomach becomes too distended, it will rupture.
- Food can take up to 60 hours to pass the entire length of the digestive tract.
- Always introduce new foods slowly, preferably taking up to a month and mixing them with the old feed.
- Horses do not have gallbladders but do have cecums (see page 21).

digest, the horse, being a trickle feeder, thrives on a steady intake of small quantities of forage; in this way, the stomach is never completely full, or totally empty.

Little but Often

In simple terms, the speed with which the stomach empties depends on the volume of matter entering it. The greater the volume, the faster it empties, and the secondary effect of this is that the food passes quickly through the intestines, thus diminishing the actual nutritional value that the horse receives from its food. This is a significant fact when determining feeding routines, and explains the cardinal rule of feeding — "little but often." By feeding small amounts at regular intervals, the horse will benefit from a much more efficient digestive process, which, in turn, increases the nutritional value absorbed.

Bacterial fermentation of the feed matter starts in the first section of the horse's stomach. The matter then passes to the second section, where it mixes with the acidic gastric juices. It then enters the small intestine, where the digestive process really kicks off.

There is nothing small about the small intestine; it measure approximately 65 feet (20 m) in length and is the major organ of digestion. Here digestive enzymes break down proteins, fats, starches and sugars. Bile, which acts on fats and alkalizes the feed matter, is continually secreted through the intestines because, unlike humans, horses do not have gallbladders. The feed matter passes through the small intestine relatively quickly and can reach the cecum within an hour.

The cecum is a long dead-ended pouch. Matter enters and leaves the cecum through the same opening, and here microbes continue to break down the feed matter, especially the more fibrous matter, such as hay and grass. The cecum has a

similar function to the rumen in a cow. The microbial population in the cecum is fairly specific as to what it can break down, which is why the introduction of new feeds should be done very slowly, in order to allow the microbial culture to reestablish itself.

The feed matter will remain in the cecum for approximately seven hours before passing into the large intestine, or the colon. The final digestive processes occur here, and they can take up to 50 hours. Water, vitamins and fatty acids are absorbed and the eventual waste products form into balls of fecal matter, which are then passed from the rectum.

Left: If feeding hay from a haynet, make sure the holes are small and the net is tied nice and high. Right: Grazing is more natural and is the most beneficial for a horse's digestive system and teeth. However some horses will "gorge" on grass and will have to have their grazing limited (see page 99).

2

CHOOSING A HORSE

The best way to find a horse is by word of mouth; an animal that can be personally recommended by someone you know and respect — your riding instructor, the manager of your local riding club, for example — is well worth considering. Breed associations are other good places to target.

Equestrian magazines and the Internet are other avenues that can be used, but be sure that any ads you see really do fit the bill. If there are vast distances involved, ask the seller to send a video of the horse. That will give you a rough idea about the horse and help you decide whether or not it is worth pursuing.

Many dealers will work with you to identify exactly what you are looking for. If you approach a dealer, make sure he or she is reputable. Many "training" barns (competition yards) also will have horses for sale, and generally the owner is more concerned with his or her good reputation than with ripping you off.

Horse sales and auctions are a gamble. If you know what you are looking for, it is possible to pick up a super horse for a good price. However, there is generally a reason why a horse is being sold through a sale, and you have to ask yourself why.

There are two main rules for the first-time buyer:

1 Always take someone more experienced than yourself with you when looking at and trying out a horse.
2 Generally, you get what you pay for.

Consolidating Your Requirements

It is very important to be absolutely clear what exactly it is that you are looking for in a horse. You should make a list of criteria, and stick to them. There are thousands of horses on the market every week, and it is easy to get sidetracked. If you persevere you will find the right horse, but it is a process that can take months. It is pointless to rush into buying a horse that is not entirely suitable and hope it will work out. Inevitably, an emotional attachment will arise, and once that attachment is formed, it makes passing on an unsuitable horse even more traumatic. When talking to sellers be very specific about what you are looking for so that no one's time gets wasted.

First and foremost, decide on a ceiling price. This price must be realistic for the type of horse you want, and once set, don't look at any ads for anything that exceeds it. If you are working with a dealer make sure that he or she knows your limit, and make it clear that you are not interested in anything over and above that; it is easy to be coerced into spending more than you intend to.

Assess your ability and your ambition. What do you want to do with your horse? Are you aiming for riding club-level competitions? Do you want to compete at affiliated competitions? Do you want to compete at all? If you are inexperienced, go for a "schoolmaster" type — a horse that has already seen and done everything that you want to do. The horse will teach you and give you confidence. Some schools of thought favor the pairing of a novice/young horse and rider together on the premise that you learn together, but generally this is a disaster unless you have continual training.

If you are looking at a horse that is said to have won X or Y at competitions, try and follow this up and find out if it has, in fact, won what it is supposed to have. With affiliated competitions you can contact the governing body, but with unaffiliated competitions you'll have to expand your enquiries. However, you can often track competition results through the organizing riding stables or pony clubs.

Safety is paramount; if you intend to hack out you must make sure that a horse is 100 percent in traffic, and ask if it hacks alone and in company. Some horses are great when with others, but a nightmare on their own.

Consider your situation and your facilities. Do you have stabling available? Would you be better off with a mare or a gelding, or does it matter? Find out how easy a horse is to catch, shoe, clip and load. You must think about all these things and apply them to your own situation.

Temperament is vital, especially if the horse is to be kept in a yard or family environment. Ask what the horse is like in the stable and in the field. Is it a bully, or does it get bullied? Most horses have their quirks, but usually temperament is reflective of their general attitude.

Many horses will have a set of faults. Though these are likely be the product of poor care and management at some point in their histories, once established they can be problematic. When looking at horses be very clear on what you are able to cope with and what you are not. A horse that is very difficult to shoe, for example, will require extensive handling to overcome the problem; are you and your farrier prepared to put in the necessary time and groundwork?

Once you have created a list of ideal-sounding horses, start making appointments to view them. From the moment you arrive at a seller's stables, pay attention to the horse and the seller. Watch the horse; see how the seller approaches it and how the two interact. Ask to see the horse without tack first, and watch as it's led up and trotted away on a hard surface in a straight line and in a circle. Look at the way the horse moves. Observe how the horse reacts to being tacked up and make sure that the seller rides the horse

before you do. If he or she is reluctant to do so, it would indicate a problem. If possible, ask to ride the horse in the field, arena and on the road. If you are buying a horse that you wish to jump, be sure to try it over fences, preferably colored and natural ones. Make sure that the horse has not been worked earlier in the day — check for sweat marks, or simply ask the seller. If the horse has already been worked, find out why. If the horse has been worked prior to being seen it may suggest the horse is difficult.

The ideal way to buy a horse is to be able to take it for a trial period first. Many sellers will not agree to this, but some will, and it is always worth asking. Make sure that you have insurance coverage if you are doing this. Generally, trial periods last for a week, and during that time you need to try the horse in as many different situations as possible.

things to consider and ask when buying a horse

- **Price.** Set a ceiling price and stick to it.
- **Age and ability.** Very generally, up to 6 years a horse could be considered novice or green, and from 8 years upward, experienced. Pair a novice rider with an experienced horse.
- **Temperament.**
- **Track record.** Check up on competition results.
- **Mare or gelding.** Does it matter?
- **Traffic.** Does it hack out alone and in company?
- **Good to shoe?** Load? Catch? Clip? Tie? X-tie? Bath?
- **Does it have vices?**
- **Does it hunt?** And if so, what type of bit does it go in?
- **Does it jump?** Over ditches? Water?
- **Why is the horse for sale?**
- **How long has the present owner had the horse?** If only for a short time, then investigate why.
- **Where has the horse come from prior to the present owner?** Tracking a horse's history can be interesting and illuminating.
- **Make sure that the horse has the correct identification papers** (see page 52). Ask to see them (if registered).

Considering Conformation

Conformation describes the way in which a horse is put together; it determines its athleticism, soundness and potential to do the job for which it is designed. When evaluating horses and judging their conformation, it is important to bear in mind the type of work the horse is required to do. The heavy muscular frame of the draft horse, for example, with its short, thickset neck, upright shoulders and massive hindquarters, is ideally suited to pulling heavy loads but not for the racetrack. Every breed, no matter its function, should be balanced and well proportioned.

Decide what you want your horse to do. This horse, for example, does not have particularly good conformation, especially for dressage, but would make a nice horse for hacking out.

Trainer's Tip
Take your time when assessing a horse. Be methodical and thorough, and don't allow a seller to rush you.

When evaluating conformation it is helpful to be systematic, starting at the head and gradually working your way back through the body.

Make sure that the horse is standing on a flat and level hard surface. Step back from the horse and assess it from a short distance. Look at the horse as a whole and try to ascertain its overall symmetry and balance. Does anything in particular strike you as out of proportion? If so,

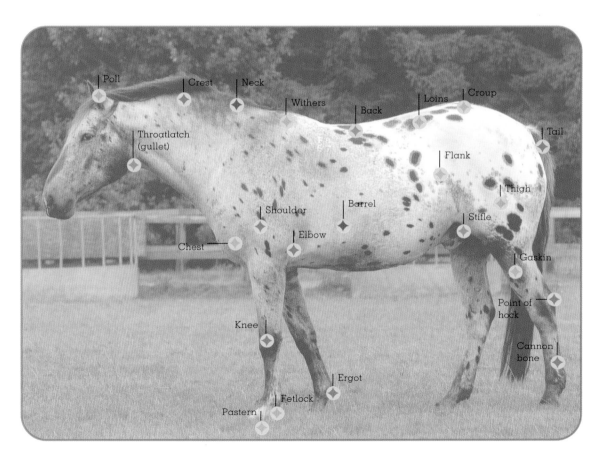

Ask to see the horse led away from you and then past you and watch the way it moves. From behind, make sure the horse is level and has even footfalls. Check to see how the horse places its feet and how it travels.

why? Try to judge the actual frame of the horse, and not the condition. If a horse is overweight or underweight, for example, as long as its skeletal structure is sound, it still may be worth considering. Weight can be gained or lost, but if the "structure" is not correct, there's nothing you can do. Temperament, as mentioned before, is extremely important, and as you work around the horse assessing it, be aware of how it is reacting to you. Try to establish a measure of the horse's attitude by observing its ears, its interplay with you and the handler, and its behavior.

Once you have assessed the horse as a whole and have determined the overall balance and proportions, you can start to evaluate the head.

Head

The head should be in proportion to the body, being neither too big and heavy nor too small and snippy. A horse with a large, heavy head is often inclined to be heavy in the hand, and the balance through the forehand is upset. The forehead should be wide and flat and the eyes large, soft and well positioned. The eyes are great windows on a horse's character — small piggish eyes invariably reflect a similar temperament! Some

horses, especially Appaloosas and skewbald or piebald (paint) horses can have pink skin surrounding their eyes and noses. This can be a problem in very hot climates, or in areas that receive a lot of snow followed by bright sun. The skin can become chapped and sunburned.

Generally, a clean, straight profile is preferable, especially for horses that are to be shown. Arabians are an exception to this as they have a dished, slightly concave, profile. A Roman nose — where the profile is slightly convex — often denotes a horse of "honest" character, but is generally frowned on in the show ring, with the possible exception of working hunter classes. The nostrils should be a good size, and equal. Very small nostrils are a disadvantage for any horse that is to be worked hard and fast as they restrict airflow. The jawline should be clean, smooth and level. Check that the top and bottom jaw meet correctly; undershot and overshot jaws cause problems with eating and chewing, wear on the teeth and are unsightly. As a guide, you should be able to fit a balled fist between the two bones of the lower jaw. Again, with the show ring in mind, small neat ears are preferable. Very large or lop ears are often frowned on, and it's an old wives' tale that long-eared horses are capable of great speed. Arabians in particular are expected to have small ears, which curve inward at the tip.

The way the head sits on the neck is extremely important, and will denote the ease with which a horse will be able to work through and into the bridle. The throatlatch (gullet) should be clean and smooth. A thick throatlatch makes it difficult for the horse to flex from the poll. If the head is set too steeply onto the neck, the airways will be restricted and it will be difficult to encourage the horse to lower into the bridle.

Neck

The neck should be in proportion to the body, and of sufficient length. It should be set well onto the shoulders. A neck that is set too low onto the shoulders will make the horse on the forehand and unbalanced. Equally, a neck that is set too steeply onto the shoulders will incline the horse to travel above the bridle, and it will be difficult to make the horse work through his back and into the hand.

The neck should be well muscled through the topline, but do not let a horse in poor condition put you off. Providing the set of the neck is correct, muscle can be built up, but if the set of the neck is incorrect, there is little you can do to compensate.

Shoulders and Withers

For riding horses, the shoulders should have an ideal slope of around 45 degrees from the top of the withers to the point of the shoulder. This degree of slope will allow the horse to have a long, low and free stride. A more upright shoulder, which is quite acceptable in draft breeds, will limit the freedom and length of stride in the riding horse. An upright shoulder will also increase the amount of concussion, which can have a negative long-term effect. The angle of the shoulder should match the angle of the pastern joint, which in

Ask to have the horse led past you in walk and trot. Watch for any uneven strides. See how freely the horse moves from the shoulder and how well it uses its hindquarters.

turn should be reflected in the angle of the hoof. The withers need to be well defined, which gives the saddle a place to rest. Rounded withers make saddle-fitting difficult, and will inhibit the length and freedom of stride. Similarly, excessively prominent withers also make saddle-fitting difficult. In the mature horse, the height of the withers and the croup should be level.

Chest and Body

You must view the chest from in front of the horse. The chest needs to be sufficiently wide to allow good, clean action without interference (brushing), but not so wide that it produces a rolling action.

It is very important for a horse to have a good depth of girth — this allows plenty of room for the heart and lungs. As a guide, the measurement from the top of the withers to just behind and below the elbow should equal the distance from that point to the ground.

Horses have eight pairs of true ribs that are attached both to the vertebrae of the spine and the sternum, and 10 pairs of false ribs that are only attached to the vertebrae. The length of the true ribs determines the horse's depth of girth, and you want good, long ribs that will provide ample room for the huge lungs and the heart.

Trainer's Tip

Be cautious when working around a horse with
which you are unfamiliar. When assessing the
horse from behind, stand back far enough to be out
of kicking reach, and make sure the horse knows
where you are so that you don't startle it. Most
horses become nervous when someone is standing
behind them, primarily because you are in their
blind spots.

These true ribs are generally flatter than the false
ribs, which are rounded or "well sprung." The false
ribs also need to be long and protect the horse's
vital organs. There should be no more than a
hand's width between the last false rib and the
hip bone; any more distance than this is a serious
conformational flaw, and will result in weakness
through the structural frame.

Arabians generally have one less vertebra than
other breeds, which, in turn, means they have one
less rib, making them shorter in the back than
other breeds.

Back and Loins

The back must be in proportion to the rest of the
horse — strong, muscular and not too broad.
Mares are prone to having slightly longer backs
than geldings and stallions. Swaybacks, which dip
deeply behind the withers, are weak and prone to
stress problems, and should be avoided. Roach
backs, in which the spine is slightly convex from
the loin to the croup, are not desirable in the
show ring, but horses with roach backs often
make good jumping horses.

The loins are a core element in the strength of
a horse's frame, providing key support to the
spine; the muscles of the loins run from the bones
of the neck to the sacrum. Loins should be short
and muscular as it is here that the propulsion
from the hindquarters is realized. Weak loins are a
serious problem.

Croup and Hindquarters

In a mature horse, the croup should not be higher
than the withers as this automatically makes the
horse on the forehand and unbalanced, both of
which will put excessive strain on the front legs
and feet. The hindquarters are the horse's
powerhouse, and should be muscular and well
rounded. An excessively sloping croup with a low-
set tail is a sign of weakness through the
hindquarters. The hindquarters should be
assessed both from the side and behind. With the
horse standing square, they should appear level
and well rounded from behind. If the horse seems
to be higher on one side of the croup than the
other, it could indicate a problem.

Front Legs

Looking at the forelegs from the side first, they
should appear straight and true. There should be
room between the point of elbow and the ribs. In
cases where the elbow is tight in to the rib cage,
the horse is described as "tied in at the elbow,"
and this will limit the forward action of its leg. The
forearm needs to be long and well muscled, while
the cannon should be short and strong. The
measurement of the cannon bone below the knee
determines how much "bone" a horse has; as a
guide, 8 inches (20 cm) of bone for a 16-hands-
high riding horse is acceptable. A long cannon
bone is a weakness, as is an excessively long
pastern bone. On the other hand, a very short
pastern will be prone to concussion problems. The
pastern bone should have a similar angle to that of
the shoulder, and both pasterns should be of equal
length. The knees need to be large, flat and
symmetrical. From the front, there should be good,
but not excessive width between the forelegs, and
you should be able to draw a straight line from the
point of the shoulder, down through the middle of
the knee, the middle of the pastern and the middle
of the hoof.

Hind Legs

The hind legs are a key element in the forward
propulsion of a horse, and correct conformation is

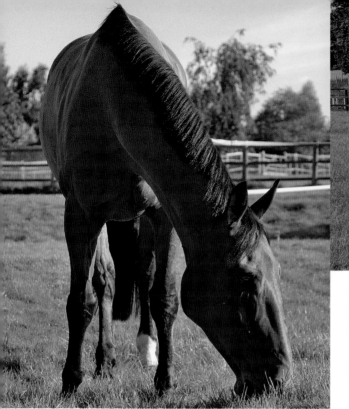

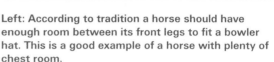

Left: According to tradition a horse should have enough room between its front legs to fit a bowler hat. This is a good example of a horse with plenty of chest room.

Above: This is a nicely put together horse that would be suitable for any discipline.

very important in the equine athlete. The thigh should be long and well muscled, and the hocks "well let down" — meaning low to the ground. Looking at the horse from the side, you should be able to draw a horizontal line from the chestnut above the knee on the front legs to the point of hock. The hocks should be large, free from lumps, bumps or swellings, and should appear to be a pair. Looking at the horse from behind, a vertical line should fall from the point of the buttock through the point of hock and down the middle of the back of the cannon bone. (For deviations of hind leg conformation see pages 32–33.)

Feet

The saying "no foot, no horse" is one of the truest expressions in the equine world. It doesn't matter how great a horse is, or how perfect the rest of its conformation is, if it has lousy feet, you're wasting your time. The front feet and the hind feet must be equal in size and shape. They must be straight and forward-facing, the quality of the hoof wall must be good, and the feet must be of proportionate size to the size of the horse. Feet

that are particularly upright and boxy are often seen in horses that go on to develop navicular disease (see page 235). Similarly, when one foot is boxier than the other, it can indicate potential problems with the internal structures. The front feet should be rounded without appearing platterlike, and the hind feet oval.

Always pick up all four feet and check the quality of the frog, the heels and the sole. The frog should look healthy and prominent, the heels should be equal and level, wide and balanced. Watch out for underslung heels — ones that grow forward at an acute angle compared to the angle of the pastern and wall. This really is a problem and requires continual attention from a farrier. Horses with very flat soles will be prone to corns and bruising. Horizontal rings on the feet indicate a nutritional deficiency or trauma, such as laminitis (see page 232), or an acute illness. It takes the hoof wall about nine months to a year to grow from the coronary band to the ground, so you can estimate how long ago the trauma occurred by how low the rings are to the ground.

Poor Conformation of the Limbs

The following conditions are all ones to look out for when evaluating conformation.

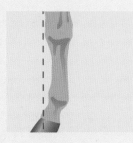

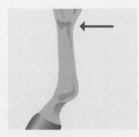

BACK AT THE KNEE
This is a serious weakness. The cannon below the knee is concave at the front, which puts enormous stress on the tendons and will invariably lead to tendon problems and lameness over a period of time.

OVER AT THE KNEE
This does not put the same amount of strain on the tendons and so is less serious than back at the knee, however, it is still undesirable and is not acceptable in the show ring. The knees appear to be curved forward, and the cannon bone slopes back below the joint.

TIED IN AT THE KNEE
This is another very serious weakness. Here the cannon measurement is narrower directly below the knee than further down the leg. This again can lead to tendon problems.

TOED-IN (PIGEON-TOED)
Either one or both of the front feet appear to turn inward when looking at the horse from the front. This is not desirable, especially in a show ring, but many horses are slightly pigeon-toed, and cope very well. Strain occurs on the lateral tendons and ligaments.

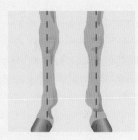

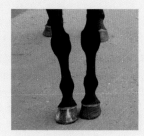

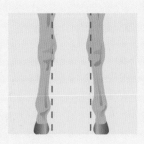

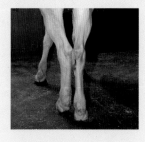

TOED-OUT
Either one or both of the front feet appear to turn outward when looking at the horse from the front. This causes some strain on the tendons, and toed-out horses are often likely to brush (one foot knocks into the opposite leg during movement). Strain occurs on the medial tendons and ligaments.

BASE NARROW
Here the forelegs slope inward and are closer together at the base than they are at the chest. This type of conformation pre-disposes a horse to action faults such as brushing.

BASE WIDE
Here the legs are wider at the base than at the chest. This again often means the horse will have action faults such as "dishing" or "plaiting" (see next page).

COW HOCKS
Looking at the horse from behind, the hocks appear to point inward. Again, not appreciated in the show ring, but generally this does not seem to affect a horse's way of going.

BOW HOCKS
This is the opposite to cow hocks — the hocks bow outward. This is considered a poor conformation problem.

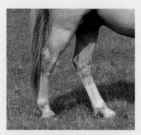

SICKLE HOCKS
The hocks are overbent so that the leg is curved inward under the horse and has a sickle-like profile. This is generally considered a serious weakness, although for horses that are used for "reining" in competition riding, this type of conformation aids the horse in carrying out the "sliding stop."

POST-LEGGED/STRAIGHT THROUGH THE HOCK
This describes a horse that has insufficient angulation through its hind leg, which gives the leg the appearance of being very straight, or "postlike." This type of conformation can lead to concussion-related problems, and would indicate a lack of athleticism in the hindquarters.

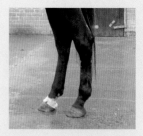

CAMPED-OUT BEHIND
The hocks and hind legs are behind the vertical, which is undesirable in the dressage or jumping horse. As it can aid some different gaits, some gaited breeds are predisposed to it. Similarly, horses shown at in-hand classes for Arabians, national show horses and American saddlebreds are often trained to stand in a "camped out" position.

ACTION FAULTS

DISHING
One or both front feet are thrown outward during movement. This can cause some strain to the fetlock joint but is otherwise not very serious.

PLAITING
The horse throws its feet inward during movement so that each foot ends up being placed virtually in front of the other. This can lead to stumbling.

FORGING
This occurs when the toe of the hind shoe catches the inside of the front shoe during movement. It is often caused by an unbalanced pace and is generally correctable.

OVERREACHING
This happens when the toe of the hind shoe catches the heel, or higher up, of the front leg. This is a problem, and can cause serious injuries. Overreach boots and protective leg gear will greatly help.

Teeth

Being confident about looking in a horse's mouth and assessing its teeth is a great advantage; it enables you to ascertain that a horse is the age it is said to be, and it allows you to regularly monitor the shape and state of wear of the teeth.

Just like its hooves, a horse's teeth grow constantly throughout its life. In the natural environment, horses wear their teeth at a fairly constant and efficient rate. The modern horse, however, is basically kept on a very different diet to the one it evolved on, and consequently teeth do not wear as evenly as they need to. Interestingly, there is a marked difference in the wear on the dentition of horses depending upon where they live. In some places, the grass has a high water content and is very soft and nonabrasive; in certain areas of the western United States, however, the grass is very tough, and becomes "sun cured," with a high nutritional value. The teeth of horses there are subject to greater wear through grazing; this leads to a slower rate of growth, less likelihood of sharp points developing and invariably less frequent attention from the equine dental technician.

Adult males have 40 teeth — 24 molars, 12 incisors and 4 tusks — and there can be wolf teeth on both upper and lower jaws, but these are not always present.

Adult females have 36 teeth — 24 molars and 12 incisors — and they may or may not have wolf teeth.

Opening the Mouth

Not all horses appreciate having their mouths opened, so always treat the exercise with caution. Never stand directly in front of a horse, and be careful that the horse does not throw its head and hit you in the face.

When looking at the teeth you must look at both sides of the jaw. If the tongue is in the way gently move it to one side.

You also must look at the front teeth — the slope, how they meet, and the coloration.

Trainer's Tip

When looking at a horse to buy, gently feel inside the corner of its mouth with your finger. If the skin either feels very thick, or is broken, cracked or sore, it would indicate that the horse has a hard mouth and pulls against the bit, or that it has been ridden excessively aggressively.

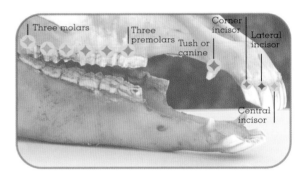

To look into a horse's mouth, face the horse standing slightly to one side and follow the procedure demonstrated on page 35. It is also useful to have a small flashlight on hand, and someone to shine it carefully into the mouth. This allows you to see the teeth really well, but be careful not to alarm the horse.

Assessing the Teeth

Before thinking about aging the horse, quickly assess the teeth themselves. The following are useful questions to ask yourself when evaluating the horse. "Do the teeth appear even? Are there any rough edges on the outsides? Does the horse appear to have any sores or wounds in its mouth? Are there great chunks of wadded feed at the back of the mouth and what does the horse's breath smell like?" Chunks of wadded half-chewed feed at the back of the horse's mouth can

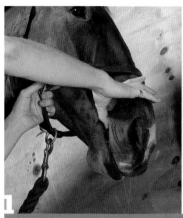

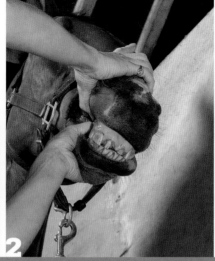

opening the mouth

1 Steady your horse's head by keeping one hand on the headcollar and the other over the nose. Slide your thumb into the corner of the mouth.

2 Move your hand from the headcollar to cradle the lower jaw. Apply gentle pressure with your thumbs to the top and bottom jaws.

3 Your horse should be encouraged to open its mouth. The looser the headcollar around the nose piece, the more it can open.

indicate a problem with the teeth, and foul-smelling breath generally indicates a severe problem with the teeth and/or gums.

Teeth as a Guide to Aging

Aging a horse by its teeth is difficult. The best way to become accomplished at it is by looking at as many different horses as possible with someone who knows their actual ages.

Horses, like humans, have temporary or "milk" teeth that are replaced with permanent teeth. By the age of nine months, foals will generally have a

Trainer's Tip

The surface of milk teeth are white and often have grooves in them. Milk teeth are smaller than permanent teeth and have a more upright angle to them.

TOOTH TERMS

- **Table.** The top of the tooth or grinding surface.
- **Crown.** The section of tooth above the gum.
- **Neck.** The part of the tooth in the gum.
- **Milk teeth.** Similar to humans, horses have milk teeth before their permanent teeth erupt.
- **Wolf teeth.** Premolars.
- **Infundibulum or mark.** A dark mark, actually a small hole, which runs partway down the (permanent) tooth.
- **Dental star.** A dark brown horizontal line between the front of the incisors and the mark, which appears at around 6 years.
- **Hook.** A small jag of tooth that first appears on the corner of the upper incisors at 6 or 7 years.
- **Galvayne's groove.** A dark line that appears on the upper corner incisors at 10 years.

full set of temporary teeth — six incisors on the top and bottom jaw and three premolars on each side of the top and bottom jaw — for a total of 12 incisors and 12 premolars.

At approximately 2½ years of age, a horse loses its temporary central incisors. These are replaced with permanent teeth; it also gets two permanent molars on both sides of the upper and lower jaws.

At approximately 3½ years, the temporary lateral incisors are replaced with permanent teeth and the horse will now have four permanent molars on both sides of each jaw.

At approximately 4 years, the four tusks start to appear in males, and the last permanent molars erupt. A horse will now have six permanent molars on each jaw.

By 4½ to 5 years, the horse should have a full set of permanent teeth.

From 5 to 6 years the corner incisors are full length and begin to wear against each other.

At approximately 6 years, the infundibulum has gone from the central incisor tables, is getting smaller on the lateral incisor tables, and will be just appearing on the corner incisor tables. The dental star will now start to appear on the central and lateral incisor tables.

At approximately 7 years, the hook appears on the top of the corner incisors; horses also get a hook at 11 years, so consider the slope and angle of the teeth as well. In the 7-year-old horse, the teeth should be fairly upright; by 11 years, they will be more sloping and longer. At 7 years, the tables will be quite oval in shape.

At approximately 8 years, the hook will have disappeared and the tables will become triangular in shape. From now on, it becomes increasingly difficult to accurately age a horse by its teeth alone, and you also should consider the horse's external appearance.

By 9 years, the infundibulum will have disappeared from all the teeth.

At approximately 10 years, Galvayne's groove will start to appear on the upper corner incisors and work its way down the crown.

At 11 years a hook will appear on the upper corner incisors.

By 15 years, Galvayne's groove will be approximately halfway down the tooth, and the tables will start to become more rounded.

By 20 years, the teeth will be sloped at quite an angle and Galvayne's groove will have reached the bottom of the tooth.

Between 20 and 30 years, Galvayne's groove will have disappeared.

Poor Conformation of the Jaw

Any conformation abnormality of the jaw is highly undesirable as it contributes to problems with eating and digestion.

Parrot mouth conformation is when the top jaw is longer than the bottom. This means that the incisors do not meet and so the "plucking" ability of the horse is compromised. It also means that the last molar on the lower jaw protrudes up behind the last molar on the top jaw. The tooth then grows excessively long because it has nothing to grind against and wear it down.

Sow mouth (undershot jaw) refers to the lower jaw being longer than the upper jaw, which causes similar problems to the parrot mouth horse. Both these conditions can be effectively maintained by regular trips to the equine dental technician, but they are to be avoided if possible.

Routine Care of the Teeth

It is vital that your horse has its teeth checked every six months to a year by a professional. If there are any mouth problems, they will affect the horse's health and attitude to work.

The Equine Dental Technician

By law, equine dental technicians are not allowed to remove teeth, perform any kind of dental surgery or administer sedatives. If your horse requires this attention, it must be done by a veterinary surgeon. Unlike human teeth, equine teeth continue to grow throughout a horse's life, and are worn down through eating.

After "plucking" or cutting forage with the incisors, food is moved back into the mouth and chewed with a grinding action by a horse's molars. However, the upper jaw is slightly wider than the lower jaw, so there is invariably uneven wear on the teeth. This can result in sharp points forming on the inside of the cheek teeth on the lower jaw, and on the outside of the cheek teeth on the upper jaw. These sharp ridges will affect a horse's grinding ability, and also can lacerate the sides of the cheek and the tongue.

The equine dental technician removes any sharp edges by floating (rasping) the teeth. He or she also will check to see if there are any abnormalities with the teeth, especially relevant with young horses who may experience problems with their permanent teeth coming through, and with very old horses whose teeth require special attention to keep them in good order.

From left to right: An equine dental technician first rinses out the horse's mouth. She then gets the horse used to the rasp before starting to work on the teeth. She then applies a mouth gag (or speculum) so that she can feel for any sharp edges on the teeth and to have a good look at the inside of the mouth, gums, teeth and jaw.

Different Breeds

Some breeds are better suited to certain jobs than others, and there are distinct differences between the different breeds. Here is a brief outline of some of the major breeds, and what you can expect from them.

THOROUGHBREDS (HOTBLOODS) have great stamina and speed, and are far tougher than their often slight and aristocratic appearance may suggest. Apart from racing, they make excellent eventers, having the endurance, speed and athleticism needed to compete at three-day tracks.

THE ANGLO-ARABIAN is a cross of Thoroughbred and Arabian with characteristics from both breeds. They are larger than pure Arabians, and make excellent eventers. There are many great horses that are not registered with a breed society; they are called "grade horses."

WARMBLOODS, of which there are many, generally exhibit similar characteristics. They tend to make good dressage and show-jumping horses, while lacking the speed and stamina for three-day eventing. Temperament-wise they are easy to get along with.

IRISH DRAFT Although technically a draft breed, the modern Irish Draft makes a great riding horse. They are surprisingly athletic for their size and weight. Crossed with lighter breeds, they make fantastic competition horses.

DUTCH WARMBLOODS make fantastic dressage horses, and show great athleticism over fences. They tend to not have the speed and stamina to excel as eventers unless their breeding contains a high proportion of Thoroughbred blood.

PONY BREEDS Ponies are famous for their intelligence and problem-solving abilities! Crossing some pony breeds with Thoroughbred horses produces fantastic small competition horses. Notable pony breeds to use as crosses are the Connemara, Haflinger and Welsh Section B, C and D.

Breeds

- Hotblooded breeds such as Thoroughbreds and Arabians have great stamina and speed, and often a "sharper" temperament than warmbloods and coldbloods.
- European warmblood breeds typically have tractable temperaments and good paces. They make excellent dressage and show-jumping horses.
- Pony breeds crossed with Thoroughbred horses make good small competition horses.
- Quarter Horses are highly intelligent and make great family horses.
- Irish horses, although not a distinct breed, are renowned for their athletic ability, equable temperament and honest nature.

ARABIANS are also hotbloods and again possess great stamina and speed. They are also very tough, and cope well in extreme climates. They are extremely intelligent and trainable, with great memories and, again, tend to act and react quickly. They are naturally small horses, rarely exceeding 15 hands high (h.h.), and are very athletic. In particular, Arabians excel at endurance competitions, although they make good all-around competition horses.

THE QUARTER HORSE is the most prolific of the American breeds, and generally has a superb temperament. On average, they are small in height, often around 15 h.h., and tend to be large-framed and muscular through the body. They excel at all riding disciplines, and make good horses in the show ring and for hacking. Generally, the pure Quarter Horse lacks the athleticism and sustained speed to excel at eventing and show jumping. They make excellent family horses.

Vetting

Before purchasing a horse it is vital to have a pre-purchase examination (PPE) done on the horse by a veterinary surgeon. During the course of this exam, the vet will assess the horse and try to determine whether or not there are any underlying problems.

PPEs, however, are not concrete evidence; there are conditions that may not present themselves in the small window of time that a vet has to examine the horse. Increasingly in times of litigation, more and more vets are reluctant to even conduct PPEs, and it is important that you as the purchaser do everything you can to elicit as much information and past history as possible from the vendor.

Most vets prefer you to be present at the vetting so you can exchange information and be aware of the process. The vet will need to know what you want the horse for and your situation and experience. Vets can only carry out the appropriate PPE with the right facilities. They must have somewhere where the horse can be

Trainer's Tip
You should insure your horse to help cover veterinary fees that might arise. Some insurance companies require proof of a five-stage veterinary examination before they will offer you coverage.

lunged on a hard surface and an area where the horse can be worked strenuously. You must make sure that, if the vendor does not have these facilities, the horse is taken somewhere where they do exist for the vetting.

The PPE

Stage One The vet will examine the horse in the stable without tack or rugs on. The heart, lungs, teeth and eyes will be examined, and the general body condition and initial temperament assessment will be made.

Sample Horse Purchase Warranty

Owner details: • name • address	Length of time horse has been owned by vendor	Purchaser's intended use for horse? Any reason why the horse might not be suitable for this use?	Does the horse suffer from any recurrent lameness? Back problems? Disease? Seasonal problem?
Agent details (if applicable): • name • address	Reason for sale Work history of horse, including competition results	Any official or legal reason why the horse may not compete in certain disciplines?	Has the horse suffered from any of the following: • persistent cough
Horse details: • name • description • identification • documents/passport • details/freeze branding/microchip number, etc.	Is the horse insured? Has it ever been refused coverage? Why? Has loss of use been paid on it?	Has the horse been off work due to injury or ill health in the past 12 months?	• colic • laminitis • sweet itch • neurological disorders • azoturia

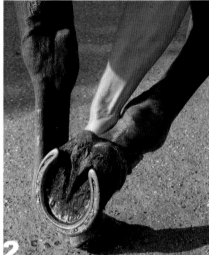
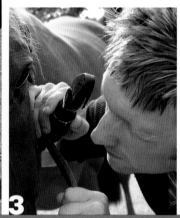

elements of the pre-purchase examination

1 Flexion tests on all four legs will be used to check for signs of stiffness, arthritis or other leg problems. Each leg is held up high, for 1–2 minutes, and then released. The horse is asked to move off immediately at a trot. Any problems will be revealed.

2 All four feet will be carefully checked to make sure that there are no abnormalities in the foot structure, that the frog is healthy, the heels in good order, and that there are no signs of bruising. If there is soreness within the foot, using a hoof tester will produce a flinching response from the horse.

3 The eyes will be carefully examined with an opthalmo-scope to check that there is no inflammation, scarring or damage to the retina, or cloudiness on the cornea, or any evidence of cataracts or other abnormalities. The pupils should react properly to light.

Does the horse have allergies to any of the following:
• food
• drugs
• bedding
• vaccines

Has the horse had surgery?

Has the horse been on medication within the last month? What for?

For mares:
• Is she in foal?

• Does she cycle normally?
• How does she behave when cycling?
• Has she had a foal?
• How easily did she conceive?
• How easily did she foal?

Is the horse good to:
• catch
• clip
• groom
• tie up
• load
• shoe
• tack up

Has the horse ever:
• bucked
• reared
• kicked
• bitten
• bolted
• rolled
• napped

What is the horse like in traffic?

Has the horse ever been seen to:
• weave
• crib
• windsuck

• box walk
• chew its blankets
• chew its flanks
• rub its tail
• chew the woodwork

Is the horse aggressive to dogs, people or other horses?

To your knowledge is there anything in the horse's history, and its physical and mental state, that may be relevant to this purchase?

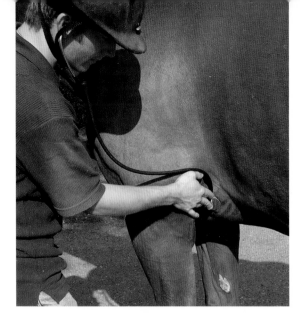

The vet will listen to the heart using a stethoscope, before and after exercise to check for faults.

Stage Two The horse will be examined in daylight and standing square. The vet will ask to see the horse walked away in a straight line, and trotted back toward, and then past him/her. The vet will observe the horse being trotted on a hard surface in a circle, on both reins.

Stage Three The horse will now be ridden (or lunged if a youngster) and worked hard on both reins and in canter. The heart rate and lungs will again be monitored.

Stage Four The horse is allowed to rest for a short period to see if any stiffness sets in. The vet will do further examinations on the legs and feet. The identification of the horse will be verified.

Stage Five When the heartbeat returns to normal, the horse will then be trotted up on a hard surface again. Flexion tests will be carried out, and generally a blood sample is taken. This will be stored for up to six months and will be used if there is any question about the horse having been drugged during the PPE.

The purchaser can request to have X-rays of the lower limbs and feet, tendon scans or have further blood tests done.

After the PPE, the vet will provide his or her opinion of the horse's soundness and suitability for your requirements. Most vets will recommend that you draw up a warranty (see pages 40–41) for the vendor to fill in. This covers aspects that the vet is not able to ascertain through the PPE.

When vetting a horse the vet will need to see it standing and run on a hard, flat surface.

quick reference

Vetting

- Always have a horse vetted before purchasing.
- Remember that a pre-purchase examination (PPE) is not infallible and the vet can only go by what he or she sees on the day of the vetting.
- Always draw up a warranty with questions that cover all bases should a legal situation occur. Make sure the vendor signs it!
- Before organizing a vetting, make sure that the vendor has sufficient facilities for the vet to be able to carry out the PPE.
- Try to be present at the PPE if possible.

Financial Arrangements

Although it can be a great alternative to purchasing a horse, leasing is not without its pitfalls. Whether you are contemplating leasing a horse for your own use, or leasing out your own horse to someone else, you must, of course, have a contract drawn up. The contract should cover every eventuality, and be fair to both the owner and the leaser. If the horse is being leased without a financial commitment, it is generally referred to as "loaning" or "free leasing."

The benefits of either leasing or loaning mean that you are able to remove yourself from the contract if, for example, you wish to progress to a more advanced horse, or your circumstances change and you are no longer able to keep a horse. In these instances you don't have the hassle of having to sell your horse, and can simply return the leased/loaned horse according to the

quick reference

Leasing, Loaning or Buying

- Leasing generally incurs a financial commitment.
- Loaning is generally without financial commitment.
- If buying, it is worth making a sensible offer below the asking price but don't if the ad specifically says "no offers."
- Always sign a contract whether you are the lessee or the owner.

contractual stipulations. The downside is that the owner of the horse can also change his or her mind and decide to have the horse returned (again, according to the contract).

Contracts are drawn up by the horse's owner in order to protect his or her interests and the well-being of the horse. Most owners who are trying to lease or loan out a horse will be keen to make a situation work. If there are aspects of the agreement that you, as the lessee, feel need adjustment, the majority of owners will work with you to come up with an agreement that suits both parties. However, the welfare of the horse is always the most important consideration.

When entering into a horse deal, it's always worth making an offer slightly below the asking price. Often the vendor will split the difference and meet you in the middle. If the ad stated "no offers," then you must be prepared to pay the full asking price. Occasionally, the vendor will enter into an agreement whereby you make a down payment followed by regular payments until the balance is paid. This is happening more frequently, and it must be supported by a legally binding contract.

3
IDENTIFICATION AND SECURITY

A horse's coat is one of the easiest methods of identification. There are a myriad of different coat colors found in horses, and in the United States there are a number of colors rarely seen in other parts of the world. Colors come in and out of fashion and some people actively search for a horse based on the color of its coat (which I don't advise). Some breeds of horses and ponies only exhibit certain colors; the Friesian, for example, is always black with minimal if any white markings, while the Lipizzaner is generally gray, although the occasional bay is found.

Coat colors originally evolved to provide the horse with good camouflage to help its survival in the wild. The dun coat is one of the most primitive; it still can be seen in Przewalski's (Asiatic wild) horse, which is the oldest surviving breed, and was undoubtedly one of the forebears of modern horses. Spotted coat coloring is also ancient; wonderful examples of this can be seen in the prehistoric spotted horse paintings discovered at Pech-Merle in France, which date back to around 25,000 BC. Interestingly, the ancient Spanish horse, which also contributed to the foundation of many breeds, was often spotted. Paintings of the famous Spanish School of Riding, founded in 1572, show many classically trained spotted Spanish horses, although today the Spanish horse appears to have lost its spots, and is predominantly gray or bay.

Colors, Whorls and Markings

Colors

Bay The body hair is brown, the mane and tail black. Bays are referred to as having black points. This means that the lower legs are black and there are black markings on the tips of the ears and the muzzle. Body hair can range from dark brown, when the horse is referred to as dark bay, to a bright reddish color, known as a bright bay or blood bay.

Chestnut The body hair is reddish brown, the mane and tail brown or flaxen. The horse does not have black points. Chestnuts can range from a dark brown, called a liver chestnut, to a very light reddish brown, called a bright chestnut.

Sorrel A light chestnut horse.

Black The body hair is black with no trace of brown hair. The mane and tail are black, but white markings can occur on the legs or face.

Brown The body hair is a mixture of black and brown, the mane and tail are generally dark brown, and the lower legs can be black.

Brown

Black

Chestnut

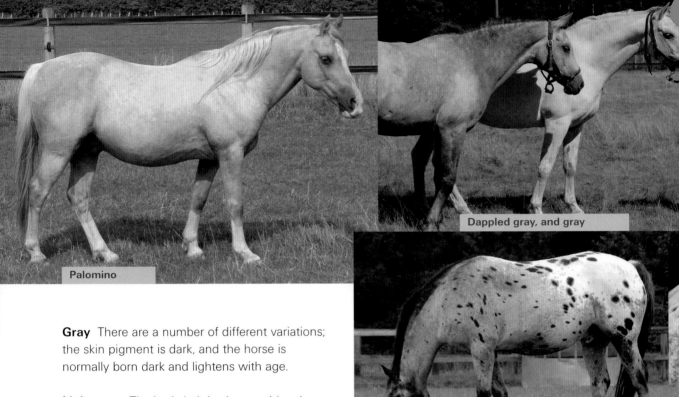

Palomino

Dappled gray, and gray

Leopard-spotted Appaloosa

Gray There are a number of different variations; the skin pigment is dark, and the horse is normally born dark and lightens with age.

Light gray The body hair is almost white, the mane and tail are white. Light gray horses tend to become flea-bitten with age. This is when brown flecks of hair appear across the coat.

Steel gray The body hair is a mixture of white and black, though the overall color appears to be a dark gray; the mane and tail are generally lighter than the body.

Dappled gray Dark gray rings cover a lighter base; the mane and tail can be lighter or darker.

Palomino The body hair is golden yellow and the mane and tail are pale cream. There can be white markings on the lower legs and face. Palominos range from a rich, dark golden through to a lighter yellow.

Spotted The body hair is white/gray and covered partially or totally with darker brown spots, or the body hair is dark and covered partially or totally with white spots. The Appaloosa is a breed that characteristically displays a spotted coat. Within the breed, there are six main patterns of spotting with nine accepted colorings.

Spotted blanket The forehand is dark with white hairs over the loins and hips, which are covered in spots.

Leopard The body hair is white and the entire body is covered in dark spots.

Near leopard The body hair is mostly white and covered in spots. The head and legs are darker.

Frosted The body hair is dark with white spots across the hips and loins.

Snowflake The body hair is dark and covered in white spots.

Blanket The forehand is dark with white across the hips and loins, which may be spotted.

Skewbald The coat is covered in large irregular patches of white and any other color except

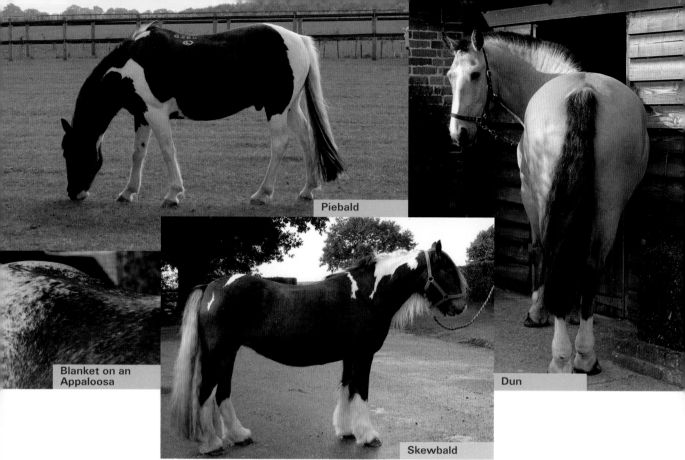

Piebald

Dun

Blanket on an Appaloosa

Skewbald

black. The mane and tail are often bicolored, and the color of the mane will correspond to that on the neck.

Piebald The coat is covered in large, irregular patches of white and black; the color of the mane will again correspond to the markings seen on the horse's neck.

Split coloring In the United States, colored horses are referred to as Paints or Pintos, and there is a breed registration for both.

Tobiano Generally have white legs and dark coloring covering one or both flanks. The dark coloring extends down over the horse's neck and chest in a shieldlike pattern. Generally, the patches of color tend to be oval or round. The tail is often two colors, and the predominant body color can be either white or colored (brown, bay, black, dun, etc.).

Overo Generally have dark legs and a single color tail. White markings are generally irregular with a broken outline and tend not to cross the back between the withers and tail.

Tovero Tend to have dark coloring over the ears, sometimes extending down the face, and dark pigmentation around the muzzle. Either one or both eyes are blue. They have colored patches that extend up from the chest through the neck, and can have colored patches and spots extending up the loins and flanks.

Dun The body hair ranges from a dark golden to pale honey and even to a reddish brown and is accompanied by black points. Duns have a dark dorsal stripe and can have shoulder markings and zebra stripes on the legs.

Buckskin There is some debate about the official difference between a dun and a buckskin

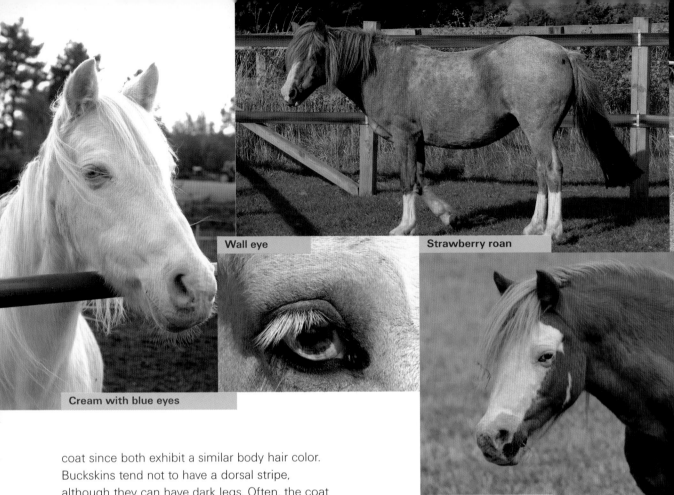

Wall eye

Strawberry roan

Cream with blue eyes

White face

coat since both exhibit a similar body hair color. Buckskins tend not to have a dorsal stripe, although they can have dark legs. Often, the coat has a slightly "metallic" sheen to it. Buckskin horses are primarily found in the United States and tend to be highly sought after.

Grullo This is a coloring that has become increasingly popular in recent years. The body hair is slate colored, smoky or mousy; each individual hair is the same color, and there are no white hairs in the coat (unlike a roan). They have dark sepia to black points, and can have a dorsal stripe, shoulder markings and leg stripes. Grullo comes from the Spanish word "grulla," which means gray crane. Also known as cremello.

Roan White hairs are mixed evenly throughout the coat with chestnut, bay and black. The mixture of the white and colored hair gives the "roan" effect. There are a number of different roan classifications: strawberry roan has white and chestnut hair; blue roan has black and white hair; and red roan has white and brown hair.

Trainer's Tip

According to old wives' tales, chestnut mares can be tempermental, gray horses honest and dun horses generous.

Cream The body hair is very pale cream, the skin pigment is pink and the eyes generally blue. These horses can be susceptible to sunburn.

Whorls

Also known as "cowlicks," these are small patches of irregular hair growth. The hair grows in a rosette type formation, spiraling out from a central point. All horses have whorls, though some have more than others. The most obvious whorls are

Blue roan

A stripe and a snip

Blaze

Mealy muzzle

those seen on the forehead, normally directly between the eyes; many horses will have another whorl under their forelocks. Whorls are also commonly found around the throat area, along the crest of the neck, across the chest, under the belly and on the underside of the neck. There are lots of superstitions attached to the number and location of whorls; primitive Indian and Arabian cultures laid great store by a horse's whorls, and if they appeared in the wrong place, they would not buy the horse.

Facial Markings

Star A small white marking on the forehead, often in a diamond shape.

Stripe A narrow white marking extending down the front of the face.

Blaze A broad white marking extending down the front of the face from forehead to lip.

White/bald face Similar to a blaze, but the white area is larger and may extend to encompass the eyes and cheeks.

Snip A small white marking between the nostrils.

White nostril Small white markings around one nostril.

Mealy muzzle Light brown and mousy muzzle, often seen in Exmoor ponies.

White muzzle The whole muzzle is white.

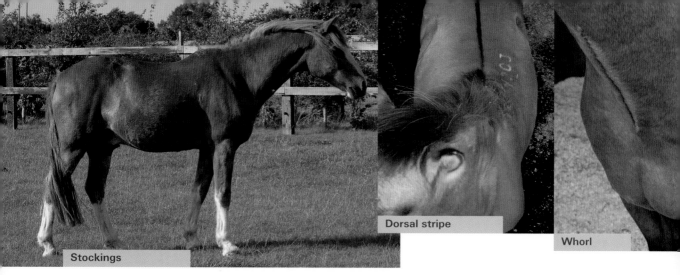

Dorsal stripe

Whorl

Stockings

Wall eye White or pale blue and white coloring instead of the normal dark brown.

White sclera The outer membrane of the eyeball is white — unlike the majority of horses, which have a dark sclera. Often seen in Appaloosa horses.

Body Markings

Dorsal/eel stripe A dark stripe runs from the withers along the backbone to the tail base.

Shoulder/wither stripes Usually accompanying a dorsal stripe, they are dark lines that extend from the wither down toward the shoulder.

Black points The legs, mane and tail, muzzle, and tips of the ears are black.

Dapples Rings of darker hair that appear over lighter body hair. Dapples are most often seen on grays or bays although they can occur on any coat coloring.

Leg and Foot Markings

Stocking The legs are white from the coronary band to the knee or hock.

Sock Similar to the stocking but the white only reaches halfway between fetlock and knee/hock.

Trainer's Tip

If a horse is described as having lots of "chrome," it means it has white leg and face markings. This is considered advantageous in the show ring because they stand out. In some countries, however, horses with white lower leg markings and pale hoof horn were traditionally thought of as undesirable and more likely to develop foot problems — which is not proven.

White coronet White markings around the coronary band.

Ermine marks Dark spots of color appearing around the coronet or pastern on a white sock or stocking.

Zebra stripes Dark rings of hair appearing around the legs with the look of zebra markings.

Blue hoof The hoof wall is dark gray/black in appearance.

White hoof The hoof wall is made up of pale horn; often seen where there are white leg markings.

Striped/zebra hoof The hoof wall is made up of vertical stripes of dark and pale horn.

Papers and Passports

Identification documents are very important, and there are different rules in different countries.

In the United States, any horse that travels across a state line, and sometimes a county line, must have a brand inspection form, health papers and an Equine Infectious Anemia (EIA) form.

Brand inspections include the horse's identifying details and must accompany it if it is moved or sold.

Health papers are temporary: they are filled in by the vet and allow a horse to travel with a clean bill of health. They usually remain valid for 30 days after issue. Brand laws and health certificate requirements vary from state to state. An EIA form will show the date of the negative blood test result and an identifying diagram of the horse.

In Canada, Equine Canada is the nationally recognized organization; it works in close contact with representatives from the Provincial Sports Organizations (PSOs) across the country. Horses competing at the majority of Canadian competitions are required to have a passport and a horse license. As with U.S. passports, the identification pages must be filled in by a veterinary surgeon. Passports and licenses are available through Equine Canada.

Microchipping, Tattooing and Branding

Equine crime is on the increase and the more precautions and anti-theft measures you are able to make, the better.

Microchipping

Microchipping has really started to take off in the last few years, and is now one of the leading forms of equine identification. The major microchip companies have also expanded their services to include microchipping everything from tack to vehicles.

So how do they work? The microchip is inserted into the nuchal ligament on the left side of the horse's neck through a hypodermic needle (a relatively painless procedure). The chip, which is tiny (about the size of a grain of rice), is made of silicon and encased in a glass capsule. Once inserted, the unique identification number on the chip can be read using a scanner, which then traces the number through a database to locate your contact details and the details of the horse.

There are several advantages to microchipping: It provides the horse with a permanent traceable identity; it cannot be seen (advantageous for show horses), and the link between a horse and owner is of great benefit in animal welfare cases.

On the other hand, there have been instances of microchips "disappearing," where the scanner is unable to pick up the chip. This can occur in cases where youngsters are chipped too early; they continue to grow and bulk out, and the chip becomes too deeply embedded under the skin to be read. Horses that are particularly thick crested and heavy through the neck can also "lose" their chips. In some cases, the chip becomes damaged, and the scanner is not able to read it correctly — although according to the manufacturers this doesn't happen very often. The microchip also does not offer any kind of deterrent, since it is invisible.

On the whole, microchipping is a good idea. It provides a good form of identification with which it is impossible to tamper.

Tattooing

Lip tattooing is used widely as all Thoroughbred and Quarter Horse racehorses have to be tattooed. The tattoo consists of a combination of letters and numbers applied to the inside of the horse's top lip. The process can be painful, although sedation makes it less traumatic. The tattoos are not always particularly easy to read, they often fade over time and can be altered.

Branding

Freeze branding is a popular method of identifying and securing a horse.

Freeze brands are usually applied on the back, under the saddle area. The area must be close clipped and thoroughly cleaned before the brand is applied. The brand, usually a combination of letters and numbers, is applied using branding irons that have been chilled with liquid nitrogen. The extreme cold destroys the pigment cells in the skin and the hair grows back white.

It is very important that the horse remains absolutely still while the brand is being applied, otherwise the brand can become blurred. The process is not particularly painful, but does cause some discomfort. The owner's name and details, along with those of the horse, are registered.

If you buy a horse with a freeze brand, it is very important to make sure that you change the details on the database.

Freeze branding is a deterrent because it is an obvious security measure; the downside is that brands can be altered, and the numbers and letters changed.

Hot-iron branding is popular among the warmblood breeds such as the Hanoverian and Oldenburg, and some native British pony breeds. Hot-iron brands fall into two categories — breed brands that identify the horse to a breed society, and personal brands for owner identity and tracking. The hair on the branded area is generally slightly darker than normal, and the area is slightly raised. Hot-iron branding is painful, although the process is very quick.

Hoof branding is another form of hot-iron branding, but the brand is applied to the hooves, and is therefore painless. However, due to the hoof growth, the brand needs to be redone every six to nine months. This is a visible deterrent, but at the same time its visibility can be undesirable in the show ring.

Other Methods

Blood and DNA tests are also used to identify horses. These are not deterrents, but provide conclusive evidence about the horse and its pedigree. Blood testing has been used for some years, especially in the Thoroughbred racing industry. New technological developments have made DNA testing a viable prospect that is very accurate and less costly than blood testing. The vet removes several mane or tail hairs with the root or hair follicle attached. This is then tested and a DNA pattern established. Some breed societies such as the Arabian Horse Association require this for registration, and it may be that in the long term, DNA tests will replace the identification drawings in identity documents.

Trainer's Tip
Once you have bought your branding irons for hoof branding, your farrier will be able to re-brand the feet for you.

Security Marks

- Microchips are inserted into the neck using a hypodermic needle; they provide a permanent, nontamperable record of the horse and owner details.
- Freeze branding is a cold-iron brand; hair in the branded area grows back white.
- Hot-iron branding is used with some warmblood breeds as a breed brand and as a personal brand; the process is quick, but painful.
- Hoof branding, a hot-iron technique, is painless but needs to be redone every six to nine months.
- Lip tattoos can be difficult to read and fade over time.
- Blood testing to ascertain parentage is quickly being replaced by the more efficient and economic DNA testing.

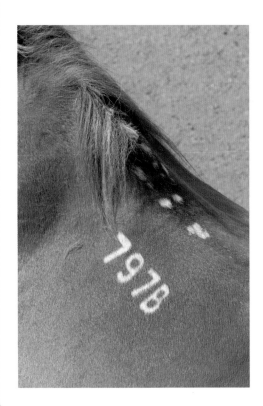

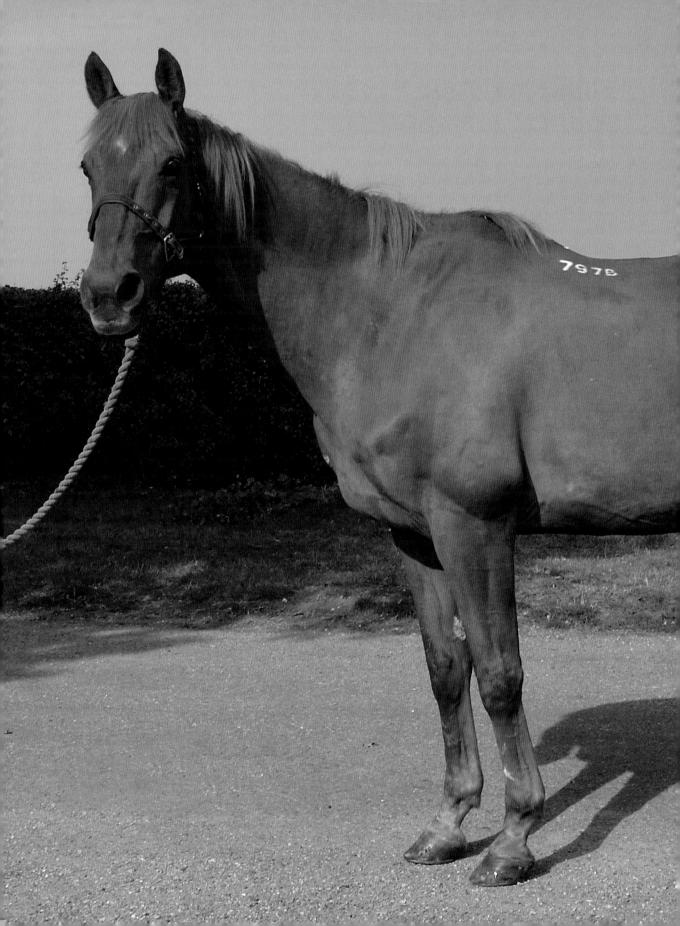

Securing Your Property and Anti-theft Measures

There are a number of ways you can secure your property and deter would-be thieves, and one of the best is to install burglar alarms and motion detector lights.

Alarms

There are many different types of alarms available, ranging from the do-it-yourself variety to the highly technical types that require professional installation. Some alarms come with security lights as a package. It is important to make sure that at least two people know your alarm keypad number, or have alarm keys, and it's preferable for a close neighbor to be one of these. If an alarm bell rings for any length of time without being shut off, a burglar will assume that the premises are unmanned and therefore easy pickings — alarm or not. If alarming stable doors, make sure that there are no wires or other key elements of the alarm that can be demolished by your horse. Keep all alarm wires and hardware as hidden as possible; it is easy for burglars to cut power wires and disable the alarms.

Security Lights and CCTV

Security lights are a great deterrent, and very useful on long, dark winter evenings. When placing security lights, make sure that the sensors are high up on buildings and as inconspicuous as possible. Enthusiastic thieves will attempt to swivel the sensors to the sky if they are able to get to them, which renders the lights useless. Keep any dark corners and your driveway lit. If there are any other routes into and out of your premises, light these, too.

CCTV (closed-circuit television) is a great bonus, but is also expensive. There are some more reasonable packages available now, but by and large, installing CCTV is quite an investment. Having said that, it acts both as a deterrent and as a means for identifying thieves.

Trainer's Tip

Make sure the structural quality of your doors is sound — there is no point padlocking something that is on the verge of collapse!

Common Sense Pays

Keeping everything locked goes without saying; however, make sure that if you are locking stables, there is always someone on hand who either knows the combination or has a key. This is vital in case of fire or emergency, and it must be possible for someone to get your horse out in a situation such as this. Leaving keys or combination numbers with neighbors is good, but if you are going to be away for a night, make sure

CCTV in action providing several different views of a horse establishment. These cameras also are useful for breeding facilities where pregnant mares and foals can be monitored without being disrupted.

that the neighbors will be in. Padlocks vary in quality and it is worth buying reinforced ones that are difficult to saw through. Chaining and padlocking both ends of all your perimeter field gates, and turning the top hinge upside down when hanging gates further prevents people from simply lifting them off their hinges.

Try to keep as few loose valuables as possible in your yard, and all tools and equipment locked away. If this is not possible then at least chain them up. Don't have a big sign on your tack room announcing what it is! Try to keep all of your outbuildings looking much the same, so that thieves are not able to target the tack room specifically. This makes their job harder, increasing the chance of their being discovered.

The power of a dog should never be underestimated. No one knows if your barking dog is fierce or not. Keeping a guard dog on a yard undoubtedly puts many thieves off. Failing that, a recording of a barking dog on a time switch in one of your outbuildings can be effective, too.

Having people around is one of the best deterrents. Always having some level of activity in your yard is a great advantage.

Security on the Move

Trailers and trucks are great targets for thieves. Painting your zip or postal code on the outside of their roofs is a good deterrent, and makes tracing them easier. Other measures for securing them are wheel clamps, alarms and immobilizers. It is also possible to get your vehicle microchipped, and tack can be chipped, too. This won't deter anyone, but will help you trace your belongings in the event of a burglary. Label everything — rugs, tack, buckets, etc. — it all helps.

Bear in mind there are often burglars who specifically target horse shows and competitions. Never leave your vehicle unlocked, even while you just run to the secretary's tent, and try to keep all blankets, tack, etc., out of sight and locked in the truck or trailer.

quick reference

Security and Anti-theft Measures

- Burglar alarms, security lights, motion detectors, CCTV and a barking dog are all options.
- Lock everything with decent padlocks.
- Label everything with zip or postal code or name.
- Put zip or postal code on the roof of the truck or trailer; use wheel clamps and immobilizers.
- Chain perimeter field gates at both ends, and turn top hinges upside down.
- Have someone around as much as possible.
- Microchip vehicles and tack.
- Keep everything locked up at competitions; often, vehicles are left open, ramps down and equipment lying in full view. A dog in the trailer/truck or tied to it can be a great deterrent.

4

HOUSING

Horses can be kept at grass or stabled. Keeping a horse that is in work stabled is more convenient; however, the stabled horse is in a very unnatural environment (see Chapter 1) and its movements are greatly restricted. It is essential that a stabled horse, unless it is stabled for veterinary reasons, is turned out every day for a period of time — simply exercising them is not enough. Horses need the release of being able to wander around, graze, roll and "be a horse": when denied this, often a horse will develop bad habits, borne out of boredom and frustration.

Some horses and ponies do well kept at grass on a year-round basis although it may be necessary to supplement feed during the winter months, or restrict grass in the spring. All fields should have good shelter, clean water, feed, adequate fencing and a safe environment. It may be necessary to rug the horse in the winter, and provide fly sheets and fly sprays in the summer. The ratio of pasture per horse varies across the United States, depending on the climate — in some parts of Wyoming, for example, it takes 20 acres (8 ha) to run one horse, while in parts of Virginia you might expect to allocate 1½ to 2 acres (0.6 to 0.8 ha) of pasture per horse. The grass-kept horse will not be able to undertake the degree of work that a stabled horse can, and will not maintain a similar level of fitness. Horses can be worked lightly off grass, but if the work increases, then their feed must be supplemented in ratio to the work.

Basic Stable Design

There are two basic types of stable blocks – the traditional brick or wooden single row block, and the barn. Barns are buildings that contain a series of stables, or stalls, down each side, and offer a "weather friendly" method of stable management.

STABLE BLOCK

Choosing the right location for your stables is important. They should be placed on level, well-draining land out of prevailing winds. There needs to be good vehicular access as well as a supply of water and power. The yard area should be enclosed with a solid post-and-rail fence. Above all else, stables need to be safe for your horse and safe for you to work in and around. Therefore, make sure you keep your main hay storage away from the stables to cut down fire risk and also keep the muck heap at a good distance to prevent flies and odor.

The roof of the stable should be pitched for drainage (with gutters) and needs to provide ample head room — the walls of the stable should be at least 8 feet (2.4 m) from the ground to the bottom of the eaves. It is preferable, though not essential, for the roof to extend out over the doorway as this provides added shelter.

In my experience, the larger the stall the better. The doors should open outward, or slide, but never open inward. Proper stable latches and

On average a 1,000-pound (450 kg) horse will produce roughly 2 gallons (8 l) of moisture a day from air breathed out — a staggering statistic when considering condensation buildup in barns.

bolts always should be used, and a top bolt with a secondary bottom kick bolt installed for extra security. The height of the bottom half of the stable door should be in relation to the size of your horse or pony. It is a good idea to have a strip of smooth metal casing covering the top of the bottom half of the door, which will discourage your horse from chewing.

Ventilation

Stables and horse barns are predisposed to be dusty and often damp — both of which are leading causes of respiratory irritation — so good ventilation is always a major consideration.

Windows are usually on the same wall as the door. All windows should be barred on the inside to keep the horse away from the glass and latches. Some windows hinge from the bottom and open outward, which tends to cut down on drafts, while others hinge from the bottom and open inward, although these take up more space in the stable.

I like to have a further opening on the wall opposite the door: during the summer this provides excellent airflow through the stable, and in winter it can be securely closed to prevent drafts. This system is particularly good for horses that are stabled for long periods and are on short turnout schedules as it gives them an extra outlook and view.

Walls and Floors

Traditional stable blocks were built of stone or brick, both of which look good, but are expensive. Wooden stable blocks are popular, as are

STABLE SIZE

Pony stable 10 x 12 feet (3 x 3.7 m)
Horse up to 16 h.h. 12 x 14 feet (3.7 x 4.3 m)
Horse over 16 h.h. 14 x 14 feet (4.3 x 4.3 m)
Foaling stable 16 x 16 feet (4.9 x 4.9 m)

DOOR DIMENSIONS

Total doorway height at least 8 feet (2.4 m)
Bottom half of door 4½ feet (1.4 m)
Top half of door 3½ feet (1.06 m)
Door width 4 feet (1.2 m)

combination wood and brick, but the wood must be treated with a fire retardant, and will require annual weatherproofing and minor repairs.

Cinder block and concrete stables are relatively inexpensive and last well. A stable should be built on a concrete base and the floor should be angled slightly toward either a central drain or a long drain running lengthwise down the front or back of the stable block. The floor also should be slightly ridged, with the ridges running in the direction of the drains. Good drainage is paramount, and will save money on bedding.

Drains require maintenance, and should be swept out and cleaned regularly. They can be situated either along the front or the back of the stable, or in the middle, although these are harder to keep clean. Those that run parallel to the front are generally the easiest to maintain.

It is helpful to have a margin of concrete extending in front of the stable block, which provides a hard standing for tying up, and is easier to keep clean.

Recently there have been great advances in flooring materials. A particularly good floor, which would be laid on top of the concrete base, is one of solid rubber bricks. This is a warm base and provides better cushioning than concrete. Many indoor barns will have rubber brick flooring extending through the central alleyway, which is also excellent, but is difficult to sweep. Alternatively, thick rubber mats can be laid over concrete. One of the advantages of rubber mats is that they can be lifted, and the floor beneath

thoroughly cleaned. This is especially useful for cleaning following illness, or in between new horses moving into a stable.

Roofs

Tiles are good but expensive; they are fire retardant and can be easily replaced. Roofing felt must be treated with a fire retardant. It is a good "quiet" roof, unlike corrugated metal, which can be noisy and has poor insulation properties. Clear panels in the roof that act as skylights are great for providing extra natural light.

Fixtures and Fittings

For safety reasons these should be kept to a minimum, and all light switches, wiring and lights should be completely out of reach of the horse.

Automatic water dispensers are excellent and labor saving, but they must be installed along with a water consumption gauge. Many of them have removable bowls for easy cleaning, and built in heaters to prevent them freezing in the winter.

If you are using a manger it should be securely put up in a corner, with no sharp edges. Hayracks are now rarely used, and tie-up rings for haynets, or tying up, should be positioned high on the wall, never below the level of the withers. When tying

up haynets, remember that when the net is empty it will hang lower than when it is full.

BARNS

Horse barns are user friendly, airy but well insulated and provide a beneficial social environment for the horse. Their major drawback is the lack of ability to provide isolation facilities for new or sick horses. Another consideration with barns is dust, so good ventilation and stable management is essential.

Barns vary in construction, materials and layout, but should include a door at each end; these help with ventilation and can be important in emergency situations. Barns should be built with an anti-condensation lining, and roof and gable vents to keep clean air flowing through.

The stalls are generally made of adjustable panels that come in a variety of designs — either solid panels that allow no contact between adjoining stalls or half-height wooden panels topped with closely set vertical metal bars. The doors can either be sliding or open like a conventional stable door. This adjustable system allows you to put up different-sized stalls with relative ease, useful if you are housing everything from a pony to a hunter to a broodmare.

Many barns are designed so that the stalls have doors both facing into the barn and on the exterior wall. Runs can then be attached to the outside of the barn, which allow the horse added room for movement. These runs are great if you have the room. They must be constructed of heavy-duty metal panels or railings that are a minimum of 6 feet (1.8 m) high. The central alleyway should be no less than 10 feet (3 m) wide, preferably 12–14 feet (3.5–4 m).

Exterior and interior views of a beautifully maintained barn showing roof ventilation and clear skylights, stables running down the sides, suitable access doors, and sliding doors installed for each stall.

Bedding Options

When choosing a bedding material for your horse, you need to consider a number of factors (see right). Whatever type you decide to use, it should be dust-free, clean, absorbent, warm and nontoxic.

FACTORS TO CONSIDER
- Does the horse suffer from allergies?
- Does the horse suffer from RAO (recurrent airway obstruction)?
- How cost effective is it?
- Will the horse eat the bedding?
- How warm or cold are your stables?
- Are you going to be deep littering, semi-deep littering or mucking out daily?
- Does your horse get cast often?
- Does your horse suffer from capped hocks or elbows or sore pressure points?
- What facilities do you have for the muck heap?
- What storage do you have for the bedding?

STRAW
- Is economical.
- Is not very absorbent; moisture runs through it to the floor, so drains must be kept clean.
- Some horses will eat it.
- It can be dusty.
- It takes up a lot of room in the muck heap.
- It is best to use wheat straw; the stalks are light and long and the horse will be less inclined to eat this than oat straw, which is more absorbent, but can be heavy and smell when wet.
- Barley straw must not contain awns, the barbed parts of barley that can cause skin irritations.

WOOD SHAVINGS
- Are expensive.
- Can now be dust extracted.
- Are very absorbent and warm and work well for semi-deep or deep littering.
- Can be used in conjunction with rubber matting.
- Are easy to store and make a relatively small muck heap that will rot down quite quickly.

PAPER
- Can be expensive but is increasingly popular.
- Is dust-free and very absorbent.
- Can be difficult to manage; it tends to blow around, and muck heap control can be difficult.
- Using recycled paper is environmentally friendly.

HEMP
- Is quite expensive.
- Comes from the flax plant and is dried and compressed to form a dust-free, absorbent bed.
- Is light, easy to muck out and is warm and insulating.
- If the horse eats the bedding, hemp has a tendency to swell, which can cause severe problems in the digestive system, leading to colic.

COMPRESSED WOOD FIBER PELLETS
- Are expensive.
- Provide a good clean, low-dust and high-absorbency bedding.
- They are easy to clean – the damp areas of the bed clump together, in the way some cat litters do.
- Similar to hemp, if a horse ate much of this bedding it would cause swelling and digestive problems, however it is unlikely to be eaten.

PEAT MOSS
- Virtually dust free.
- A warm bedding
- Can be expensive and difficult to muck out.
- Useful for laminitic horses on stall rest.
- Makes stalls appear dark.

WOOD FIBER
- Can be quite economical.
- Is very absorbent and drains well.
- Is suitable for daily cleaning or deep littering.

Hemp

Paper

Woodchip

Rubber matting

RUBBER MATTING

- Is expensive.
- Makes excellent flooring and bedding, used in conjunction with wood chips or paper.
- Is designed to "give" under the weight of the horse, so when the horse lies down the mat contours to the body — in theory.
- Relies on good drainage, and it may be necessary to alter the slope of the stable floor so that the drainage works.

ANTI-CAST CUSHIONS

Some horses have a tendency to become cast in the stable, which can make them panic and lead to them damaging their legs as they struggle to stand up. Anti-cast cushions are padded, extend part way up the stable walls from the floor, and are contoured so that a horse can push itself away from the cushion and so stand up. They are a very good idea, but are expensive. They are completely removable and easy to clean, and are of particular benefit in veterinary yards.

Above is an old farm building used as a stable with a deep litter bed. If a horse doesn't have sufficient bedding, it may get capped hocks (right).

Trainer's Tip

Horses hate to urinate on a hard surface due to "splashing" up their legs. If you are using mats in your stable be sure to use at least a small amount of conventional bedding to allow the horse a "soft" place to urinate.

quick reference

Bedding

- Before choosing your bedding, assess whether your horse has any particular special needs.
- Always choose a dust-free bedding.
- Consider rubber matting, but provide your horse with a layer of conventional bedding on top.
- Always bank your bedding up around the walls to provide the horse with extra cushioning.

Muck Control

Daily mucking out takes longer than deep littering, but by and large is more hygienic. If you are deep littering, manage your bed well to prevent ammonia and mold spores building up, and watch out for foot problems such as thrush.

THE MUCK HEAP

Muck heaps should be positioned well away from your stables to cut down on flies and smell, but should be easily accessible by wheelbarrow and a tractor for ease of use. Solid three-sided structures are the best design for a muck heap. Keep piling the muck up, making sure the outside edge is square. It is important to have a well-compressed heap to aid the decomposition process, and to keep the temperature high enough to kill larvae and parasites. You need to let a heap rot for at least 12 months before using it on your fields, to ensure that any eggs or larvae have died and to prevent spreading worms across your pastures. In very dry climates, heap decomposition will be severely delayed.

When you construct your structure, make sure that the opening is wide enough for a tractor loader to fit into it. That way if you are not able to utilize your muck heap yourself, you can organize for a local farmer to haul it away for you.

Deep littering is when only the droppings and immediate wet areas are removed daily with fresh bedding added on top. Then once monthly the entire bed is removed, the floor thoroughly cleaned, and a new bed started. Deep litter beds provide excellent cushioning and are warm, but must be well managed to avoid ammonia and mold spores developing.

Semi-deep littering is when the entire bed is removed and cleaned weekly. It is easier to manage and less work than the monthly clean out.

Mucking out is when the entire bed is cleaned daily. Clean bedding is swept to the side and the floor is exposed through the day, before the bed is put back down at night. This takes longer on a daily basis, but is more hygienic.

Trainer's Tip
Respiratory problems can be caused by dusty unhygienic environments — dust-free bedding is essential for a healthy horse.

daily mucking out

- Remove the horse from the stable when mucking out to prevent it inhaling any dust or spores during the disturbance of the bed.
- If you are not able to move the horse, tie it up and make sure you always use the fork away from the horse. Never leave any tools in the stable.
- Remove the water buckets from the stable, wash out and clean.
- Remove all the droppings.
- Starting at the front and working backward, go through the bedding, moving clean bedding into one pile and removing any wet patches.
- Sweep the floor clean.
- Leave the bed up to air through the day, and replace at night ("setting" the bed), adding any extra bedding if needed.
- Remove any droppings during the day.
- Replace the water buckets after mucking out.

Above: A well maintained and tidy muck heap is shown. This type of muck heap, with its three walls and hard standing is ideal. Left: Mucking out a deep litter stable. Be sure to either remove the water buckets, or cover them, as seen here, so they remain clean.

Pastures

The safety of the field is vital when considering pasturing. There is, of course, the "perfect field" just as there is the "perfect stable" and occasionally the "perfect horse"; however, all of these are hard to find, and most of the time we have to work with what we have.

TYPES OF FENCING

All important for safety and security, there are many factors to think about when choosing fencing. Among the considerations, make sure you are able to undertake the maintainence and keep the fence in good order.

Post and Rail with Hedge

This is the best form of fencing as the hedge provides a good windbreak. Post and rail fencing is safe, sturdy and aesthetic, but is very expensive and requires annual maintenance such as weatherproofing and worn rail replacement. The disadvantage is that many horses will chew this type of fencing, although you can overcome this by painting the rails with anti-cribbing products.

If you have a hedge surrounding your field, make sure that it is not poisonous.

Post and Smooth Wire

This is a relatively economic type of fence and can be very effective, and it is possible to build these fences using an insulation system that allows the wire to be electrified — which is ideal. The tension of smooth wire must be maintained at all times — a loopy smooth wire fence is very dangerous, and a horse can sustain horrific injuries if a foot becomes trapped in the wire.

Synthetic Fencing

Solid post and rail synthetic fencing is generally white and attractive to look at, but very expensive.

Synthetic fencing also comes on a roll and can be nailed to the fence post. This has a degree of flexibility, so that if a horse runs into it there is a slight cushioning effect. Many of these types of fences are sold with tension devices that allow you to easily tighten the strands.

Mesh and Rail

Small hole mesh fencing is very useful, especially for foals and "escape artist" ponies. The mesh is generally nailed to posts with a single top rail, and extends from the top rail down to the ground. It is semi-flexible, and if a foal hits it at full speed, it tends to "bounce." It is very safe, and will not be chewed, but is expensive. It is important to get the right tension when putting it up, and to make sure that the mesh is small enough to prevent even the smallest of hooves from becoming entangled in it.

Electric Fence

This is one of the best types of fencing for horses, and can be used with an existing fence by

Different fencing Top: Wire. Right: Electric. Middle: Post and rail; to service more than one field, site water tanks along the fence line and well away from gate ways or corners; the best fencing has a hedge behind. Far right: A substantial fencing perfect for stallions.

running it around the inside perimeter. This can keep your horse safe, contained and out of danger. Electric fencing varies enormously, from the movable to a semi-permanent form. Where possible, a "tape" fence is better than wire because the horse can see it more easily. Horses will quickly learn to respect an electric fence and will stay well away from it. It is expensive initially, but you can take it with you if you move, and is well worth the money. If you decide to make the investment, go for a good-quality brand name, and remember to keep the battery charged or the power switched on.

OTHER CONSIDERATIONS
Gates

These should be wide enough to safely move horses through, and to accommodate machinery such as tractors for fertilizing, mowing, etc. Generally, 5 feet (1.5 m) or more will work. It is easier to have the gate open into the field, and try

FENCING KNOW-HOW

- All fencing must be safe and well maintained.
- The top of your fence should theoretically be the height of your horse's back — however, this is not always practical, and a good solid fence of at least 5 feet (1.5 m) high will generally contain all but the most ambitious of horses.
- The bottom rail should be a minimum of 1 foot (30 cm) from the ground. This will prevent the horse from catching a foot on it. If only using a two-rail fence, the bottom rail can be higher.
- Make sure rails are attached on the inside of the posts, not the outside.
- It is a good idea to "round off" corners in your field, especially when you have several horses turned out together. Nail a long rail diagonally across the corner — this prevents a horse becoming trapped or cornered.
- Never, ever, use barbed wire, sheep netting or any kind of pointed metal fencing.

to hang the gate so that it only opens as far as you push it. Gates need to be safe, with equine-friendly latches, bolts and openings. Keep both ends of your gate chained and locked, and put the top hinge on facing down so that it is not possible to lift the gate off its hinges.

Shelter

Fields must provide shelter for horses and be sufficient to accommodate the number of horses in the field without injury. A natural stand of trees, or a thick hedge, provides good shelter from the wind, but does not protect from driving rain.

- Site a shelter on the highest point of your field so the ground will drain away from it, and place it out of the prevailing winds. Try to locate your shelter so that it can serve more than one field.
- Make sure the shelter is big enough: allow roughly 12 x 12 feet (3.7 x 3.7 m) per horse.
- Three-sided shelters are good because there is lots of escape room for the horses.

Trainer's Tip
It is useful to have a shelter that you are able to close and turn into an impromptu stable if necessary. Slip rails work well.

- Four-sided shelters must have a doorway 10 feet (3 m) wide minimum at *both* ends.
- Doorways and the shelter itself must be high, wide and safe.
- Consider the footing of your shelter, and always bed it down — and clean it out.
- Some shelters now are movable, which is useful when rotating your fields.

Water

A clear, clean flowing stream is the best source of water for any field, although a very sandy river bottom can cause colic if the horse ingests large amounts of grit. If using a natural water source, make sure that the horses can easily get down to the stream to drink without slipping, and that the water gap area is large enough to prevent squashing and barging. A stagnant source such as a pond is not adequate; the water quality will be poor, and if the pond freezes over during the winter it can be dangerous for the horses if they attempt to walk out onto it.

Automatic water tanks are great but, as with any water container, need to be regularly cleaned out. Tanks should have thermostats on them so that they can be heated in the winter – especially in areas where temperatures drop below freezing

for months on end. They should be on a solid base to stop the ground from becoming poached; the concrete needs to be ridged for traction, otherwise broken up brick or gravel works well. Also, make sure that the ballcock and other working components of the tank are safely covered and out of the reach of curious horses.

If automatic tanks are not an option then any clean, safe receptacle such as a large rubberized bucket will work. Rubber withstands greater extremes of temperature and is less likely to become brittle and crack than plastic. Make sure that the water tanks are big enough to accommodate the number of horses in the field without drying up before you can refill them. Also, try to secure the tanks so that they are not knocked over. To keep them upright, place the containers in large tires.

Remember to keep all faucets securely covered so that horses cannot damage them or injure themselves. Make a simple wooden box to cover the faucet, and fill it with insulation material to help prevent freezing in the winter. Use good-quality hoses that won't split and crack, and drain them after use in winter to keep them from freezing up, and in summer to prevent a buildup of algae on the inside of the hose.

POSITIONING A WATER TANK

- Place your water tank along a fence line.
- Keep the tank away from gateways.
- Do not put your tank in or near the corner of a field where a horse might get trapped.
- Keep the tank away from trees (which will drop leaves and debris into it); and any low branches that might cause injury to the horse.

Trainer's Tip

Rain scald is a nasty skin condition caused by an organism that lives in the soil and thrives in wet conditions. If a horse has a dirty or dusty coat, and then gets soaking wet, the organism grows. The hair starts to fall out in large clumps, and the skin will become inflamed and painful. Bathing the area with antiseptic shampoo and treating the skin with salve or mineral oil will clear it up, but the best cure is prevention — provide your horse with shelter, or a waterproof rug to prevent the onset of rain scald.

SAFETY IN THE FIELD

Regular maintenance checks must be made of your pasture to make sure that it is a safe environment for your horse.

Poisonous Plants

The majority of poisonous plants have a bitter taste and most horses will avoid eating them unless they are very hungry. Luckily, many poisonous plants tend to grow in horse-poor pasture and on neglected land. So by keeping your fields in good shape, and providing your horse with extra forage if grass is short, you will help to avoid the chance of your horse ingesting toxic material.

Trainer's Tip

Some poisonous plants are as toxic when they are dead as when they are alive. For this reason, if possible, digging up poisonous plants, rather than spraying them is preferable.

Poisonous plants and weeds should either be sprayed with a suitable weedkiller or dug up by the roots. If buying weedkiller, read the instructions to make sure it will kill the plants you need to clear and that it won't kill your grass. Keep your horses off the pasture for at least a day after spraying, **or for whatever period your product recommends.** If spraying weeds, keep a watch on the weather: most weedkillers need to be on the plant for at least seven hours before being rained on.

Make sure that your field does not contain poisonous trees or hedges, and if it does, fence these off so your horse is not able to reach them.

Below and on page 77 are some poisonous trees and plants to watch for.

- Laburnum
- Yew
- Oak — the acorns are toxic
- Horse chestnut — the conkers are toxic
- Deadly nightshade
- Foxglove
- Hemlock
- Rhododendron

- Laurel
- Privet
- Buttercups
- Bracken
- Potato plants (and any other plants that contain nicotine-related compounds)
- Horsetail
- St. John's wort
- Oleander
- Tansy ragwort. Extremely poisonous and very difficult to eradicate. If it is ingested in any quantity, irreparable liver damage usually results. While the plant is alive, it is bitter to taste, and most horses will avoid it. However, when it dies and dries out, it loses its bitter taste and a horse will eat it (especially if mixed in hay).
- Yellow Star Thistle
- Larkspur
- Locoweed
- Ground Ivy

Bear in mind that poisonous plants also can be mixed with something else, such as hay. Check hay thoroughly before you buy it and, better yet, visit the fields from where you intend to purchase your hay to see what state they are in. It is much easier to spot weeds while they are growing than when they have dried.

HAZARD CHECK

- Rabbit holes, or other holes — fill in with rocks and soil.
- Walk the fence line at least once a week to check for weak spots, broken rails or loose wire.
- Make sure there are no relics left in the field from previous owners, i.e., dangerous farm equipment such as harrows, rolls of wire or anything else hidden in the grass.
- Watch for poisonous plants in your own field, and in neighboring pastures — seeds can be windblown and travel for miles.
- Keep any very boggy areas, dangerous ponds or other "hot spots" fenced off.

Looking After Grass

Horses are picky eaters and hard on fields; they will eat some areas down to the dirt, while leaving other areas — mostly where they urinate or defecate — to grow long and lush. Add to this the natural damage that occurs to the ground during winter and poor grass growth, and it makes for a rough-looking field by spring.

Ideally, pastures should be rotated. Choose your winter pasture, taking into account the shelter, drainage and type of grass, and rest it through the summer. At the end of the summer, move your horses to the winter pasture. Harrow and fertilize the summer paddocks and leave to rest over the winter.

Divide your land into three or four paddocks. Rotationally graze the paddocks for three to four weeks at a time. After moving your horses to the next field, ideally graze the previous pasture with cattle for two weeks before allowing a period of three weeks to rest and regrow. Cattle will eat grass the horses leave and help to keep the worm burden down — worms that harm the horse gut are killed in the cattle gut. If cattle are not available, keep the grass topped with a tractor, which will help keep weeds down and improve the overall quality of the grass.

During regrowth time you can lightly harrow and fertilize if necessary. Harrowing in the early spring is also beneficial; it removes any dead grass and aerates the soil.

If patches of your pasture have suffered, it is possible to reseed, but seek professional advice on the mix of grass seed you should use.

Trainer's Tip

A horse will often find a favorite chewing spot on a fence, and come back to it again and again. To stop this, paint the spot with hot sauce or Tabasco. This is more economical than having to pay for a large pail of anti-cribbing liquid, and is just as effective.

ABOUT GRASS

- Grass has its highest protein content during the early growth period of May through June. Donkeys, ponies and overweight horses are most at risk from laminitis at this time.
- Over the summer the nutrient value of the grass gradually decreases, although in the autumn there is often a short burst of growth.
- By winter the grass is basically only a fiber provider.

Pastures

- A pasture must have strong, safe fencing, a good clean water supply and shelter large enough to safely house all the horses in the field.
- Keep field gates locked and chained.
- Check fields constantly for poisonous plants; dig up rather than spray, if possible. Fence off any poisonous trees or hedges, or other dangerous areas in the field.
- Check fields weekly for hazards.
- Droppings should be picked up at least once a week to prevent contaminating the pasture with worm eggs.
- Try to rotate your pastures.
- Try to graze cattle or sheep on your pastures with your horses.
- Keep the grass mowed, if necessary, to prevent it growing too long.
- Harrow fields in early spring and autumn.
- Fertilize pastures in the autumn, if necessary, and do not graze for at least four weeks after fertilizing. Always seek professional advice before fertilizing — serious damage can be done to the land and, more importantly, your horses by improper use of fertilizers.
- Pastures should be rested for a minimum of three weeks during the growing season and longer over the winter.
- Roll pastures in early spring to flatten out poached ground from the winter.
- If reseeding grass mix, do so in the early spring and it should be ready by autumn, or reseed in the late summer for the following spring.
- After reseeding you can roll the ground, which will help the seed to take. Rolling can only be done when the land is dry enough that the tractor doesn't tear it up, but still wet enough that the roller has effect.

It is beneficial to have a soil sample taken in your pastures, which will tell you the relative acid or alkaline content of the soil. This will guide you on the type of fertilizer to use. As a general rule, acidic soil benefits from lime or ground chalk, while very alkaline soil benefits from good old-fashioned farm yard manure.

For pastures that have become poached and uneven, harrowing followed by rolling can help to flatten out the ground. Rolling only works if the ground is just wet enough to be smoothed over, but not too wet that the roller and tractor tear it up even more. Try not to roll more than once or twice in the early spring because it also compresses the ground surface, which can discourage the grass growth.

Some good grasses for horse pasture are shown on page 76. Two others are creeping red fescue and crested dog's tail. Wild clover is lower nutritionally than cultivated clover, and is preferable in the pasture because it doesn't cause as many digestive problems if ingested in large amounts.

Horses also love wild herbs, which also have a good nutritional value. You can seed certain herbs around the edge of your pastures if there are none naturally occurring in your fields. Good herbs for horse pasture are chicory, garlic, sheep's parsley, comfrey, burnet and yarrow.

GOOD GRASSES FOR THE PASTURE

The best pastures consist of palatable and nutritious grasses with a mix of herbs as listed on page 75 and some white clover. Perennial rye grass combined with creeping red fescue, timothy, meadow grass and some cocksfoot provides a good dense sward.

Meadow grass
This tends to grow quite densely, which helps to prevent weed growth. It is palatable to horses, nutritionally good and important for a mixed pasture.

Cocksfoot
A good horse grass but not especially favored by horses.

White clover
Highly nutritious, its root nodules provide nitrogen to the soil, increasing its fertility and quality.

Timothy
Very palatable and nutritional. Good for grazing and haymaking.

Rye grass
Palatable and highly nutritious, it grows quickly and well.

POISONOUS PLANTS IN THE PASTURE

It's important to rid your pastures of these noxious flora, which can be very dangerous to your horse. Fence off any poisonous trees and either dig up the roots of poisonous plants or use weedkiller on them. Proper pasture maintenance should decrease their incidence.

Buttercups
These have a bitter, acrid taste and are generally not consumed. If ingested in quantity, however, they can cause mouth blisters, gut pain, convulsions and, occasionally, death.

Oak trees
If ingested in quantity, acorns may cause kidney damage.

Bracken
Large amounts can cause convulsions and death.

Ragwort
Exceptionally poisonous to horses and extremely virulent.

Yew
All parts are poisonous. Can cause sudden death a few hours after eating.

5

FEEDING

In recent years there have been huge developments in the science behind equine nutrition, and this has led to more information and a greater range of products. While this is beneficial, it can also make deciding what to feed your horse confusing. If in doubt, consult an equine nutritionist, but bear in mind that many nutritionists work directly for feed companies, and their advice will be to recommend one of their products! Having said that, most top feed companies offer similar products, which promise the same results, only market them under different names.

Despite the science, feeding basically comes down to common sense. Proper feeding is vital to the fundamental health of the horse, and also allows the individual to reach its maximum athletic ability. Overfeeding is as dangerous as underfeeding, and finding the right balance is the key.

In theory, a horse should obtain all the vitamins and minerals it needs from good grass.

There are three functions that feeding should cover:
1 **Maintenance** Keeping the horse in a healthy condition. When weight loss or weight gain occurs, the level of feeding is not correct.
2 **Growth and repair** Enabling the body to renew and repair tissue and cells during growth, normal wear and tear, and build muscle.
3 **Energy** Providing the horse with the "fuel" to work.

The Feed Room

The feed room must be secure, free from dust and moisture, and able to be barricaded against any uninvited equine guests. Ideally, it should be easily accessible and close to the stables. It is preferable to have a water supply including a sink, but if this is not possible, then situate your feed room near an outside tap. The room needs to be vermin-proof, horse-proof and insulated. If you have to store bags of feed, keep them off the floor on pallets; however, it is better to bring in what you need as you need it, as feeds have a shelf life.

Each horse's feed program should be clearly marked — whiteboards or blackboards work well — and any changes made to the diet must be noted on the board. In busy yards with lots of horses, each horse's stall should be labeled with the name of the horse, its feeding ration and any other relevant information (allergic to oats, etc.) to cut down on the chances of a horse receiving the wrong feed.

One person should be responsible for overseeing the feeding — making up feeds, ordering feed, monitoring individual diets and maintaining the feed room. This cuts down on any confusion.

The earliest evidence of supplementing horse feed with grain dates to 800 BC. The Assyrians first fed barley, using it to boost the energy of their war horses.

Trainer's Tip
Keep feeding simple and methodical and, most importantly, consider the needs of the individual horse.

MATTERS AFFECTING INDIVIDUAL REQUIREMENTS

- **Size** The bigger the horse, the more food that's needed.
- **Temperament** Some horses are more excitable than others. Horses that live on nervous energy can find it hard to keep weight on.
- **Work** How much, how often and how hard.
- **Age and Sex** Youngsters, seniors, lactating or pregnant mares, and stallions during breeding season require special feeding.
- **Season** The horse expends more energy in the winter just to stay warm so it will need more food.
- **Breed** Arabians, Quarter Horses, many pony breeds, and often warmblood breeds are "good doers": they convert their food highly efficiently and maintain their weight well on smaller rations.

RULES OF FEEDING

- The horse should have free access to water at all times apart from right before or right after hard work.
- Make changes to the diet very gradually; when introducing a new feed you should do so over at least a month to allow the microbial culture to adapt.
- Feed according to the individual's requirements (see box, page 79).
- Feed the correct ratio of roughage to concentrate (grain and grain byproducts).
- Always weigh your feed, never "guesstimate" amounts or feed by the coffee can!
- Feed quality feeds.
- Never feed a meal that is over 4 pounds (1.8 kg) in weight.
- Feed little and often, allowing at least four hours between feedings.
- Feed at regular intervals and establish a feeding routine.
- Allow at least one hour (and preferably more) after feeding and before working. Never feed a horse directly after work.
- Always feed moistened feeds.
- Feed salt as a supplement, or supply a salt lick, especially during the summer.
- Feed succulents whenever possible.
- Do not keep soaked beet pulp longer than a few days, and less than this in extreme heat.
- Ideally feed the horse in a rubber bucket on the ground — this is the most natural position for a horse to eat in.
- Clearly label your feed bins so that there is no confusion between feedstuffs that may look similar, i.e., horse and pony nuts and unsoaked beet pulp pellets.
- Keep all feed receptacles clean, and wash mangers after every feeding.
- Always finish all the feed in the feed bins before adding more on top.

The Feed Room

- The feed room must be horse- and vermin-proof.
- Keep written charts of every horse's feed ration.
- Keep feed sacks in vermin-proof bins (old chest freezers work well). Alternatively store off the ground on pallets.
- If possible have a tap and sink in the feed room.
- Make sure all feed bags and supplements are clearly labeled.
- Introduce new feeds slowly.
- It helps to install a cat!
- Try to keep one person in charge of feeds and the feed room to cut down on confusion.
- Keep a large sign up with notice of any horse's allergies.
- Label stables with the name and feed ration of each horse.

Methods of Feeding

The horse as a grazing animal naturally eats with its head down, and studies have shown that by eating in this way, its teeth actually wear more evenly. If possible, feed your horse from the ground. Concentrates can be offered in heavy rubber feed pans. If the horse is inclined to paw and scatter its food, then place the pan in an old tire. If using a bucket, stick to the heavy rubber type. Though initially more expensive, rubber is more durable than plastic. Remove any handles from buckets to prevent the risk of a foot becoming caught. Never tip the grain on the ground to feed, as much is wasted in this way.

If you prefer to feed using a manger, the best design is the corner variety. It must be removable for daily cleaning, and free from any sharp edges. Fit your manger at a sensible height for the height of the horse. Many modern internal stalls have sliding mangers that allow you to pour the feed in from outside the stall, and rotate the manger inward. These can be useful, although some designs do not have removable troughs, which makes them hard to clean.

When feeding grain to a large number of horses in the field, place your feed pans a long way apart. If feeding out of long troughs, make sure that you use at least two to three depending on the number of horses. They will generally sort themselves out so that everyone eats. If a horse is not able to eat due to bullying, or has special requirements, it will need to be separated from the rest to feed.

HAYNETS
Always hang haynets high to prevent the chance of a caught foot; bear in mind that an empty net will hang lower than a full one.

Keep troughs turned upside down after feeding to prevent them from filling up with water.

Feeding Hay

Hay for the stabled horse should be soaked, and is most efficiently fed in small-holed haynets. These make the horse work harder to get the hay, which makes the hay ration last longer. These nets also cut down on waste, and minimize the chance of a horse getting its foot caught.

It is possible to buy and install low-level troughs for feeding hay in the stable. These allow a horse to eat with a natural stance, but can be difficult to clean. There is also a new design of hay feeder for the stalls that fits into the corner and is shaped like an upside-down cone. It also allows a horse to eat with its head down. It is made from sturdy plastic and has no sharp edges or corners. It is easy to install and works well. Some versions have drainage holes in the bottom, which allow you to feed wet hay.

Avoid hayracks in the stall; hay and dust will fall into the eyes causing irritation. They also take up a lot of space and increase the chance of injury. Feeding hay from the ground is good for the horse, but it does result in a lot of waste and will get kicked around the stall. In the field, feeding hay on the ground is quite effective, although there will still be some waste. Feed in small piles set a good distance apart, and put out a pile for each horse, plus one extra. Hayracks in the field have similar problems to those in the barn, and there is a danger of crowding around them, with some horses being pushed out. Round bale racks where you put out a whole bale at a time are labor-saving, but not ideal. Avoid large bales; it is impossible to tell the quality of the hay in the middle. There is also a danger of mold, and of small rodents being baled; this creates a very serious risk of botulism, which can be fatal.

quick reference

Methods of Feeding

- Feed at ground level if possible.
- Use rubber rather than plastic feed buckets.
- Always remove handles from buckets in the stable.
- Mangers should be removable.
- Keep mangers at a reasonable height for the individual horse.
- Use small-holed haynets.
- Hang nets high.
- Avoid hayracks.
- Place piles of hay in the field a long way apart, and put out the same number of piles as horses, plus one.

Feed

The horse's diet must include all of the following elements: water, carbohydrates, fat, protein, vitamins and minerals. A deficiency or an excess of any of these will greatly affect the health and well-being of the horse.

Water

This is the most important aspect of feeding and also the most overlooked. In extreme cases, a horse can survive for weeks on starvation rations, but only for a couple of days if deprived of water. Water is an essential part of the diet and is fundamental to the body's functioning. Horses must have a good, clean supply of water at *all* times, other than directly before and after hard work. Horses will drink more during the summer, and a stabled horse will drink more than one kept at grass. Pregnant mares also will need more water. Dehydration causes serious problems in horses, and it is essential to make sure that your horse is drinking properly.

Water tanks must be kept clean and free from leaves, which produce bitter-tasting tannin, and algae, which can contain toxic compounds.

Carbohydrates

Carbohydrates are a horse's main source of energy and should make up the majority of its diet. There are two types of carbohydrates — simple and complex. Simple carbohydrates, which include sugar, glycogen and starch, are digested in the small intestine and absorbed into the

Trainer's Tip

Horses become accustomed to the taste of their own, local water. If traveling and staying overnight, try using a flavored drink powder in the water to encourage the horse to drink. Get the horse used to drinking this at home, before you travel.

WATER CHECKLIST

- Keep tanks and buckets clean.
- Take your own water and buckets when traveling; never use "foreign" tanks at show grounds, etc., to avoid the spread of disease.
- Always travel with electrolyte supplements to replace the salts lost in sweating, and to prevent dehydration.
- Keep water at a moderate temperature — extreme chilling and heat will put the horse off drinking.
- Use automatic water dispensers with a measuring gauge on them.
- Avoid using sandy-bottomed streams for your water source due to the risk of sand colic.
- If using a natural water source, ensure the footing is solid and that there is a large enough access to it to prevent crowding.
- If using a tank with a water flow system, catfish or goldfish work wonders at keeping the algae down.

bloodstream. Glucose, a simple sugar, is the major source of energy. It is converted to glycogen in the body, and any excess is converted to fat.

One of the main complex carbohydrates is cellulose. This is found in all plants and grasses, and is a horse's major fiber source. Fiber is vital to a healthy digestive tract. Cellulose is broken down by the bacteria and microbial culture living in a horse's hindgut (cecum and large intestine). This microbial culture is extremely important to a horse's health — a sudden change in food, some wormers, and many oral antibiotics upset this delicate balance, which is why changes to the diet must be made slowly. It can be beneficial to put a horse on a course of probiotics following antibiotics. Probiotics help to stabilize the microbial culture.

Fat

Another source of a horse's energy, fats, actually contain higher levels of energy than carbo-hydrates, but are harder to break down. The energy derived from fat is useful in "slow release" instances, such as when a horse is doing slow,

Trainer's Tip

If you are feeding low-quality protein your horse will have increased urine production, and the urine will have a strong smell.

steady work. The energy from carbohydrates is "fast release" energy, needed by horses in hard and fast work like jumping and racing. Fats also provide the horse with an insulation layer, and contribute to a healthy coat and skin.

Protein

Protein is instrumental in tissue and cell growth and repair, and in muscle building. Proteins are made up of a series of amino acids. Horses need 22 amino acids; 12 are synthesized by the liver and the remaining 10 have to be ingested through the diet — the latter are referred to as "essential amino acids." The "quality" of a protein is determined by how many essential amino acids it contains. However, labels on bags of feed that refer to a protein value are misleading. First, they do not specify the "quality" of the protein, which is important; and second, they refer to a "crude protein value," *not* the digestible protein. This means that the protein value you are actually feeding your horse is probably less than you think.

A deficiency in any essential amino acid causes major problems. The most common deficiencies are of lysine, methionine and threonine. All straight cereal crops are low in lysine, but mixed horse feeds should be balanced.

Vitamins

Vitamins are present in good, green grass and sunlight, so if your horse has access to both, it should be provided with an adequate vitamin

Trainer's Tip

Biotin as a supplement should be fed along with methionine and sulfur.

supply. Good quality hay also should provide the essential vitamins, and it is now possible to have hay samples tested to determine their nutritive values. Horses that are in very hard work, and pregnant or lactating mares, will benefit from a vitamin supplement. It is possible to overdose on vitamins, so exercise caution when supplementing feed, and always feed according to the manufacturer's guidelines.

THE MAIN WATER-SOLUBLE VITAMINS

VITAMINS	SOURCE	FUNCTION	DEFICIENCY
Vitamin B_1 (Thiamine)	Synthesized in the hindgut or ingested through green grass and plants, peas, beans and alfalfa	Nerve functions	Deficiency is rare, but will include signs of nervousness, excitability and weight loss
Vitamin B_2 (Riboflavin)	Good, green grass	Aids protein and carbohydrate metabolism	Loss of condition and energy
Folic acid linked to B_{12}	Good, green grass and cereals	Red blood cell production	Anemia
Biotin	Good, green grass and corn	Protein, fat and carbohydrate metabolism and associated with methionine and sulfur in hoof growth	Poor hoof growth and poor hair quality
Vitamin C (Ascorbic acid)	Synthesized in liver and green grass and legumes	Boosts immune system; tissue and cell maintenance and repair; thought to aid stress and nervousness	Weight loss and poor wound healing

MAIN FAT-SOLUBLE VITAMINS

VITAMINS	SOURCE	FUNCTION	DEFICIENCY
Vitamin A (Retinol)	Good, green grass and high-quality hay	Night vision, fertility, fat and carbohydrate metabolism, and healthy skeletal structure	Weight loss, sometimes lameness
Vitamin D	Sunlight and colostrum. It is also stored in the liver	Healthy bones and the uptake of calcium from the body	Bone deformities and lameness
Vitamin E	Good, green grass and some cereals	Works with selenium to maintain tissue and cells; antioxidant	Problems with skeletal frame, heart and red blood cells
Vitamin K	Green, leafy grasses	Blood clotting	Slow clotting time

There are two types of vitamins: water soluble and fat soluble. The water-soluble vitamins are B_1 through B_{12}, and vitamin C. These vitamins are metabolized in the hindgut, and horses receiving an adequate fiber content in their diets should be in no danger of a deficiency. The main fat-soluble vitamins are A, D, E, and K. Horses kept on good, green grass with access to sunlight should not be deficient, but horses that are stabled for much of the time may be in danger of a vitamin deficiency. Fat-soluble vitamins can cause problems if fed in excess, so always consult a veterinarian or nutritionist before supplementing the diet.

Minerals
There are macro- and microminerals. Macro-minerals are required in a higher volume and are measured as percentages or parts per hundred (pph). The main ones are calcium, phosphorus, magnesium, sodium and potassium. Micro-minerals are required in much smaller quantities and are measured in parts per million (ppm). The main microminerals are selenium, zinc, copper, iodine, iron, molybdenum, manganese, cobalt, fluorine and chromium. The best way to supplement the diet with these minerals is by using a mineral block.

Different Types of Feed
There are two different ways to feed, either by using conventional feeds or by using compound feeds. Compound feeds can either be in nut or pellet form, or found as a coarse mix, also called "sweet feed."

Trainer's Tip
The calcium-to-phosphorus ratio is vital to the healthy well-being of the horse, and must be 2:1. Many cereals are high in phosphorus, especially oats. If the 2:1 balance is upset, the phosphorus actively prevents normal uptake of calcium, which has severe side effects. Horses on high cereal diets must be fed a calcium supplement — limestone flour is effective and economical.

MAJOR MACROMINERALS

MINERALS	SOURCE	FUNCTION	DEFICIENCY
Calcium	Good, green grass, leafy plants and legumes	Maintenance of healthy bones, nerve functions and blood clotting	Problems with skeletal frame, linked to azoturia, slow clotting times
Phosphorus	Cereals and grains	Essential to nearly all enzyme functions, and linked to calcium functions	Skeletal problems, weight loss, hair loss and lameness
Magnesium	Good, green grass	Involved in many of the body's functions including bone hardening, metabolism and regulation of insulin	Muscle spasms, weak skeletal frame, nervous disorders, and linked to laminitis
Sodium	Salt should be added to the diet in the form of blocks or loose salt	Regulation of body fluids and healthy nerve functions	Dehydration, lack of energy and poor growth
Potassium	Good, green grass	All cellular functions, nerve muscle contractions, and nerve transmissions	Muscle fatigue, tying up, and associated nervous and muscular disorders

Compound feeds are designed to provide all the basic nutrient values that your horse requires, including its vitamin and mineral intake. The feeds are graduated and specific to different levels of work, i.e., a competition or racehorse mix will be of obvious higher energy content than a leisure mix for the horse in light-to-medium work. If you are planning on using a compound feed, make sure you select the right grade of feed for the level of work your horse is in.

Compound feeds are convenient but expensive. They have the obvious advantage of being nutritionally worked out for you. Providing you feed according to the guidelines, your horse should receive a balanced diet. If you have any specific

questions, most feed companies employ equine nutritionists who are generally very helpful.

Conventional feeds are the old-fashioned cereals and grains. If feeding using conventional feeds, you will need to work out the exact nutrient content of each individual element.

Oats

One of the most popular grains, oats are an excellent feed, particularly for horses in hard work. A good batch of oats should consist of four parts carbohydrate to one part protein and one part fat. In general, oats contain 12 percent protein, and are high in fiber. They are a valuable energy food. Oats are high in phosphorus and low in calcium, so if feeding them, it is necessary to add a calcium supplement. Oats have a hard outer husk, which accounts for their fiber content. For the horse to get the most nutritional benefit from oats, this husk should be cracked open; however, once the oats have been cracked, or rolled, their shelf life is limited to approximately three weeks. Feeding whole oats is best avoided. Huskless oats have recently been developed. These have a higher energy density than normal oats but lack the benefit of the fiber. Caution must be used to avoid overfeeding.

Electrolytes are an essential combination of minerals required for normal bodily function. Electrolytes are lost when the horse sweats excessively through work or stress. They must then be replaced through feeding an electrolyte supplement.

Barley
Less palatable than oats, barley is still a useful feed. It can be fed rolled, flaked, cooked, boiled or micronized, but never whole. Cooked barley is more digestible and can be a good feed to tempt a horse with a poor appetite. It has a similar protein value to oats, approximately 12 percent, and a good fiber content. Barley is often added to compound feeds to "pad" them out.

Wheat
Wheat is not suitable for horses because it has a high gluten content, which is thought to contribute to impaction colic.

Bran
A byproduct of the milling process of wheat, bran is useful when fed in small quantities. It should

consist of large, flat, creamy-colored flakes and be free from dust. It is high in fiber and phosphorus, but a calcium supplement should be fed with it. If fed dry, bran has a binding effect; if fed damp, it is supposed to be a laxative. There is, however, little scientific evidence to back these assertions! A warm bran mash does make a tempting feed for a horse that has lost its appetite, and can be a good feed for sick or resting horses.

Corn
Corn, or maize, has a higher energy value than oats, but is lower in protein and fiber. It is also a fattening feed. It should be fed cooked and flaked or micronized to make it more digestible; it should not be fed whole.

Beet Pulp
This is a valuable source of fiber and is almost always enjoyed by the horse. It can be a useful

Rolled Oats

Flaked Barley

Corn

how to make "the perfect" bran mash

- 1–1.5 pounds (0.7–0.9 kg) bran
- half a scoop of soaked beet pulp, or 3 tablespoons (45 ml) of thick, dark molasses, or 3 tablespoons (45 ml) of applesauce.
- 1 teaspoon (5 ml) of salt
- 2 chopped (lengthways) carrots, or chopped apple
- hot tap water

1 Mix the first four ingredients in a bucket. Slowly stir in the hot water until the consistency is on the wetter side of damp.

2 Cover the bucket with a cloth and allow to steep for five minutes.

3 Check the middle of the mash to make sure it is not too hot, and present to your grateful horse.

Note: Never feed your horse more than 1–1.5 pounds (0.5–0.7 kg) of bran a day. Avoid feeding bran to youngsters until they are over 4 years old.

feed to tempt poor eaters. Beet pulp *must* be soaked before it is fed. It comes in pulp or pellet form, and each will vary according to the time it needs to be soaked. The traditional beet pulp had to be soaked for 24 hours before feeding, but there are now quick-soak varieties that require much less soaking time. It is also possible to buy unmolassed beet pulp, which is useful for horses on a calorie-restricted diet. Beet pulp has the added advantage of being high in calcium and low in phosphorus, which helps to address the imbalance if feeding it with oats. Once soaked, beet pulp will spoil quite quickly, and should be used within a few days.

Molasses
Molasses is derived from the sugarcane and is a sweet addition to the diet. It is often added to compound feeds and to chaff, but can be added separately if feeding conventional feedstuffs.

Almost all horses will readily eat molasses and it makes a good cover for slipping wormer or medicated powders into the feed.

Linseed
Highly nutritious, being a good source of protein and oil, linseed is an excellent way to put condition on a horse, although it should only be fed in small amounts. Before feeding it *must* be soaked overnight, and then boiled and simmered until the seeds burst open — this can take up to eight hours. If linseed is not boiled it is poisonous. It is now possible to buy ready-prepared linseed oil, which is convenient to use.

Peas and Beans
Peas and beans are very "heating" and should only be fed in small amounts and to horses in hard and fast work. They must always be split before being fed.

Chaff

A 4:1 mixture of chopped hay and straw, chaff is not commonly used in the United States. It is a valuable source of fiber when added to a meal, and also acts to slow the horse down, preventing it bolting its food and increasing the amount it chews. Chaff can be bought with molasses.

Oil

The addition of a tablespoon of either cod-liver oil or vegetable oil to the meal keeps the coat shiny and is a good source of vitamins.

Hay Cubes

These are densely compressed small cubes of good-quality hay that is primarily alfalfa. Cubes can be added to the feed to act in a similar capacity as chaff. They should be well soaked so

The old expression "full of beans" used to describe a lively individual came from the practice of feeding peas and beans to workhorses to give them extra energy.

Left: Unsoaked beet pulp pellets and shredded beet pulp. Right: Horse and pony nuts, chaff (blue container), and coarse mix or "sweet feed" — all menu choices for your horse.

that they start to crumble. They also can be useful for old horses that are not able to eat conventional hay, and for horses that have dust allergies — providing they have been soaked.

Hay

Any hay is only as good as the pasture it was cut from, and the way in which it was baled!

Making hay is a fine art, especially where farmers have to constantly battle unpredictable weather. It is important to learn how to recognize good hay from poor, and any hay should be carefully evaluated before you buy it. It is now possible to have nutrient value readings taken on some hay, which cuts out the margin of error.

The price of hay will fluctuate dramatically depending on the weather and subsequent crop — cheap hay is often cheap for a reason! It is better to pay a little more and get good quality.

New hay is rich and should be allowed to sit for several months before being fed. Some farmers put up "seed" hay. This is specially seeded hay that generally has a higher nutritional value than meadow hay (cut from permanent pastures). The grasses tend to be harder, which the horse likes, but are less digestible.

Alfalfa hay is popular. Alfalfa is a legume and very high in protein — it is so high in protein that the horse is not able to utilize all of the protein properly, and much of it is passed in the urine. Alfalfa hay is rich and green; horses love it, but it must be fed sparingly and should only be fed to broodmares or horses in hard and fast work. It should not form the entire hay ration but should be fed in addition to regular grass hay.

HOW TO EVALUATE HAY

- It should smell clean and sweet.
- There should be no visible signs of mold or dust.
- Reach into the middle of the bale and remove a handful of hay to check it.
- The bales should not be warm, which would indicate fermentation and mold.
- There should be no obvious signs of weeds.
- Small grass hay bales should weigh 30–50 pounds (14–23 kg) — if they are more than this check that the hay is not wet and moldy.

The protein content in hay will vary according to the different grasses, but all hay will start to lose its nutritional value after a year.

working with hay

1 First check your hay to make sure there is no mold, weeds or dust inside. Grab some hay from the center and make sure it smells clean and sweet and is not warm to the touch.

2 Place your hay in small-holed nets to cut down on waste and make it harder for your horse to bolt down its food. Hang the net sufficiently high in the stall so the horse does not catch its foot. Use a hay scale to measure the quantity the horse is getting.

3 Soak the hay in a large tub of water for no more than 20 minutes to eliminate dust spores before feeding. Old milk crates are ideal for draining. Lift the hay out of the tub and place on top of the crate(s).

Hay should be fed dampened — soak the net in a clean barrel or large bucket for no longer than 20 minutes, then drain. Soaking the hay for any longer leaches out the nutrients. Spraying the net with a hose is ineffective as only the outside of the hay is dampened and the middle of the net remains bone dry.

Haylage

Haylage, also known as silage, is the topic of much debate, and has both advantages and disadvantages. It is currently more widely used in Europe than North America, although it is starting to become popular in California. After cutting the pasture, instead of being allowed to dry as with conventional hay, the grass is baled while in a semiwilted state and placed in airtight plastic bags.

The grasses use up the remaining oxygen in the bag and undergo fermentation, which lowers the pH value. When it reaches pH 5, the fermentation stops and the grass remains in a suspended state.

Among the advantages of haylage is its higher nutritional value due to leaf preservation and nitrate reduction. It is also dust-free, and therefore great for horses with allergies. It is easier for farmers to bale, cuts down on baling time, and is clean to store. Maybe most importantly, horses like it.

On the minus side, if the bags are punctured and oxygen reaches the grasses, a secondary fermentation occurs, which results in the formation of dangerous mold. It can't be examined before purchasing, so the buyer has no way of determining the quality of the grasses.

The moisture content of the grass is crucial when baling haylage. If it is too wet, feed value will be lost, and if too dry, the fermentation process is reduced, and mold is likely to occur.

Haylage in small bales is very expensive, and large bales are only suitable for yards with lots of horses. It has a short shelf life, and once opened needs to be used quickly.

One of the myths about haylage is that you should feed less of it than your conventional hay ration, based on its higher nutrient value. However, haylage has a very high water content, so its weight is disproportionately high compared to dry hay. As a rough guide, aim to feed the same amount of haylage in bulk (not weight) as you would feed dry hay; this will compensate for the difference between dry and wet weight.

Trainer's Tip
Haylage should be baled when the grass has a 45–50 percent moisture content, as opposed to hay that is baled with 15–20 percent moisture content.

HAY OR HAYLAGE?
Many horse owners find haylage (shown left) easier to store and use than hay (shown inset, left), and it cuts down on their working time. However, when buying, its condition can't be assessed because it is bought sealed.

Feeding and Feed

- A balanced diet must include water, carbo-hydrates, fats, proteins, vitamins and minerals.
- Water is the most important and most ignored element of feeding.
- Horses should have access to water at *all* times other than directly before or after work.
- Always bring electrolytes when traveling long distances (see page 83).
- Carbohydrates are the biggest energy provider for the horse.
- There are two types of carbohydrates: simple and complex.
- Glucose is a simple carbohydrate and is stored as glycogen; excess glucose is turned into fat.
- Cellulose is a complex carbohydrate. It is found in all grass and plants and is the main source of fiber.
- Cellulose is broken down by the bacteria and microbial culture of the hindgut.
- This microbial culture can be easily upset, i.e., by sudden changes in food and some wormers and oral antibiotics.
- Fats have a higher energy value than carbo-hydrates, but are harder to break down.
- Proteins have little energy value but are needed to maintain and repair tissue and cells, and build muscle.

Supplements

There are literally hundreds of supplements on the market that promise a range of miraculous results; the only certainty, however, is a hole in your paycheck! Before diving into the supplement trap there are a few things to consider:

• Does your horse really need a supplement?
• What exactly is the supplement supposed to do?
• What exactly is in the supplement?

Any horse that is on a balanced diet and has access to good, green grass and sunlight, and that has no special requirements or problems should, in reality, not need its feed supplemented, other than with salt and calcium (limestone flour) if it is on a diet high in oats.

If you are feeding a compound feed and sticking to the manufacturer's guidelines, then all the essential vitamins, minerals and feed components will be included. Feeding a balanced diet is by far and away the best approach to preventing the onset of diet-related problems.

MINERAL BLOCKS
These can be scattered around the field or placed in the stable.

Mineral Block   Flavored Mineral Block   Salt Lick

There are, however, many horses that genuinely do require a supplement, and if this is the case with yours, then you need to thoroughly research the product. Find out what the actual ingredients are, not just what it promises to do. The ingredient list is particularly relevant if competing; you must make sure that there is nothing that would be classed as a banned substance.

With herbal supplements, the ingredient list must be approached with even more caution. The herb valerian, for example, contains a compound with the same chemical makeup as Valium, which is a banned substance. A product labeled "herbal" or "natural" is not without side effects and risk, just as synthetic products are not.

Treat product promises with caution. Supplements that offer muscle-building, topline development, increased athleticism, etc., may well help the horse to achieve this, but at the end of the day, nothing replaces work and exercise.

Some supplements are extremely expensive; others share similar-sounding names, so make sure that you are buying what you think you are and not something you don't need or that does an entirely different job.

On the next two pages, you will find just a selection of the many products available — all of which are marketed under many different names. Try to choose a well-known and reputable company to buy from and, if you are in any doubt about using a supplement, consult either your veterinary surgeon or an impartial equine nutritionist.

One last word on supplements; products that imply that they actually take some action against a condition are often referred to as nutraceuticals. However, since these products don't actually fall under the heading of "medicine," they are not subject to the same rigorous testing and research that medical items are, and are not subject to the same laws.

Salt

Most compound feeds will have sufficient salt already added into the mix, but in very hot weather, or if the horse is in hard and fast work and sweats profusely, then 1 to 2 teaspoons (5 to 10 ml) of loose salt can be added to the feed. Alternatively, provide a salt lick in the stable and the field.

Calcium

This can be added to the feed in the form of limestone flour, which is relatively economical. Pure calcium supplements are also available, but are more expensive.

Oil

Cod-liver oil is high in vitamin D and produces a good shine on the coat, but does have a strong smell. Corn oil or sunflower oil will also improve the appearance of the coat, although some horses can have an allergic reaction to corn oil.

quick reference

Supplements

- Unless your horse has a specific requirement/problem, and providing it is on a balanced diet and has access to grass and sunlight, it shouldn't need supplementing.
- Be sure to thoroughly check the ingredients listed on the supplement and make sure they are not considered a banned substance if you are competing.
- Herbal supplements are not without their side effects and reactions.
- *Never* overdose on supplements, but feed according to the manufacturer's guidelines.
- Give supplements time to work — at least two months, and longer for foot supplements.
- Only buy supplements from well-known, reputable companies.

Limestone Flour

Garlic

Foot Repair Formula

B Vitamins and Iron

This is a useful supplement for horses in hard and fast work; vitamin B_{12} is thought to be particularly beneficial. Iron helps horses prone to anemia.

Biotin, Methionine and Sulfur

These will help to improve the condition of the hoof wall and are a useful supplement for horses with poor feet. It takes at least eight weeks to really see any improvement, but through continual use, not only will your horse's feet improve dramatically but so, too, will the quality of its hair.

Selenium and Vitamin E

This is a combination to be treated with caution. Selenium is a trace mineral that causes severe problems if deficient *or* in excess — and it is a fine balance to get the proportions right. Selenium is gained through the soil and plants, so have your pastures tested. Areas low in selenium require supplementation. The benefits of selenium and vitamin E are in maintaining normal muscle function and fertility. This is a supplement that is often given to horses that have a history of azoturia (see page 233).

Glucosamine and Chondroitin

This is marketed under a number of different names and is the new "wonder" product that combats joint inflammation and pain. In my experience, it works well on some horses, and has no effect on others — not the most scientific evidence, but it is worth giving it a try.

Check the products carefully; for the supplement to do any good at all, it must provide at least 3,600 mg of glucosamine and 1,200 mg of chondroitin daily.

Yeast and Probiotics

These can be fed in supplement form and are intended to help keep the bacteria in the hindgut healthy and balanced. It is particularly worth feeding these after a course of antibiotics, and in times of stress, such as after a bout of colic or traveling.

Problem Feeders

Some horses require special attention and feeding either due to workload, or because of other problems such as age, temperament or weight.

Horses in Hard and Fast Work

Racing, eventing and jumping incur a much higher energy requirement than moderate work for a horse. They require fast-releasing energy, which is in the form of glycogen stored in the muscles. Glycogen comes from simple carbohydrates, so the horse needs to be on a high-carbohydrate diet. The drawback is that starch produces higher stomach acidity, which increases the chance of ulcers. Ulcers are also related to stress, and invariably the competition horse in this degree of work is subjected to a certain amount of stress as well. To combat the effects, feed a calcium and magnesium supplement, which acts like an antacid.

Fiber requires a lot of digesting, and the digestive process uses energy, which the horse in this type of work cannot afford to spare. Therefore, although it is not ideal for their digestive tract, horses in this type of work should not be fed large amounts of fiber. Beet pulp for example, is highly fibrous, and should not be fed to racehorses or advanced eventers. Their diet must be balanced between concentrates and roughage, and they will need to be carefully monitored for digestive problems. Due to the high requirement of concentrates, the horse in hard and fast work will need to be fed at least four or more times a day, with no one feed exceeding 4 pounds (1.8 kg) in weight. A supplement containing the B vitamins and iron can be useful.

Seniors

Old horses require special care and attention, especially when it comes to feeding. Invariably their teeth are poor, rocky or in some cases missing, and the effectiveness of their digestive tracts is diminished. They need highly digestible foods, and if grains are being fed, then cooking them first increases their digestibility.

For horses with poor teeth, feed softened foods, wet-chopped hay or soaked hay cubes.

There are several compound feeds available specifically for the senior horse, and these work very well. Old horses are less able to process protein well so it is best to feed them a small amount of high-quality protein, rather than a lot of poor-quality protein. As horses age, their metabolisms slow down, which means that many old horses maintain their weight well. However, if a horse's digestive system is not working

Placing a large stone (about the size of a brick) in the feed bowl can prevent a horse bolting down its food. The horse has to eat around the rock and work to get its food.

efficiently, it will lose weight. Adding calories to the diet in the form of rice bran, flax or whole roasted soy can be helpful.

Bolters

Some horses fall on their food and practically inhale it in their enthusiasm. This can be a problem as a horse needs to chew its food properly to start the initial digestive process, and to stimulate the production of saliva. Bolting down food also can lead to choking, which is highly distressing for a horse and its owner.

You need to try to get to the root of the bolting problem. Some horses bolt down their food because they feel threatened, believing that their food will either be removed or eaten by someone else. If you suspect this, separate the horse and allow it to eat undisturbed in a quiet environment. Other horses bolt down their food if they think they are going to be left. When feeding in a stable block, make sure that everyone has finished before moving horses in and out of the area. Adding chaff or soaked hay cubes to the feed greatly helps to slow a horse down. Another good method is to place a large rock in the bottom of the manger (see picture on page 97). Using a small-holed haynet will help to slow down hay consumption.

Off Food

Some horses are poor eaters, while others lose their appetite due to sickness or stress. First determine the cause of the problem.

- Check the teeth to make sure they are in good condition and that there are no mouth problems such as pain, infection or blistering, etc.
- Address the stress situation and resolve it if possible.
- Make sure the manger is clean.
- Make sure the food is not moldy, dusty or old.
- Call the vet if you suspect there is a medical problem.

To tempt the horse to eat, reduce the ration and try offering small amounts of food more often. Offer the horse a "perfect" bran mash, sweetened with molasses, beet pulp, or applesauce – most horses like sweet food. Sometimes adding chopped up carrots and apples to the feed helps. Allow the horse to see its neighbor being fed; often this will encourage it to eat.

Sometimes a change of scenery peps a horse up enough to want to eat. Providing it is well enough, lead the horse out of the stable for a five-minute walk and on its return offer feed again. Using a new bucket also helps. Decant the feed into the bucket and leave it in the corner of the stable; a horse will invariably go over and investigate.

The Thin Horse

Again address the reason why the horse is thin and first deal with the cause.

---

quick reference

Problem Feeders

- Horses in hard and fast work need a diet high in carbohydrates and low in fiber.
- Old horses lose their ability to digest properly; they have a decreased ability to process protein, and often their teeth are in poor shape.
- Feed soft feeds to the old horse.
- Horses that bolt their food often do so due to stress. Look to the root of the problem and address it.
- A large rock in the manger can help to slow down a bolter.
- Bran mash with molasses, beet pulp, or apple-sauce is a tempting meal for a horse off its food.
- High-fiber soaked feeds such as beet pulp, are good for putting weight on thin horses.
- Increase the amount of feeds a day to several small ones.
- Feed the overweight horse "light" products without sugar.
- Increase exercise – it almost always works!

Trainer's Tip

An outbreak of hives that may or may not be itchy and can spread across much of the body *can* be caused by an allergy to a specific protein in the feed. Barley, oats and beet pulp are the most common feeds to cause this.

- Does the horse have a nervous temperament?
- Is it stressed?
- Are other horses keeping it on the run in the field (bullying)?
- Are its teeth okay?
- Has it been wormed regularly?
- Is its conformation poor, i.e., is it herring-gutted, which would give it the appearance of thinness?

Never make sudden changes to the diet, and introduce new feed slowly, especially if it has a high nutritional value. Increase the amount of feeds a day to four small ones, and feed high-fiber soaked feeds such as beet pulp with boiled flaked barley or oats. Any feedstuff high in fat, such as linseed, roasted soy and milk pellets, are good weight-gainers. Feed the best quality hay you can find on an ad lib basis and add some haylage in with it.

The Fat Horse

Some horses are easy keepers — particularly ponies, warmblood breeds, warmblood crosses and Arabians. Try to restrict the grazing and find a good turnout area with minimal grass. Increasing exercise, if possible, is always the best method of keeping weight down. Exercising twice a day, even if one session is only on a horse walker, can really help.

Feed a high-fiber diet with a low fat and sugar content. It is possible to buy sugar-free beet pulp and unmolassed chaff, both of which are good fiber providers. Make sure that the bedding is not remotely edible — many horses will munch through a straw bed! Use a small-holed haynet to make the horse work for its hay.

Feeding Formulas

An adult horse needs to eat 2.5 percent of its body weight a day. This includes concentrates and roughage, which in turn includes hay and grass. Ponies require 2 percent, and growing youngsters 3 percent. First, work out how much your horse weighs. Use a livestock scale or "weigh station," a weight measuring tape or a weight table. Weight tables are only estimates; some horses vary dramatically from the average weight listed.

Approximate Weight Chart		
HEIGHT IN HANDS	**WEIGHT IN POUNDS**	**WEIGHT IN KILOGRAMS**
11	260–550	118–250
12	525–640	238–290
13	640–780	290–354
14	780–930	354–422
15	930–1,180	422–535
16	1,100–1,400	499–635
17	1,300–1,600	590–725

how to weigh your horse with a measuring tape

Weight tapes are cheap to buy and generally available through feed outlets or manufacturers.

- Place the tape around the horse, so that it sits just behind the wither and around the girth.
- Read the weight marked on the tape. It's as easy as that.

Determining Appetite

Use the following formula to find the "appetite" of the horse:

- Body weight ÷ 100 x 2.5 = appetite.
- For example, a 16 hands high (h.h.) hunter type weighing 1,200 pounds (544 kg) would need 30 pounds (13.6 kg) of dry feed a day or 1,200 (544) ÷ 100 x 2.5 = 30 (13.6).

Working Out Ratio of Concentrate Food to Roughage (Forage)

As an example, let's take the 16 h.h. hunter type in medium work. Its overall feed ration is 30 pounds (13.6 kg), of which (according to the chart), 60 percent should be hay and 40 percent concentrate.

- 30 (13.6) x 0.60 = 18 pounds (8.2 kg) hay.
- 30 (13.6) x 0.40 = 12 pounds (5.4 kg) concentrate.

The horse's feed ration then needs to be divided into at least three, and preferably four meals a day, with the bulk of the hay ration being at night. The ration will need to be changed according to increasing or decreasing workload, and will constantly require monitoring.

All tables are approximate only, and many horses will require an alteration of both the amounts of feed and the ratio of concentrate to roughage.

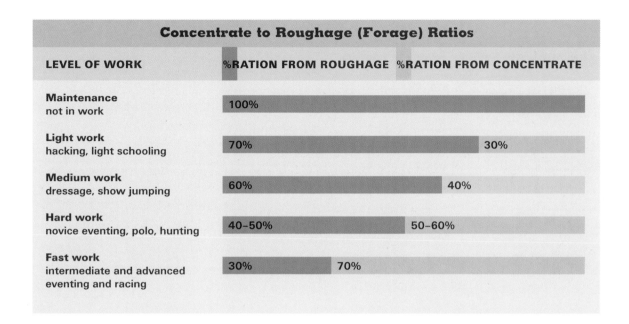

Concentrate to Roughage (Forage) Ratios

LEVEL OF WORK	%RATION FROM ROUGHAGE	%RATION FROM CONCENTRATE
Maintenance not in work	100%	
Light work hacking, light schooling	70%	30%
Medium work dressage, show jumping	60%	40%
Hard work novice eventing, polo, hunting	40–50%	50–60%
Fast work intermediate and advanced eventing and racing	30%	70%

There are further formulas for calculating the energy requirements of your horse and for determining the nutrient value of different feedstuffs, which are particularly relevant if feeding conventional rather than compound feeds. In this case it is a good idea to consult with an equine nutritionist to make sure that the balance is correct, and your horse is receiving sufficient protein and energy in its diet.

Whenever the roughage portion of the feed ration falls below 40 percent, the horse's digestive system is compromised. While this is a necessary evil for horses in hard and fast work, it is worth being aware that the horse's digestive system is designed around the intake of fiber, and when that is restricted, digestive complications can result. Horses on rations such as this need very careful monitoring.

A last word on hay: Although it goes against the traditional feeding formula, the feeding of ad lib meadow hay to the stabled horse can be beneficial in certain circumstances. Provided the horse is in light-to-medium work and is not overweight, keeping a steady supply of hay in front of it allows its digestive tract to work in a more natural manner.

quick reference

Feeding Formulas

- A horse needs to eat 2.5 percent of its body weight every day.
- Weigh your horse using a livestock scale, weight tape or a weight chart.
- Work out in pounds (kg) how much your horse needs to eat per day.
- The ratio of concentrates to roughage varies according to the level of work the horse is in.
- Work out the percentage of its feed ration that should be concentrate and should be hay.
- Plan to split its feed ration into at least three, and preferably four meals a day.
- Always feed the bulk of hay ration at night.
- Compound feeds already have the nutrient levels balanced for you.
- If feeding conventional feeds consult an equine nutritionist to work out the digestible energy and crude protein of your feeds.
- Feeding ad lib hay can be beneficial providing the horse is not in hard or fast work and is not overweight.

6

FOOT CARE

At present, in the United States and Canada, there is no legal requirement for a farrier to be licensed, which means that anyone can present themself as a farrier. There are programs that offer training and exams, such as the American Farrier's Association (AFA). Check to make sure that your farrier is a member of one of the registered bodies such as the AFA, and that he or she has recognized qualifications. The AFA currently offers five levels of competence.

Before choosing your farrier, do some homework on who is working in your area, and check on his or her reputation. Local veterinary hospitals or horse establishments should be able to offer you an opinion. If you have young, green or nervous horses, it is especially important to find someone who is competent, patient and is a "horseperson."

Be aware of how your horse travels across the ground. Does it stumble or forge (see page 33)? How does it pick up and put down its feet? It is a good idea to study the way your horse moves so that you become aware of any potential problems before they occur. If you are able to turn your horse loose in an arena, this is an ideal opportunity to watch how it moves from the ground. If you are unable to do so, get someone to run your horse for you.

If you are having problems such as forging, let your farrier know so that he or she can make adjustments when shoeing the horse. Don't be afraid to discuss things, but remember that your farrier is not a vet, so limit any questions to shoeing-related concerns.

The Structure of the Foot

EXTERNAL STRUCTURES

The foot is made up of insensitive and sensitive structures. The external components — the horny wall, sole, frog and bars — are tough and insensitive and protect the sensitive structures of the foot.

Periople

This is a thin cover of soft horn that helps to restrict the evaporation of moisture from the hoof wall. The periople extends from the coronary band part way down the outside of the hoof wall. Excessive rasping by the farrier, or continual work in an abrasive sand arena will damage the periople and can contribute to dry and brittle feet.

Hoof Wall

Tough horny tubules that run vertically from the coronary band to the ground surface of the foot make up the hoof wall. The hoof wall grows continually down from the coronary band at a rate of approximately ½ inch (1 cm) a month, and so it takes between nine months and one year to grow a completely new wall. Normally the wall is smooth, but when the horse has suffered a dietary change or poor health, ridges or rings may develop around the hoof. These rings will gradually move down the hoof as the wall grows, so it is possible to estimate how many months previously the change or trauma occurred by the height of the ring on the hoof.

The hoof wall is divided into three areas, the toe (where the wall is at its thickest), the quarters and the heel. At the heel the wall turns inward and traverses part way along the sides of the frog, forming the bars.

Frog

The frog is a wedge-shaped pad of elastic horn that is in contact with the ground. It functions to provide traction, to aid in the reduction of concussion and to help the circulation of blood through the foot and back up the leg. As the frog

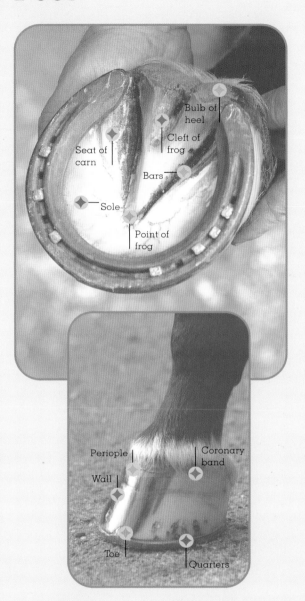

Bulb of heel

Cleft of frog

Seat of carn

Bars

Sole

Point of frog

Periople

Coronary band

Wall

Toe

Quarters

Trainer's Tip

It's useful to work with your horse's feet daily so that it is well mannered and used to having its feet handled. Your farrier's job is to shoe your horse, not to train it.

hits the ground it depresses, putting pressure on the sensitive digital cushion that sits above the frog and pumps blood back up the leg.

Sole

This forms the ground surface of the foot and protects the sensitive structures above it. The sole should be gently concave and is non-weight-bearing — horses with very flat soles (flat feet) are prone to bruising- and concussion-related problems. The thickness of the sole will vary from horse to horse, with Thoroughbreds often being referred to as "thin soled." The thinner the sole, the more prone the horse will be to bruising. The white line (which is actually yellow in color) shows the junction between the wall of the foot and the sole, and it marks out the position of the sensitive structures within the foot. This line is used by farriers to show where they are able to drive their nails, and also indicates the thickness of the horny wall.

INTERNAL STRUCTURES

The inside of the foot is a very complex structure. While a complete rendering of the parts is outside the scope of this book, the following will acquaint you with the most common elements.

Digital Cushion

This wedge-shaped structure sits above the frog and is a central component in blood circulation within the foot. As the foot hits the ground the digital cushion expands, forcing the heels apart and driving blood back up the leg.

Bones and Joints

The small navicular bone, the pedal bone and the bottom two-thirds of the short pastern bone lie within the foot, and between these bones is the coffin joint.

Sensitive Laminae

These attach to the surface of the pedal bone and interlink with the insensitive laminae that connect with the inside of the hoof wall. The bond

between the sensitive and insensitive laminae is incredibly strong and supports the pedal bone in place.

Lateral Cartilages

Important in the reduction of concussion, the lateral cartilages attach to either side of the pedal bone. They are normally soft and elastic, and can be palpated above the coronary band. It is not uncommon for the lateral cartilages to harden with age, especially in horses that have been worked hard, and for bony deposits to occur along their length. This syndrome is referred to as "sidebone" (see page 237).

Hoof Angles

Viewed from the side, there should be an angle of approximately 45 degrees between the wall of the front feet and the ground; in the hind feet this angle should be between 50 and 55 degrees. The angle of the wall of the feet should be the same as the angle of the pastern; in instances where this does not occur it is referred to as a "broken hoof/pastern angle," which is serious and should be rectified by the farrier. The angle of the hoof wall should remain parallel through the foot from the toe to the heel.

Maintenance of the Feet

Sound, healthy feet make the horse, and it is important to maintain their condition through regular care and attention.

Picking Out

The stabled horse should have its feet picked out at least twice a day — when bringing it in from the field, and when leading it out of the stall — and the grass-kept horse at least once a day. Feet should be picked out from the heel down toward the toe, with particular attention being paid to the clefts of the frog. While picking out the feet check the state of the shoes for risen clenches, sprung or slipping shoes, wear and tear, and hoof growth.

Hoof Supplements

Some horses naturally have "poor" feet and will benefit from an oral hoof supplement containing biotin and methionine, which will also improve the quality of the coat. Oral hoof supplements take a long time to work, so be prepared to allow at least three to four months before a noticeable improvement occurs in the quality of the horn.

There are many topical applications available to condition and moisturize the feet but most are fairly ineffectual. Two products I have found to

Excessively upright feet, where the angle is 60 degrees or more (sometimes referred to as a club foot), will lead to severe concussion within the foot, and can cause the horse to stumble. It may lead to the development of ringbone and arthritis.

work with continuous use, however, are Hoof-Alive and Kevin Bacon's Hoof Dressing.

In very dry conditions, the feet will become brittle and excessively hard and often crack so keep the horse on a good supplement and use topical dressings. It also can help to soak the feet several times a day in water for a few days prior to the farrier's visit. An easy way to do this is to stand the horse in a stream or spring if you have access or on a wet, boggy path of land.

In very wet conditions, the feet will become soft and mushy and will have a higher risk of developing seedy toe and thrush (see page 231). If this happens, ensure that the horse's feet are allowed to dry out daily. A grass-kept horse must be shut in for a few hours a day on a dry surface.

Horizontal rings around the hoof can indicate a previous attack of laminitis (founder), a sudden change in diet, sudden growth, seasonal changes, trauma or illness. Rings caused by laminitis tend to be wavy and widen at the heels, while rings caused by other factors are generally more regular and evenly spaced.

When picking out the feet as part of the daily routine, work from the heel to the toe using the pick in a downward motion toward the toe and be careful to clean out the areas surrounding the frog really well.

A Visit from the Farrier

The rate of foot growth varies from horse to horse and will also be affected by nutrition and, to a certain extent, climate. Horses should, however, have their feet reshod or trimmed every six to eight weeks.

It is essential that your horse is used to having its feet picked up and handled before the farrier arrives. I can't stress this enough. It is not the farrier's job to train your horse, and he or she can't be expected to do a good job if your horse is being difficult. By the same token, however, some horses can be particularly hard to shoe, often as a result of poor care and management. If you know that your horse is particularly nervous, or does have problems, explain to your farrier so that he or she can behave accordingly and allow extra time in scheduling if necessary.

The Shoeing Area

To do a good job, the farrier needs a safe working area. This must be somewhere flat and hard, preferably either on rubber matting or concrete and under cover. The farrier will need good light and there should be enough room for him or her to be able to work safely around your horse. If you are not able to provide a safe, flat area then it is worth taking your horse somewhere else to be shod.

The Farrier at Work

Each farrier will work in a slightly different way using different techniques, but basically the procedure for shoeing a horse is the same.

Stage One: Assessing and Removing

First the farrier will assess the horse and its feet. The horse should be led up, and the farrier will evaluate the way it is traveling in order to make any necessary adjustments to the shoeing.

Then the farrier will remove the old shoe. The clenches will be cut off, either using the clench cutter (buffer) and hammer, or the rasp. The farrier now will take his or her "pull offs" and

Trainer's Tip

If holding your horse for the farrier don't let it swing its head around, and don't let it put its head down to eat. This affects the horse's balance and the distribution of weight through its body, which will make the horse lean on the farrier holding up its foot — making the farrier's job much harder.

carefully lever the shoe off the foot. Starting at the heel, the farrier pulls inward and downward from one side of the foot to the other, gradually working toward the toe. This must be done carefully so that none of the horn is damaged or pulled off as the shoe comes off.

Now the shoe is off, the farrier will prepare the foot to be reshod.

Stage Two: Trimming and Shaping

First the farrier will make a "nipper run," trimming off excess horn growth with the nippers. Using the rasp, he or she will shape the foot and level the ground-bearing surface, and then trim away dead, ragged parts of the frog and cautiously trim the sole to avoid taking too much off. It is very important that the foot is balanced.

Stage Three: Fitting

The farrier will select an appropriate-sized shoe and heat it in a forge until it is hot enough to be malleable. Then, using an anvil and shaping hammer, the farrier will shape the shoe to fit the horse's foot.

The hot shoe is then carried to the horse using the fitting tongs, or pritchel, and is measured against the foot to make sure it is the correct shape.

Some farriers "burn on" — pressing the hot shoe on to the insensitive foot, which enables them to check whether they have trimmed the foot level. This process causes lots of smoke, and can be unnerving for horses that have not experienced it before.

Stage Four: Nailing

Once the farrier is happy with the shape of the shoe, it is dropped into cold water to cool off. It is now ready to be nailed on.

The farrier drives the nails using a driving hammer, and then either twists the sharp ends off with the claw end of the hammer, or bends them down on the outside of the hoof. These will eventually be made into the clenches.

Many farriers will drive one nail on either side of the shoe and allow the horse to put its foot down. They can now assess whether they have the shoe exactly how they want it.

They will then continue to drive nails, traditionally using three nails on the inside edge of the shoe and four on the outside.

Stage Five: Finishing

Now the farrier has to make the clenches and "finish" the foot. Using the edge of the rasp, a shallow groove is made for the clenches to fit in.

If the farrier has not already cut the sharp ends off the nails, he or she will now do this, and then flatten the ends with the finishing rasp.

Next, the clenches are squeezed tight using the clenching tongs, and finally the farrier will rasp the edges of the foot smooth.

Studs

Studs are a useful aid for traction and are used mainly by competition horses. The farrier will drill,

Trainer's Tip

After your horse has been newly shod, cover its hooves in hoof-conditioning salve. This will help to keep the hooves in good condition and prevent cracking, which is especially important during the summer months.

or punch a stud hole into the shoe, and then "tap" the hole, which makes the threads into which the studs can then be screwed when they are needed. Generally, stud holes are drilled in the shoe's outside heel. Using a stud on the inside and outside of the shoe has the advantage of causing less imbalance to the foot, but there is a danger with a stud on the inside heel that the horse may injure its other limbs.

Studs come in a variety of shapes and sizes, from large rectangular blocks for very heavy, muddy going, to small sharp points for use on hard, slippery going. Studs should never be used when riding on concrete or on the road, with the

STUD KIT

- A selection of different-sized studs wrapped in paper towels sprayed with oil and some plastic stud hole plugs.
- Tools – a spanner or wrench to tighten studs, a small Philips screwdriver to clean out stud holes, an Allen key for screwing in metal plugs, and a clearing tap, used to screw into the stud hole to keep the threads even and working.
- Cotton and a can of WD40.

All should be kept in a lidded plastic container away from moisture.

the shoeing process

1 The clenches of the old shoe will be removed either with a buffer and a hammer, as seen here, a clench cutter, or by rasping them off. Do not attempt to remove the shoe until the clenches have come off.

2 Next the shoe will be levered away carefully from the foot with "pull offs." Starting at the heel, the farrier will pull inward and downward from one side to the other, gradually working toward the toe.

3 Once the shoe has come off, the farrier can then make a "nipper run." Taking his nippers, he trims off excessive horn growth.

4 Next the farrier has to create a level, ground-bearing surface, and he does this using his rasp. He will rasp the underneath of the foot and also tidy up the foot's outside bottom edge.

exception being road studs. Road studs are small square studs that can be screwed into the shoe and have a tungsten steel central pin, which is very hard and provides traction. The disadvantage with road studs, however, is that they do unbalance the foot and the stud can wear down around the edges, making them difficult to unscrew.

Studs should always be used with caution. Although they are a valuable traction aid (especially for jumping), they do unbalance the

the farrier's toolbox

- Anvil – for shaping the shoes.
- Forge – to heat the shoes up to make them easier to shape.
- Buffer – to cut the clenches.
- Pull offs – to pull the shoes off.
- Hoof knife – to trim the frog and sole, and make clip notches.
- Rasp – to shape and level the foot.
- Nippers – to cut away excess hoof growth and shape the foot.
- Tongs – to carry the hot shoe.
- Shaping hammer – a large, heavy-headed hammer used to shape the shoes.
- Driving hammer – a smaller-headed hammer with a driving head and claw head used to drive nails.
- Clenching tongs – to squeeze the clenches tight.
- Finishing rasp – a finer rasp to finish off the foot.
- Magnet – to pick up any metal raspings or wayward nails.

5 The foot then needs to be smoothed and prepared for having a shoe fitted. During this process, the farrier also will trim away dead and ragged parts of the frog and trim the sole using his hoof knife. With the knife, he also will make a notch for the toe clip, side clips or quarter clips, if they are to be used.

6 Next the farrier takes an appropriate sized ready-made shoe and heats it in the forge. This makes the shoe malleable so it can be shaped to fit the individual foot. The farrier holds the shoe with tongs and uses a shaping hammer.

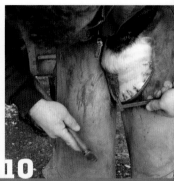

putting on a shoe

7 Using the tongs or pritchel, the farrier will carry the hot shoe to the horse and measure it against the foot to see if he has made the shoe the correct shape.

8 Once happy with the shape the farrier will cool the shoe in cold water. Next, using a driving hammer, he will begin to nail on the shoe.

9 The sharp ends of the nails that are now protruding from the wall are either twisted off or bent down on the outside of the hoof; these will be cut off and made into the clenches.

10 The farrier now needs to make a "bed" or shallow groove for the clenches to rest in on the outside of the hoof wall using his hammer and a custom-made sharp-ended tool; many farriers will use the edge of a fine rasp.

foot and can put a degree of torque on the shoe.

Stud holes must be thoroughly cleaned before a stud is screwed in to prevent dirt and grit causing pressure problems between the sole and the stud. You can buy small plastic or metal plugs that can be used to cover the stud hole and keep it clean, or wad up a tiny amount of cotton and plug the hole, or use ear plugs. It is a good idea to clean stud holes out once a week and to screw and unscrew the stud to keep the threads of the hole in good working order.

Pads

Pads are used to give temporary added protection to the sole of the foot if the horse has suffered an injury. Horses that are particularly thin soled or prone to concussion-related problems may be shod more regularly with pads, but using pads does have its disadvantages. The foot beneath the pad can be prone to thrush (see page 231) and will soften. Also, if a problem occurs in the foot it is not possible to investigate it without having the pads removed. Pads are applied between the sole

Trainer's Tip

When putting studs in at a competition, lay an old towel on the ground under the foot so that if the horse puts its foot down, the stud hole stays clean. Have everything you need ready and on hand. It is easier to hold the horse's leg between your legs — in the way your farrier does — when putting studs in.

of the foot and the shoe and are held in place when the shoe is nailed on. They are usually made from plastic or leather, although there is a new acrylic liquid pad available.

Wedge pads are used in a remedial capacity to alter the angle of the foot. They are thicker at the heels and come in a range of thicknesses.

Snow pads are plastic pads that can be used during the winter, and are designed to pop snow out of the foot as the horse travels.

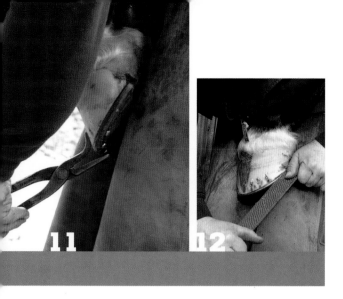

11 Once the groove is made, the clenches can be tightened with clenching tongs. These basically squeeze the end of the clench tightly against the outside of the hoof wall and keep the shoe secure.

12 Finally, the farrier will "finish" the foot. He takes a finishing rasp, which has a fine tooth pattern, and tidies up the hoof, smoothing down any rough areas.

When the shoe is a good fit, the farrier will carry it to a bucket of cold water using his tongs, and immerse it until it has cooled off. Once the shoe is cool, the farrier can handle it with his hands, and the nailing on process starts. Always have a bucket of water ready for the farrier.

quick reference

The Well-shod Foot

- The angle of the hoof should follow the angle of the pastern joint. In front feet this is roughly 45 degrees at the toe, and in the hind it should be 50–55 degrees. This is referred to as the hoof/pastern angle, and is extremely important. If the horse has a broken axis, great strain will be placed on the internal structures of the hoof and leg, and it will affect the horse's natural way of movement.
- The feet should be balanced, and should appear to be in pairs, bearing in mind conformational differences.
- The bearing surface of the foot should be level and flat to the shoe — there should be no gaps between the shoe and the foot.
- The shoe should fit the foot and there should be no excessive overhang of the shoe, unless in specific therapeutic cases.
- The clenches should be even and smooth, with no sharp points, and the same height all the way around. They should sit roughly one-third of the way up the hoof from the ground.
- There should be no evidence of excessive use of the hoof knife on the frog or sole, or the rasp on the outside of the hoof.
- The shoe should be the right weight and type for the horse and its job.
- The nails should be the right size for the shoe. If they are too large they will wear away, and more importantly they will displace the hoof wall and cause cracks and if they are too small they will come loose. They should fit snugly into the fullering (groove in the shoe).
- The clips should fit the notch made for them, and should be tight fitting against the hoof.

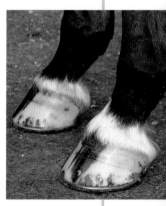

Special Shoes

Special shoes fall into two categories, the remedial or therapeutic shoe that is used to address a specific problem, and shoes designed for the show or competition horse and gaited horse to increase their movements.

Remedial Special Shoes

The bar shoe is one of the most commonly used of the remedial shoes and comes in several different forms.

Heart bar So-named because these shoes are shaped something like a heart, they apply pressure to the frog. They are generally used on horses suffering from laminitis (see page 232) and can help to prevent rotation of the pedal bone. They can also be used on horses with navicular disease (see page 235).

Egg bar These are egg-shaped shoes that provide extra support at the heels to help horses with low, sloping heels. They also can be used on horses with flexor tendon problems (see page 226–28) or with navicular disease or laminitis.

Straight bar These shoes have both heels connected through a straight bar of metal and are useful for providing heel support.

Patten bar These shoes have a raised bar at the heels and are only used for horses in stall rest. The angle of the heel bar reduces tension on the deep digital flexor tendon and so is used on horses following a severe tendon injury.

Wide web These shoes have a broader ground surface than normal and so reduce concussion. They are commonly used on thin-soled horses.

Wedge These shoes can be built up at the heels to increase the angle of the foot, which is most often seen in horses with spavins or stifle problems. As an alternative, a wedged pad can be used under the shoe to achieve the same effect.

Rocker The ground surface of these shoes is not flat but built up in the quarters. This eases the break over of the foot and is most commonly used on horses with arthritic joint conditions such as ringbone.

Feather edge Used on horses that brush during movement, the inside branch of these shoes is

From top to bottom: A wide-webbed plain punched draft horse shoe, a heart bar shoe, a straight bar shoe.

narrower than the outside, which reduces the likelihood of injury to the opposite limb.

Natural balance These shoes have an excessively squared toe, which is designed to increase the point of break over.

Glue-on Constructed from dense synthetic materials, these shoes are attached to the foot without using nails. They are useful for horses that suffer from thin and shelly hoof walls, chronic seedy toe, laminitis and other foot-related problems, and also provide good shock-absorbing qualities, which can help concussion-related problems.

Above: A shoe with a rolled toe. Right: A type of pattern bar shoe.

Non-remedial Special Shoes

Racing plate These lightweight aluminum shoes are for race horses. They are put on before a race and removed afterward.

Sliding plate These are specifically for the reining horse and are only used on the hind feet. They have a very wide web and extended heels and are designed to reduce traction during the sliding phase of the stop.

Toe-weighted Heavier at the toe than at the heels, these shoes are designed to increase the animation of the gait. They are most commonly seen on extravagant show horses such as the Arab, Morgan, Hackney and the gaited breeds like the Tennessee Walker and Missouri Fox Trotter.

TO SHOE OR NOT TO SHOE?

Not everyone believes it is necessary to shoe a horse; some believe it is detrimental and unnatural to do so. Undoubtedly, many horses in work manage just fine without shoes, although this depends on the terrain they are working on, the level of work they are required to do and, most importantly, the toughness of their feet. (A thin-soled, flat-footed Thoroughbred might struggle with barefoot trail riding over rocky, uneven terrain!)

There are horses who actively go better without shoes; their natural foot provides them with traction, and is able to expand during movement. There is, however, an increased chance of bruised soles when

riding barefoot, and the hoof wall can be worn down excessively quickly leading to sore feet.

If keeping shoes on your horse, be aware of the damage that driving nails causes to the hoof wall, and look after the feet with dressings and nutritional aids (see page 96). If a horse is off work for a period of time, pull the shoes and allow the feet the opportunity to grow and recover. If opting to keep your horse barefoot, be wary of the type of terrain over which you ride – and if in doubt, picture yourself running barefoot along similar ground! Above all, whether keeping your horse barefoot or shod, make sure that its feet are seen regularly by a farrier.

7

TACK

The effects of poorly fitting tack are profound, not just on a horse's physical health but also on its performance and attitude. Bear in mind also, that tack that fits at the beginning of the season — when the horse is not in shape — may not fit by the end of the season when it has lost fat and gained muscle. Similarly, a young horse will continue to change shape and develop significantly from the time it is backed at 2 or 3 years, until when it has finished growing, which can be as late as 5 or 6. Routine checks must be made on all tack to ensure that it is still fitting correctly, and is in good working order.

There is enormous range of tack available and choosing the right equipment can sometimes be difficult, although keeping things simple is a good rule of thumb. Certain items (particularly bits) come in and out of fashion, but try to avoid this and choose the correct equipment for your horse based on common sense.

If you are looking at new products, research them first. Some tack shops have a "bit bank," for example, and will allow you to try a different bit on your horse. If doing this, be sure to thoroughly clean the borrowed bit, soak it in boiling water then allow it to cool before putting it in your horse's mouth.

English Saddles

Construction

The traditional English saddle is built around a "tree," which is usually made from laminated beech wood, and can either be sprung or rigid. Sprung trees have steel springs fitted along their length to provide added strength, and to prevent the tree collapsing in on itself under the weight of the rider.

Trees without these steel springs are referred to as "rigid" trees. The tree provides the basic shape and dimensions of the saddle, and is its building block. Trees traditionally come in narrow, medium and wide fittings, although some saddlers will offer variations. From this basic structure, the exact shape and width of the saddle can be built up by the saddler to fit the individual horse.

The length of the saddle, or the seat size, is traditionally measured from the saddle stud to the middle of the cantle, and generally goes up in ½-inch (1 cm) increments, with 17-inch (42.5 cm) and 17.5-inch (43.75 cm) trees being the most popular sizes. The size of the seat is dependent on the size of the rider and the length of the horse's back. If the horse is particularly short coupled, a very long saddle should be avoided.

Attached to either side of the tree at the front are the metal stirrup bars, which hold the stirrup leathers and stirrups, and running across the tree on either side are the webbing attachments to which the girth pulls connect. The underside of the tree is padded with "flocking," leaving a channel, the gullet, down the middle of the saddle to keep weight off the spine. The flocking is instrumental in the fine-tuning of the saddle's fit; it is this that your saddler will alter to ensure the saddle fits your horse. The seat of the saddle is generally built up on webbing straps covered by hessian, covered by a layer of latex foam.

Types

General purpose (GP) saddle This is suitable for dressage, jumping and hacking, and is an ideal saddle for the rider who wants to do a bit of

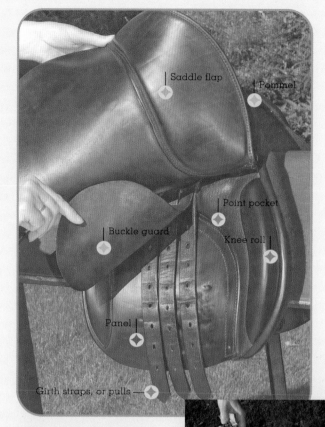

Saddle flap

Pommel

Point pocket

Buckle guard

Knee roll

Panel

Girth straps, or pulls

Traditionally, the English saddle includes three girth straps (or pulls). The front two straps are attached to the same piece of webbing that passes over the tree to the other side. The rear strap is on a separate piece of webbing.

English saddles are measured from one of the front studs to the middle of the cantle (back of the saddle), in inches.

everything without spending for separate dressage and jumping saddles. These saddles will have a moderate knee roll and a slightly forward cut flap and panel.

Dressage saddle This has a longer and straighter saddle flap and panel, with longer stirrup bars that are set further back to aid the leg position. Some designs also provide knee rolls to keep the leg in a straighter position. Generally, the seat is deeper than the GP saddle, and the girth pulls are long and extend downward so that the girth buckles below the bottom of the saddle flap. Dressage girths are shorter than other girths because of the longer girth pulls, and are often wider to spread pressure across a greater area.

Jumping saddle This has forward cut panels and flaps with large knee rolls to provide support to the leg when jumping, and a flat seat to allow the rider to shift his or her weight back and over the horse's center of gravity. Jumping saddles also can be referred to as "close contact" saddles, especially in tack catalogs, which can be confusing. In the United States, "close contact" may be used to describe any type of English saddle, as opposed to a Western one, so be warned!

Event saddle This is an extension of the jumping saddle, but generally has a slightly deeper seat, and is not as forward cut. The event saddle is suitable for all phases of the one-day event and the jumping phases for two- and three-day

Trainer's Tip

Many people sit their saddle too far forward on the withers. Make sure the saddle is sitting behind the withers, which will also allow greater freedom of movement through the shoulders.

events. A new saddle that has only one flap instead of two and brings the rider into closer contact with the horse (called the single-flap event saddle) is now available. This has become very popular, and is also lighter in weight than the conventional saddle. These saddles have long girth pulls similar to the dressage saddle, which allows the girth to be buckled below the level of the rider's leg.

Show saddle This generally has square cut saddle flaps that are long and cover small knee rolls to help to position the leg. Often, the back of the cantle is squared off, and the seat is broad and flat.

Racing saddle This is designed to keep the weight down, and as such there is little to it! Essentially, it is little more than a thick leather pad, and is usually constructed around a fiberglass tree.

Side saddle This is rarely seen now, although there is an active side-saddle association in the United States. The rider sits squarely on the saddle with her left leg in a normal position, and the right leg hooked over the "fixed head" or "top pommel," to hang on the left side.

Synthetic saddle This has become popular recently, due to its relatively low cost in comparison to the traditional leather saddle. Designs continue to improve every year, although these saddles must be treated with caution — some are much better than others. One of the

Opposite: Dressage saddle; left inset picture: GP saddle; right inset picture: suede show saddle. Below: GP saddle annotated to show the parts of a saddle.

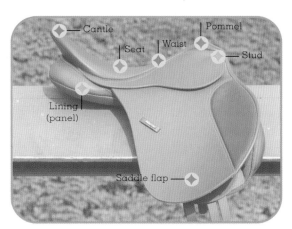

fitting a saddle

A reputable and qualified saddle fitter should carry out the final fitting. It is up to the individual to determine when his or her saddle (and horse) needs to be seen by the saddler, and to recognize when a saddle does not fit. Saddles should be checked at least once a year, and twice if the horse's condition changes shape regularly due to a changing workload.

- Place the saddle, without a numnah or pad on the horse and do the girth up.
- First evaluate the saddle without a rider.
- From the side, the saddle should appear to sit level on the back of the horse, and should not be too long.
- The tree must be the correct width, i.e., narrow, medium or wide, for the horse. If the tree is too narrow, it will appear to pinch at the withers; if it is too wide, it will sit too low on the withers.
- There should be enough room for four fingers between the pommel and the withers without a rider on.
- Standing to the front or back of the horse, there should be a clear channel over the spine.
- The saddle should fit snugly, but not tightly — run a hand down from in front of the saddle stud under the saddle panel to check the saddle is fitting closely. If the saddle is too wide it will move around on the horse and rub.
- Looking at the horse from behind, the saddle should appear to fit square so that weight is distributed evenly along both sides of the back.
- With a rider on board there should be two fingers' worth of room between the pommel and the withers, and there should still be a clear channel running along the spine.
- The saddle needs to fit the rider, too, so choose the correct seat size.
- The length of the saddle flaps can also generally be customized for particularly short or tall riders.

biggest concerns with synthetic saddles is fit. Some makes offer an interchangeable gullet system, and others the "Cair" system — special panels that replace traditional flocking, and are supposed to mold to the shape of the horse. It is possible for a saddler to alter some synthetic saddles, and it is worth finding out if your local saddler is prepared to work on a saddle before you purchase it. On the plus side, a synthetic saddle is easy to keep clean.

Holistic saddle There are a number of different types, which either have specially designed flexible trees, or are treeless. They generally have a much wider weight-bearing area under the seat to distribute the weight of the rider over a larger area and are usually flatter in the seat, which allows the rider greater freedom to move, especially relevant for the dressage rider. Normally, they are flocked with wool behind a brushed serge panel. Many horses do go better in these but they take some adjusting to, and give a different feel from the traditional saddle.

Check the Saddle

As well as the fit of the saddle, it is necessary to check the saddle itself. Sit the saddle on a block and make sure that it is even — bear in mind that some horses may be uneven in their frame, which can make a saddle look uneven.

Check it off the horse first. Look to see that the saddle is symmetrical throughout, then turn it upside down and feel the smoothness of the padding, which should be lump-free and have no

irregularities. Place the saddle facing you with the pommel on your leg and, taking hold of the cantle, gently pull it toward you to check for a broken tree. There should be some marginal give, but no more. If in doubt about the integrity of the tree, do not ride on it. Check all the visible stitching on the saddle, and look for signs of wear in the girth pulls; these can be easily replaced.

Girths

With extensive choice and lower prices now available, it is best to avoid webbing, string and nylon girths, which have a tendency to chafe, and go for a more modern option. Many synthetic girths are currently available that are soft, supple, easy to clean and hard wearing. They have the

Far left: An event saddle and a holistic dressage saddle. Above: An event saddle with surge lining and next to it a holistic treeless saddle with surge lining. Note the wider weight-bearing area on the holistic saddle in the picture on the right.

added advantage of helping to direct sweat away from the horse, which cuts down on chafing. The more traditional leather girths come in all styles, from the short, sculpted dressage girth to the three-fold, Balding, Atherstone and any number of individual contoured designs.

Dressage girth These are short girths designed to fit the long girth pulls of the dressage saddle. There are countless different styles, including those with elastic insets, shaped girths that

When fitting a saddle make sure there is a clear channel over the spine; there needs to be enough room between the pommel and the withers to provide a clear channel when the rider's weight is on board. Run your hand down the inside of the front of the saddle to make sure the saddle is not too loose or too tight.

When jumping, some horses tuck their front feet so tightly into their body that they can damage their underside, especially if wearing jumping studs. The stud girth (see left) offers protection against this. Below, from left to right, a dressage girth, Balding girth, Atherstone girth and three-fold girth.

Trainer's Tip
Try to do the girth up the same amount of holes on both sides of the horse, as this will keep pressure more evenly balanced and will help to prevent skewing the saddle.

contour to the horse, synthetic polyurethane girths that are both soft and low maintenance, girths with independent buckles, and girths with Y-like attachments for the buckles that distribute pressure more evenly.

In general, avoid girths with elastic. Although they sound good in theory they tend to stretch, put uneven pressure on the girth pulls and give a false sense of security.

Balding girth This is a leather girth with three pieces that cross over and are joined in the middle. The girth is contoured to the shape of the horse and rarely chafes.

Stud girth This leather girth has a large middle section designed to protect the horse from stabbing itself with its studs when jumping. They are very effective, but can be quite heavy.

Atherstone girth This padded leather girth is soft and contours to the shape of the horse. It can come with or without elastic insets, and is also available in synthetic materials.

Over girth This webbing girth is secured over the top of the saddle. It is used during the cross-country phase of an event only in conjunction with another girth as a safety measure.

Trainer's Tip

Never try fitting an English saddle with a
numnah underneath.

Three-fold This leather girth is one piece of
leather that is folded three times to produce a soft
but very strong girth.

Stirrups

Stainless steel stirrups The traditional stainless
steel stirrup takes some beating.

Safety stirrups These come in a number of
different designs. There are the traditional "rubber
band" stirrups, where the outside edge is a thick
elastic band designed to pop off if the foot
becomes hung up.

There are also sculpted safety stirrups where
the outside edge is curved in such a way to
prevent hanging up. Recently, a new "break loose"
design has come onto the market, where the
outside edge of the stirrup pops open under
pressure.

Flexi stirrups There are a number of different
flexi stirrups available, most of which are
designed to allow the sides to flex forward and
backward and so reduce pressure and increase
shock-absorbing qualities.

Offset stirrups These stirrups are designed to
guide the rider's foot and bring closer contact
between the rider's knee and the saddle by using
an offset design that encourages the foot to hang
a certain way in the stirrup.

Nylon stirrups These are tough and lightweight,
but not particularly attractive!

Numnahs

If the saddle is fitted correctly then a lightweight
cotton numnah is all that is required, its primary

job being to protect the underside of the saddle.
However, numnahs have come into their own
with bigger, better, fluffier versions appearing
every day. If you must invest in a serious numnah
do ask yourself why.

Cotton or wool numnahs are the best, although
wool ones can be difficult to clean. If using a wool
numnah, take a very thin cotton numnah and use
underneath; this can then be washed as
necessary. Look for numnahs that are quilted —
the quilting helps to keep the padding from
balling up in one area. Some numnahs have a
non-slip lining, which is great, and others are
specially designed for high-withered horses —
these again are very effective.

When using a numnah, ensure that it is not
allowed to pull tight over the withers, as this will
cause rubbing and soreness. Always attach the
numnah to the girth pulls or D rings to prevent it
rucking up under the saddle, and always keep
them clean.

**From left to right: Child's safety stirrup with rubber
band, curved edge safety stirrup, and traditional
heavy weight stainless steel stirrup.**

English Bridles and Bits

Traditional English bridles are made up of several elements: the headpiece, which includes the throatlatch, the browband, the noseband, the cheek pieces, the bit and the reins.

Double bridles, which involve the use of two bits together, will have a further strap (the bridoon cheek piece or bridoon slip) to hold the second bit (the bridoon), to which is attached a second set of reins.

English bridles are defined by the type of bit or bitting arrangement they have, and consist of the:

- Snaffle
- Double bridle
- Pelham
- Gag
- Bitless bridle

The combination of the bridle and the bit works by exerting pressure in one or more of the following areas:
- Corners of the mouth
- Bars of the mouth
- Tongue
- Roof of the mouth
- Chin groove
- Nose
- Poll

Bits

Bits come in all shapes and sizes, and the huge choice available can be confusing. Not only are there different styles, many of which do not fall under the traditional headings, but they are also manufactured in a number of different materials. If in doubt, always seek advice.

Stainless steel This is the traditional material, and stainless steel bits are great, but can be very heavy. (Consider using a hollow mouth bit to cut down on the weight.) They can be very cold, so in the winter warm the bit first before tacking up.

German silver Wonderful, but very expensive. They make a slightly "warmer" bit and encourage the horse to salivate nicely.

Vulcanite or rubber Good for horses with sensitive mouths, although they can be quite heavy. They also can have very thick mouth pieces, which are especially uncomfortable for a horse with a small mouth. They are warm and encourage salivation, but often will be chewed.

Sweet iron or copper These bits encourage salivation and most horses like the taste. Some horses really take to them.

Synthetic Plastic or latex bits are warm and flexible. They are good for horses with sensitive mouths, but are not particularly durable and can be chewed.

TYPES OF BITS
Snaffle Bits

These exert pressure primarily on the tongue, bars, and the corners of the mouth. Types include:

Eggbutt snaffle With eggbutt cheeks.

Loose ring snaffle With loose ring cheeks.

D ring snaffle With D ring cheeks.

> Watch out for the die-hard traditionalists who insist all horses go best in an eggbutt snaffle. While many do, some horses find snaffle bits uncomfortable.

Straight bar snaffle Straight bar, often rubber or vulcanite, and usually with a loose ring cheek.

Fulmer snaffle With full cheek pieces.

French link Snaffle bit with plate (rounded in a figure eight) in the middle that lies with the tongue. A mild bit.

Dr. Bristol Snaffle bit with angled rectangular plate designed to increase tongue pressure. A strong bit.

Bridoon A narrow snaffle bit designed to work in conjunction with a Weymouth on a double bridle.

Wilson snaffle Has two loose rings inside the bit rings. The bridle cheek pieces attach to the loose rings, and the reins to the other rings. When a pull is taken on the reins, the inside rings exert pressure on the sides of the mouth. A strong bit, generally used for driving.

Gag snaffle The bridle cheek pieces run through the center of the bit rings and attach to the reins. When a contact is taken on the reins, pressure is exerted on the poll and upward pressure is exerted on the corners of the mouth. Gag snaffles should be ridden with two reins, one on the regular bit ring and the second on the cheek piece ring. A strong bit.

American gag snaffle/European elevator/Dutch gag snaffle The three rings allow different options for severity; the lowest ring creates the greatest amount of pressure on the poll. These bits should be ridden with two reins, with one rein on the normal snaffle ring. A strong

Different Bits

There are endless new designs of bits available on the market, which can make choosing one difficult. It is best to seek advice from an expert if in doubt. The traditional bit is an eggbutt snaffle, but now there are similar bits being made that have shaped or sculpted mouthpieces, designed to fit the horse's mouth more effectively, and be more comfortable for the horse.

Top: Cherry roller bit. Bottom: Waterford snaffle.

Top: Mullen mouthed Pelham. Bottom: Kimberwick.

Left: Fulmer snaffle. Right: Synthetic Fulmer with lozenge.

Left: Eggbutt snaffle. Middle: Synthetic loose ring snaffle. Right: Stainless steel loose ring snaffle.

Wilson snaffle.

Left: Dr. Bristol. Right: French link.

American gag snaffle, also called a Dutch gag or a European elevator.

Breaking bit with keys.

Western sweet iron snaffle bit with decorative silver inlay.

Bridoon (or bradoon) This is a thin snaffle bit that sits above and behind the Weymouth. Most contact should be through the bridoon rein, with the Weymouth rein being used lightly.

Pelham Bits

The Pelham should ideally be ridden with two reins, although it is possible to buy leather couplings to allow the bit to be ridden with one rein. The length of the bit shank determines the severity of the action of the second rein, which will exert pressure on the poll and chin groove. The top rein, which is attached to the regular bit ring, will exert pressure on the tongue and the corners of the mouth. The Pelham bit can be confusing for the horse because it can send several different messages at once. However, if properly ridden it can be very effective for a strong horse. There are many variations on the Pelham, including a ported Pelham, a mullen mouth, a straight bar, a jointed mouth, a mouthpiece with a lozenge and rubber, plastic and vulcanite Pelhams.

Bitless Bridle

Also referred to as hackamores, these bridles exert pressure on the nose and the poll, and in some designs also on the chin groove. They are useful for a horse recovering from mouth problems, or for horses that are particularly sensitive in the mouth. Not all horses tolerate the action of the hackamore and, depending on the design, they can be very severe.

Bit Rings and Cheek Pieces

Loose ring This has greater movement in the mouth than a fixed ring, and so can encourage a horse to accept the bit. Often used on young horses, it is a "kind" bit. When fitting a loose ring bit be particularly careful that it is big enough to prevent pinching at the corners of the mouth.

Eggbutt The most traditional of bit rings, these are fixed to the bit and are egg shaped.

bit. There is another type of bit that is also referred to as an American Gag. It has long shanks and the bridle cheek pieces attach to the top ring and the reins to the bottom ring. Mid-shank is a section that allows the mouthpiece to slide up and down, depending on the amount of contact. A useful bit for a strong horse.

Double Bridle

Weymouth This is the curb bit from a double bridle, and is fitted with a curb chain. This bit acts primarily on the bars of the mouth, tongue, chin groove (through the curb chain) and poll. Usually these bits have a port that allows the tongue more room and increases pressure on the bars.

Full cheek Useful for starting young horses, the straight metal bar of the cheek piece will encourage the horse to turn its head. The bit cheek piece can be connected to the bridle cheek piece by a leather keeper.

D ring This is similar to the eggbutt, but the bit ring is D shaped and larger. These can also be helpful in teaching a young horse to turn its head.

Hanging cheek/baucher The cheek pieces of the bit extend upward to a small ring that attaches to the bridle cheek pieces. Below this is the rein ring, which is fixed. These will exert some poll pressure.

Mouthpieces

Straight These bits may also be slightly contoured (like a mullen mouth). They are kind bits in that they do not offer the nutcracker action, but can encourage horses to lean on the bit.

Single joint/nutcracker This is the traditional bit form, which has recently come under some scrutiny. The nutcracker action works on the tongue, and can be quite severe. There are now bits with curved sides leading to the join, which sit better in the horse's mouth.

Double joint/lozenge This is a much kinder bit than the single-jointed mouthpiece. It has a lozenge or small plate in the middle of the bit, which allows more movement through the mouthpiece, and prevents a nutcracker action. The exception is the Dr. Bristol bit where the middle piece is angled to exert pressure on the tongue. This is quite a severe bit.

Roller Some mouthpieces incorporate either a single roller, or a series of rollers. The multi-rollers were designed to prevent the horse from grabbing hold of the bit, but they are also valuable for their "mouthing" qualities and encourage the horse to salivate.

Left: This horse is wearing a double bridle. The width of the noseband and browband will vary from bridle to bridle, and this horse, who has a lovely chunky head, has been fitted with a suitably substantial noseband. It sets off the shape of its head and is appropriate for its size. The bridoon and Weymouth bits are lying correctly. Right: The corrected fitted Weymouth curb chain held in place by the slim leather lip strap.

This horse is wearing a chifney, or anti-rearing bit, which can be helpful for boisterous stallions or horses that are difficult to load. It should always be used in conjunction with a headcollar. Two lead ropes should be used, one on the headcollar and one attached to the chifney. This bit produces a severe action and should only be used if experienced.

Port Some mouthpieces incorporate a raised curve in the middle of the bit, which is designed to increase pressure on the bars of the mouth while allowing the tongue more room. Ports vary in their degree of severity, and are seen in Pelham, Weymouth and Kimberwick bits.

Keys These are small copper sections that attach to the middle of the bit and hang down loosely. They are used to encourage a young horse to mouth the bit, but can cause the horse to be overly restless in the mouth.

Twisted Some mouthpieces are constructed from twisted wire or metal. These are exceptionally severe and should only be used by experienced riders on very strong horses.

Waterford This is a multi-jointed mouthpiece that works well on very strong horses. It is a severe bit, but is effective and also encourages the horse to mouth the bit.

fitting a bridle

- Before fitting the bridle on the horse, hold it up to the horse's head and assess the size.
- Start with the bridle slightly on the big side to make it easier to put on and adjust.
- Undo all the straps from their runners and keepers so they are easy to adjust.
- Put the bridle on.
- The snaffle bit should sit high enough so that the horse has one or two wrinkles at each side of the mouth.
- The bit should project approximately ½ inch (1 cm) on each side of the mouth.
- The browband should sit snugly to the head without pulling the headpiece forward and into the back of the ears.
- The split in the headpiece should not be visible above the browband. If it is, the size of the headpiece might be incorrect.
- You should be able to fit four fingers sideways between the horse and the throatlatch.
- The cavesson noseband should sit two-finger widths below the cheekbone prominence, and you should be able to fit one finger inside it.
- In a well-fitting bridle, all the buckles should line up on both sides of the bridle, and should ideally be approximately level with the eye.
- The reins should be long enough to allow the horse to stretch its head and neck down and away, but not so long that there is a danger of the rider catching his or her feet in them.

Curb Bits

Pelham, Weymouth and Kimberwick bits fall into this category. They are all used with a curb chain (see page 130) and so exert pressure on the chin groove and, depending on the individual design, may also exert pressure on the bars, tongue, corners of the mouth and poll.

The Kimberwick is one of the mildest of the curb bits, and is ridden with one rein. It generally

The horse wears different nosebands. From the left: A flash noseband; the top part of the noseband sits two finger widths below the cheekbone prominence, and the bottom strap passes below the bit ring. Next is a cavesson noseband then a drop noseband; note the band sits a good four finger widths above the nostrils, which ensures it does not interfere with the horse's breathing. Finally, a crank noseband for horses that open their jaws to evade the action of the bit. The strap passes through a metal loop and back on itself, which allows it to be fastened more tightly than a conventional noseband.

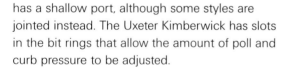

has a shallow port, although some styles are jointed instead. The Uxeter Kimberwick has slots in the bit rings that allow the amount of poll and curb pressure to be adjusted.

Curb Chains

These normally come as either a single or double-link chain, and must be fitted so that they lie flat to the horse. Rubber or leather curb chain guards can be used to diminish the effect of the chain, prevent rubbing and distribute pressure more evenly. The chain should be fitted so that it comes into play when the bit shanks are at a 45-degree angle, and should not be fitted too tightly. Curb chains should be used in conjunction with a lip strap that is attached to each side of the bit's cheek pieces and passes through the middle link

of the curb chain to make sure the curb chain is lying correctly.

Nosebands

Cavesson This is the traditional English noseband and has primarily an aesthetic function. The cavesson should sit two finger widths below the cheekbone, and should be snug without being too tight. The cavesson can also be used as the point of attachment for a standing martingale.

Drop This noseband sits lower on the nose and fastens beneath the bit rings. It is designed to keep the mouth shut to prevent bit evasion, and works by applying nose pressure. Take care not to fit the drop too low or it will interfere with the horse's breathing — it must be at least four finger widths above the nostrils.

Flash A combination of the cavesson and the drop, the flash is designed to keep the mouth shut while using less direct nose pressure.

Grackle This noseband crosses over the front of the nose, and so applies direct pressure to a single spot in the center of the nose. They are used to keep the mouth shut and prevent the horse crossing its jaw.

Mexican This is similar to the Grackle although the crossover is more steeply registered, and the top strap fastens higher up the jawbone.

Kineton Not often seen now, this is a severe noseband that loops around the bit ring and works in conjunction with the bit. It does not keep the mouth shut, but is used as a control device to slow the horse down by exerting nose pressure.

Crank This is a well-padded cavesson-style noseband that is fitted tightly to prevent the horse from opening its mouth.

Reins

Reins come in a number of different materials, styles and lengths (see page 127). It is important to choose the correct length of rein. If they are too short for the length of the horse's neck, then the rider will be pulled forward. Conversely, reins that are too long can be dangerous and loop around the rider's foot. There is no hard and fast rule for measuring the length of the rein, but common sense dictates and is based on the length of the horse's neck.

English bridle reins are attached to the bit ring most commonly through either a buckle or a metal pin, through some have metal snaps. The attachment area, whatever it is, must be routinely checked for any wear and tear, as should all tack and equipment. Most English bridle reins are actually composed of two pieces of leather, which are joined by a buckle at one end; the exception to this can be the reins attached to the curb bit in a double bridle, which are often stitched together instead of buckled.

Reins are most commonly made from leather, though they can also be partially covered in rubber, which affords the rider good grip especially in wet conditions, or webbing, which again gives good grip. Some leather reins are braided; these are attractive and give good grip, while others are smooth, these most commonly being used in show classes. There are also a number of synthetic reins (and bridles) on the market that are strong, lightweight and very easy to clean.

Western Saddles, Headstalls and Bits

Saddle Construction

Like the English saddle, the Western saddle is also constructed around a tree. The western tree was traditionally made from wood, such as yellow poplar, Douglas fir or cottonwood, covered in rawhide, which greatly strengthened the frame and prevented the wood from warping. Now fiberglass can be used in place of the rawhide, and some trees are made from a synthetic polyethylene substance, which is lighter than wood and highly durable. The two sides of the tree that rest along either side of the horse's back are called the bars, and the angle and size of these determine the fit. There are four basic sizes of tree, determined by the width and length of the bars.

- Regular; the bars are approximately 5½ inches (14 cm) apart.
- Semi-quarter horse; the bars are designed to fit a lighter weight horse than the quarter horse with more pronounced withers, and the bars are approximately 6 inches (15 cm) apart.
- Quarter horse, built to fit most stock type horses, the bars are approximately 6½ inches (16 cm) apart.
- Arabian, built to fit the wider, shorter shape of Arabian and Morgan horses, the bars are approximately 6¾ inches (17 cm) apart.

At the front of the Western saddle is the horn, which will vary in height, width and angle depending on the type of saddle. The shape of the pommel (front of the saddle), beneath the horn will also vary from a smooth "A" shape, to a more defined shape with swells.

Trainer's Tip

When saddling, always do up the front cinch first, then the back; when unsaddling, undo the back cinch first and then the front.

Opposite: This is a saddle suitable for barrel racing and cutting. It has a tall, narrow horn that gives the rider something to grip onto, and good sized swells. The seat is relatively flat. Inset top: A saddle suitable for roping, although the back cinch is not pictured. The horn is broad and strongly constructed and the seat deep. Inset bottom: A saddle suitable for pleasure riding (note the padded seat), but could also be used for reining as the horn is relatively small and the seat well shaped.

Attached to the tree is the "rigging," which can come in one of five different positions that incorporate one or two large D rings on each side of the saddle. The rigging is the system to which the cinch, or girth, is attached. Western saddles can have two cinches. The front cinch is attached to the rigging D rings on each side of the saddle via a long folded piece of leather called the latigo; the back cinch is designed to keep the saddle extra secure when roping livestock, and is fitted more loosely than the front cinch. Both cinches are connected by a short keeper strap. The back cinch is attached to the saddle via the flank cinch billet. It is fitted relatively loosely, although there should not be more than 1 inch (25 cm) between the belly and the cinch, to prevent the risk of a horse catching a foot.

Different Types

There are many different types of Western saddles with the most common being:

Pleasure An all-purpose saddle for the trail rider. These saddles are designed for comfort rather than speed and generally have a reasonably high cantle and often a padded seat. They can have either front, or front and back cinches.

Roping Designed for roping livestock, these must be very well constructed with strength, fit and durability in mind. They have a front and back cinch, a significant, strong horn, and generally a low seat and cantle with deep, wide stirrups.

Reining These are used for the Western version of dressage and so are designed to allow as much feel as possible through the saddle. The horn is small so as not to interfere with the reins, and the seat is well shaped. Normally these saddles use only a front cinch.

Barrel These are relatively lightweight, with a deep seat and often wide swells to aid the rider's security while racing around the barrels. The horn tends to be narrow and tall to give the rider something to grip onto and again they generally use only a front cinch.

Cutting These have a tall, thin horn and a flat seat to allow the rider ease of movement. The swells are usually quite substantial and cut back to help the rider's security when the horse is moving rapidly and athletically. These saddles generally have front and back cinches.

A beautifully turned out and well-trained Western horse. It wears a Western saddle with a breastplate, which helps secure the saddle in place, and a typical Western headstall (bridle). Note the lack of noseband and the long and loosely held split reins. The horse is traveling with a lowered head and neck carriage characteristic of Western pleasure riding.

Show Western show saddles are highly decorative and generally display ornate silverwork and intricate carving. Different styles come in and out of fashion, but they tend to have a short horn and low cantle, and often a padded seat.

Arabian Designed specifically to fit the shape of the Arabian horse, these saddles are shorter and wider in the bars than regular Western saddles.

Flexi saddle This is designed to allow more flexibility than the traditional fairly rigid Western tree. The structural integrity of the saddle is

Top: An old-style endurance saddle made from leather; most modern ones are now synthetic, which are much lighter and easier to clean. Bottom: It is a good idea to store Western saddles with their stirrup fenders secured (here a pole is used). This encourages the fenders to lie correctly when the rider is on board. It is particularly useful with new saddles where the leather is stiff and the fenders unwieldy.

Trainer's Tip

Due to the lever action, curb bits allow the Western rider to give an aid with a very light contact on the rein, so while the bit may look severe, it is only as harsh as the hand of the rider.

maintained through a combination of leather and a high-density polyethylene that provides flexibility, while a neoprene lining on the skirt provides added cushioning.

Endurance saddle This is designed to be comfortable for horse and rider during long rides. It differs from the traditional Western saddle in that it does not have a horn, and is not as heavy. Often made from synthetics that are lightweight and easy to clean, this saddle generally has a reasonably high cantle with small swells through the pommel. Treeless versions are popular at the moment; they offer closer contact between horse and rider and move with the horse.

fitting the saddle

The Western saddle was designed primarily to accommodate the working cowboy in his job of moving, sorting and herding cows, and as such had to be utilitarian and comfortable for horse and rider during lengthy periods. The wide surface area of the saddle transfers the weight of the rider over a much greater area than the English saddle, minimizing pressure points. Western saddles should be used in conjunction with a saddle blanket (equivalent to the numnah) or a pad.

- Select a saddle with an appropriate tree for the size and shape of the horse.
- Place the saddle on the horse without a pad and assess the length. The saddle should not be so long that it will rub the hip bones.
- Holding the horn, lightly joggle the saddle from side to side. It should fit the horse so that there is minimal movement, and so that the saddle sits securely even without being cinched up.
- The saddle should appear to sit level, and the seat itself should also be level.
- With the weight of a rider on board, there should be 2 inches (5 cm) of clearance between the withers and the saddle, and a clear passage through the gullet.
- You should be able to slide a flat hand between the saddle and horse from the pommel down.
- Make sure that the pad/blanket is long enough to completely clear the back of the saddle, and that the saddle still fits the horse with the pad. Some pads are extremely thick, and will alter the way the saddle fits.

Cinches

The Western cinch comes in a number of different materials, from the traditional horsehair to a mohair blend, cotton, nylon, felt and, increasingly, synthetic fabrics. Synthetic cinches have the advantage of being easy to clean, and wick moisture away from the girth region; they also are padded and can be contoured to fit the horse. Back cinches are leather and usually wider and more substantial than the front cinch; the two cinches should be joined by a keeper strap.

Stirrups

There are two main forms of Western stirrups available.

Visalia stirrups These provide a wider base for the foot, which some people find more comfortable. The width of the tread can vary from 1½ to 4 inches (3 to 10 cm) and is a matter of personal preference. They can be constructed from wood covered in leather or rawhide, aluminum, nylon and various synthetic materials, and can also be faced in brass and even silver. Many stirrups now come with rubber treads for comfort and grip, and some have a swivel and lock system designed to relieve knee and ankle pressure by allowing the rider to set the angle at which the stirrup hangs.

Ox bow stirrups These have a more rounded shape and a narrower tread than the visalia stirrup. Ox bows have quite an "old time" look and are usually constructed out of metal, which can make them quite heavy (and cold in the winter). Aluminum ox bow stirrups are now available, which reduces the weight.

Saddle Blankets and Pads

There are hundreds of different saddle blankets and pads on the market, available in practically any color combination. Saddle blankets are normally either thick woven cotton or wool, and provide less cushioning than a pad. When choosing a blanket make sure it is long enough to

"Running the barrels" is a competition that involves racing a horse around three barrels in a clover leaf pattern. It is a timed event and a horse must be extremely agile and athletic. The horse wears a barrel racing saddle and the rider holds the horn with one hand. Bandages and overreach boots are worn for protection.

extend beyond the front and back of the saddle. Wool is hard to beat and is durable and breathable, but has the disadvantages of being expensive and difficult to keep clean.

Cotton blankets are generally very cheap and do not last well, but are washable. Using a combination of a cotton blanket with a wool one on top can be effective, or try attaching a cotton liner to a wool blanket with Velcro; this can then be removed and washed.

Pads are thicker than blankets and again come in a variety of materials from quilted cotton to thick felt, wool, sheepskin and neoprene. Felt pads are excellent and last well and, if allowed to thoroughly dry out, they can be brushed clean with a stiff brush.

When choosing a pad or a blanket try to buy the best you can afford, as spending a bit extra is worth it in the long run.

Breast collars are often used with the Western saddle to help keep the saddle in place, which is especially relevant when roping livestock. Breast collars are traditionally leather, although nylon ones are available.

WESTERN HEADSTALLS AND BITS

Western riding involves a featherlight contact on the reins, which are held loosely in one hand. Western headstalls (bridles) tend not to incorporate nosebands (unless using a tiedown) and the reins are generally long and split, although roping reins are shorter and more similar to the English rein. Western tack can be heavily decorated with silver and intricate leatherwork.

Headstalls

Split ear This headstall, also known as a shaped ear headstall, incorporates a slit across the top of

the headpiece through which one (and occasionally both) ears may be slotted. Due to this design the bridle does not require a browband, does not have a noseband, but does have a throatlatch.

One ear Also known as a slip ear headstall, a loop of leather is attached to the headpiece through which the ear fits. This is similar to the split ear design and has the same features. There is also a double ear version with two earpieces, both the one ear and double ear tend to be popular in the show ring and are often highly decorated.

Browband headstall This is similar to the English bridle and features a browband, but generally does not include a noseband unless using a tiedown.

Bosal This is a heavy rawhide (or plastic) noseband to which the reins attach. It is essentially similar to a hackamore bridle (see page 127) but works primarily by using nose pressure without the leverage on the poll. Bosals can be ridden alone, or in conjunction with a bridle, in which case the rider uses two sets of reins.

Tiedown This is used in conjunction with a headstall and is designed to prevent the horse from raising its head above a certain level (similar to the standing martingale, see page 140) by applying pressure to the nose. A strap attaches from the middle of the front cinch, runs through a ring on the breastcollar, and attaches to the back of a cavesson-type noseband (see page 130) that can be made from rawhide, plastic/nylon, leather and, in extreme cases, chain- or metal-covered in plastic. Sometimes tiedowns are referred to simply as nosebands.

Bits

Western bits can roughly be divided into two groups, the snaffle group and the curb group. Snaffle bits are non-leverage bits and there is a

direct contact through the reins to the bit ring and the mouthpiece. Snaffle bits work by exerting pressure on the bars of the mouth, the corners of the mouth and the tongue. Curb bits are leverage bits; the reins attach to a ring on a shank to which the mouthpiece is attached. When a contact is taken on the reins there is a lever-type action through the shank that applies pressure to the lower jaw and the poll. The longer the shank of the bit, the greater the lever and the more severe the action of the bit.

There are numerous different Western snaffle bits that work essentially in the same way as the English snaffle, and a multitude of different curb bits. Some curb bits are jointed while others are straight, and some incorporate a port or a plate in the mouthpiece. Depending on the height of the port or the plate, pressure can also be exerted on the roof of the mouth when a contact is taken. Curb bits can also be ridden with a curb chain, which will exert pressure on the back of the chin when a contact is taken.

Western Reins

There are a number of different types of Western reins, and they are fitted quite differently from the English rein. The most common Western reins

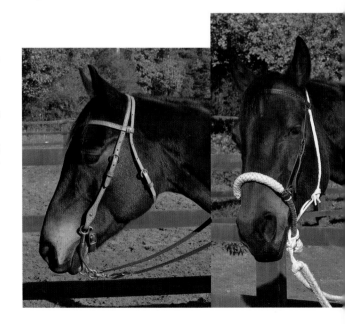

(split reins) consist of two separate reins (not joined together like English ones) and are much longer in length than the English rein. Western reins are generally held in one hand, with a much lighter contact than English ones, or in one or two hands (especially on young horses) where the reins cross over the neck at the wither and hang down each shoulder. The Western horse is primarily guided by the rider's leg pressure and shift in weight first, and through the reins being used against the neck, rather than through the mouth, the exception to this being roping horses. Western reins are much thicker than English ones and are generally made from light tan harness leather. Most often, Western split reins fasten to the bit by threading back on themselves and being tied, either with a short piece of leather or rawhide. They can also be fastened with buckles or snaps.

There are two main types of Western rein that do join together, unlike the split rein, and these are roping reins and show reins (romal reins). Roping reins are short and one continuous length,

similar, though shorter, than an English rein. They are used during roping competitions and practice and give the rider greater control, with less chance of the reins becoming entangled. Although split reins may be used in some show classes, some of the more advanced classes require show reins. These generally attach to the bit ring via a short length of chain, and at the other end are joined together. At the place where the two reins are joined there is a further single section of rein attached, which is called the romal. These show reins are often highly decorated with silver or intricate leather and rawhide braiding.

From left to right: A horse in a browband headstall with roping reins attached. A horse wearing a bosal. A horse in a one ear headstall with split reins. A horse in a double ear headstall decorated with rawhide detailing, with split reins.

Special Tack and Training Aids

There are a large number of items that fall under the category of either training aids or special equipment, and new products come on the market virtually every day.

Generally, training aids should only be used by experienced riders, or by more novice riders providing they are being taught. Training aids in the wrong hands can do great damage to the horse, while if used correctly they can be a useful addition to the training process.

Martingales

These are designed to prevent the horse from raising its head excessively. There are two main types of martingale, the running martingale and the standing martingale.

Running martingale This attaches to the girth, runs between the front legs, and connects to a neck strap, which may or may not have further straps to secure it to the D rings on the front of the saddle. From the neck strap, the martingale divides into two, the fork, and ends in a ring on each side through which the reins pass. To fit a running martingale correctly, first the neck strap must be sufficiently loose that it sits well onto the shoulders and, second, without the reins attached, the forks should be pulled back and extend to approximately 4 inches (10 cm) below the withers.

Standing martingale This attaches in the same way as the running martingale at the girth and neck strap but instead of dividing into a fork, the leather continues in one piece and is attached through the back of a cavesson noseband to prevent the head from being raised by exerting pressure on the nose. The martingale should

The horse on the left is wearing draw reins. They attach to the middle of the girth, run up between the front legs, through the bit rings, and into the rider's hands. The one on the right is wearing a breast girth with a running martingale attachment.

basic lunging equipment

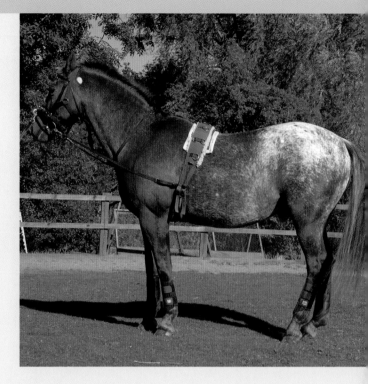

HORSE
- Lunging roller with pad or saddle with stirrups removed or secured.
- Bridle with reins removed or twisted up and secured in throatlatch.
- Brushing boots or exercise bandages on all four legs.
- Overreach boots.
- Either a lunging cavesson to which the lunge line is attached, or run the lunge line through the inside bit ring over the poll and snap onto outside bit ring.
- Side reins, if required.

THE HANDLER
- Hard hat.
- Gloves.
- Appropriate nonslip footwear.
- Lunge whip.
- Neatly coiled lunge line.

reach to just below the throatlatch when extended.

Breast girth
This comes in a variety of styles, and is designed to prevent the saddle from slipping backward. It is particularly valuable for use on jumping horses, especially in cross-country events.

Training Aids
There are many different training aids available, and all should be treated with caution. They must be introduced slowly, used only in the short term, and never by inexperienced riders.

German martingale Similar in appearance to a running martingale, the forks run through the bit rings and back to the reins, where they are attached by a snap hook. The reins have a series

Trainer's Tip
A strong supporting leg must always be used in conjunction with training aids to prevent the horse becoming bent over, on the forehand, and trailing his hocks out behind.

of D rings along them so that the tightness (and therefore severity) can be altered. If the horse raises its head above the set level then the device becomes tight and downward pressure is exerted on the bit. Also called a market harborough.

Harbridge Similar to a running martingale except the forks are elastic and attached directly to the bit ring. It encourages the horse to soften through the back and aids self-carriage.

Draw reins These should always be used in conjunction with regular snaffle reins, and *never* on their own. The reins attach to the center of the girth, run through the front legs, through the bit rings and into the rider's hands.

Side reins These only should be used when lunging. They attach to either the lunging roller (surcingle) or the girth at one end and snap onto the bit ring at the other. They also can be attached to the center of the girth, coming up through the front legs and snapping to the bit ring — this method will encourage the horse to lower its head and is often used in Western pleasure training.

Chambon This piece of equipment should only be used on the lunge. It attaches to the center of the girth or roller, comes through the front legs to the neck strap, and then splits into two long forks. These run up to and through a ring on either side of a special poll pad and down to the bit ring

where they snap on. This device encourages the horse to lower its head and neck and work through its back.

De Gogue Similar to the chambon, but this is suitable for use when riding. Instead of the forks snapping to the bit ring, they are passed through the bit rings and come back into the rider's hands, although it should be used in conjunction with the normal snaffle rein.

Pessoa Used on the lunge, this encourages the horse to work through its back and into an outline. It is made from soft cord that attaches on each side to the roller, runs to the bit, to a padded hindquarter section and back to the top of the roller. By incorporating the hindquarters, the horse is encouraged to work through from behind.

Lunging is a particularly useful exercise both for the horse alone, and as seen here for the horse and rider. Lessons on the lunge allow the rider to work on their balance and position, while the trainer controls the horse, whose own balance and way of going can be improved through moderate lunging.

Cleaning Tack

Tack should be cleaned after use to keep the leather in good condition. Wash boots, bandages and numnahs as needed, and after riding, air out numnahs and bandages. Once a week tack should be thoroughly cleaned, taken apart and checked all over.

- First wash the bit and dry with a soft cloth.
- Wash the stirrup irons and treads.
- Using warm water, thoroughly clean the tack, removing the worst of the grease and dirt. Next take a clean cloth and, using saddle soap, thoroughly go over the tack again.
- Finally, apply saddle cream using a clean dry cloth.
- Periodically polish all buckles and stirrup irons.
- After cleaning the tack, replace all straps in the runners and keepers, loop the reins through the throatlatch and do the noseband up.

Western saddles involve a bit more cleaning and a bit more time! Many have extensive "tooling" or engraved patterns across the leather. Use a soft-bristled toothbrush to clean tooled areas, and treat the saddle with a coat of neatsfoot oil once a month. The leather used in Western saddles is

Trainer's Tip

Murphy's Oil Soap, which is actually a wood soap, works well on leather, providing a leather cream is used afterward. It is an economical way to clean tack, being much cheaper than saddle soap and going further.

thicker and tougher than that in English saddles, and neatsfoot helps to soften the leather and keep it in good condition. Neatsfoot can darken the leather, so on very light saddles use leather butter instead. When the saddle has been cleaned, twist the stirrup fenders out and run a broom handle through the two stirrups — this helps to keep the fenders hanging correctly.

Saddle soap removes dirt and grease but can leave the leather looking dull and some soaps can have a drying effect. Saddle creams are a nourishing agent that feed the leather, keep it supple and add shine. Use soap and cream in conjunction for the best results. There are some "one step" products that claim to do everything — these are useful for daily cleaning, but the weekly clean should involve the use of leather creams.

When cleaning, thoroughly check the tack for signs of wear and tear. Pay particular attention to the stitching and make sure it is in good condition; also check the buckle holes, in the stirrup leathers and on the bridle.

Over time, and particularly on the stirrup leathers, the holes will stretch with continued use, and horizontal cracks may appear running outward from the holes. Be sure to replace the leathers in this instance as there is a danger of them breaking. Most saddlers will happily do repair work on tack such as renewing areas of stitching, but can sometimes take a long time, so be sure to check with them first.

Trainer's Tip

Stainless steel sink cleaner works well on steel stirrup irons.

Also while cleaning tack check the saddle lining to make sure it is smooth and firm, and has not settled out.

After cleaning the bridle, it is traditional to hang it in one of two ways, illustrated here. On the left, the reins have been looped through the throatlatch and the noseband secured around the outside of the cheek pieces.

Left: The reins are looped through the throatlatch, which is crossed over the front of the cheek pieces, while the noseband again is fastened around the outside of the cheek pieces. Presenting the cleaned bridle in these ways keeps it tidy.

Below: On a daily basis, clean the bit with a damp sponge (left). For weekly cleaning, take the bridle apart and thoroughly clean each individual part. Shown below is the bridle taken apart and cleaned, and ready to be reassembled. Do remember which holes your bit and cheek pieces should be on so that the bridle fits properly after being reassembled.

Boots and Bandages

The primary function of boots and bandages is to provide protection and support for the horse.

Boots come in all shapes and sizes, and modern boots that offer protection against brushing also can provide tendon support and protection to the fetlock. They range in design and material from leather to synthetics such as neoprene and polyurethane. Synthetic fabrics are easy to keep clean and are generally quick to put on and take off, but they do not last as long as leather. Leather boots are expensive but durable, providing they are well looked after, and cleaned and oiled regularly.

Protective Boots

Brushing boots These provide protection to the lower leg from below the knee to just above the fetlock.

Tendon boots These fit around the back of the leg to provide support and protection to the tendons, and to prevent high overreach injuries. Tendon boots can be open fronted, which is useful for showjumping, or fully enclosed. Traditionally, they fit from below the knee to the fetlock, though many now continue down through

From left to right: Open-fronted tendon boots and overreach boots, coronet ring or sausage boot, brushing boots, front event boots

Trainer's Tip

Choose boots with easy fastenings. There is nothing worse than fiddling around with fastenings in the dead of winter when your fingers are cold.

the pastern to provide support to the suspensory ligaments and superficial tendons.

Event boots A pumped-up version of the tendon boot, designed to offer maximum protection through the cross-country phase of eventing. They are also referred to as polo boots.

Schooling boots/wraps Generally made from neoprene or similar materials, these boots are designed to be easy to put on and take off and offer protection to the lower leg from below the knee to the pastern.

Fetlock boots These are short boots that just cover the fetlock joint and provide protection against low brushing injuries.

Yorkshire boots Rarely seen now, these are also for protecting the fetlock but are made from a thick felt that is tied then doubled over.

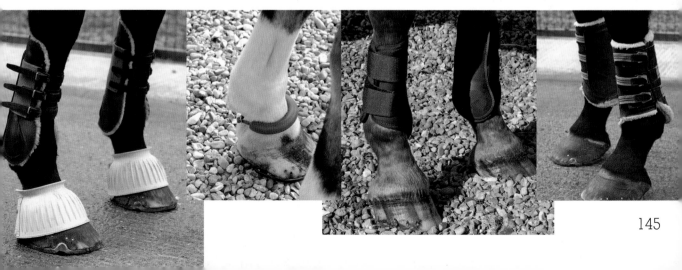

Fetlock ring and coronet ring These are thick rubber rings that are attached with a small buckle. The fetlock ring sits above the fetlock to prevent high brushing and the coronet ring sits above the coronary band to prevent low brushing. These are also used to prevent the horse damaging its elbow with the shoe when lying down. Also called donut boots.

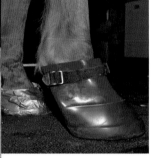

Clockwise from top: Neoprene schooling wraps provide some support and protection from below the knee down to the pastern. An equiboot, which is used for keeping dressings in place and an injured foot clean. Knee and hock boots with heavy leather knee pieces.

how to make cold boots

To keep costs down, make your own cold boots. Prepare a kaolin poultice.

1 Spread the kaolin between two pieces of cotton 10 inches (25 cm) long by 6 inches (15 cm) wide to form a sandwich. Keep in the freezer until needed, then,

2 Mold to the shape of the leg and cover with a layer of plastic (shopping bags work well).

3 Hold in place with padding and an elastic bandage. These will stay cold for approximately 15 minutes.

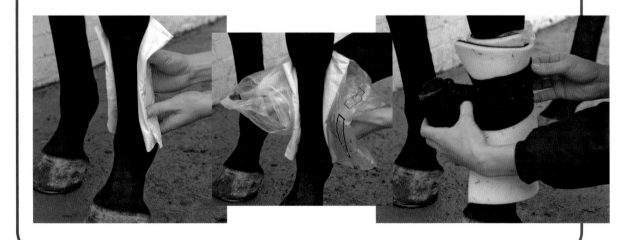

Overreach boots Made from thick rubber, these bell-shaped boots fit over the front feet and protect the heel bulbs from injury caused by a hind foot. Also called bell boots.

Skid boots These are fitted to the fetlock to provide protection to the back of the joint. They are used for Western riding, especially reining, and protect the fetlock during sliding stops.

Knee boots Generally made from leather and felt, these fit over the knees for protection during traveling and hacking.

Hock boots These fit over the hocks to protect from injury during traveling.

Traveling boots These padded boots may extend above the knee and hock to negate the use of knee and hock boots.

Therapy Boots
Ice boots These are kept in the freezer and applied to the legs to provide short periods of cold therapy.

Magnetic boots A magnetic insert can be added to provide magnetic therapy to the legs.

Water boots These boots have a hose attachment on the outside through which water is filtered. They are very useful for applying cold

Left to right: Traveling bandages, exercise bandages, polo bandages.

therapy, but the horse must not be left unattended while wearing one.

Equiboots Useful for keeping dressings on the feet and the feet clean for medical reasons.
.
Poultice boots These keep a foot poultice in place, and are also useful for soaking a foot.

Bandages
See page 218 for further information about different types of bandages.
Exercise bandages Elastic bandages used during exercise should be applied over a bandage pad to evenly distribute pressure. They are excellent for providing support to the tendons and ligaments, but many will shrink when wet, and if riding through water they can tighten.

Polo bandages Long fleece bandages that are useful when schooling but do not provide sufficient protection for use when jumping. They can be applied without a pad, but keep the pressure even when bandaging.

Cool bandages Are impregnated with cooling gel and can be kept in the refrigerator to enhance their cooling action. They are useful immediate first aid for bruising, pain and inflammation.

Rugs and Blankets

Modern materials are breathable, actively wick moisture away from the horse, and invariably have a ripstop outer membrane that prevents the inevitable snags and tears. They also come in every conceivable color combination and look pretty sharp!

Fitting a Rug

Fit is really important with rugs, as rugs that do not fit properly will rub and chafe or slip and be dangerous. Rug measurements are taken from the middle of the chest horizontally to the middle of the tailbone, apart from exercise sheets that are measured from the front of the withers along the back to the top of the tail. The measurements go up in 3-inch (7.5 cm) increments, and if your horse falls between a size, always go for the larger one. However, when fitting a hood, the size must be exact. If the hood is too large there is a danger that it might slip over the eyes and cause the horse to panic. Similarly, if it is too small, it will be uncomfortable and may restrict the horse's jaw movement.

Summer Rugs

Fly sheet This is designed to keep the flies off the horse and to block UV rays that bleach the hair. Go for a model that offers a good belly band, a detachable neck piece and fly mask. Never leave a fly mask on overnight.

Summer sheet This lightweight cotton rug is useful for keeping dust off the stabled horse and

Trainer's Tip

Pull-on rugs are quite popular. These do not have a front opening and are pulled over the head. They have the advantage of cutting out chest drafts, but can be alarming to a young horse, or a horse that is not used to them.

can be used for traveling. Summer sheets also are useful for providing an extra layer when used under a night rug in the winter.

Sweat rug The old fashioned "string vest-style" sweat rug is now virtually obsolete in the face of newer "wicking" rugs. However, they are still useful for drying a horse, but *only* work if used underneath a cotton summer sheet. There are also thicker sweat rugs with a smaller mesh that work quite well, and can be used as an extra layer under a night rug.

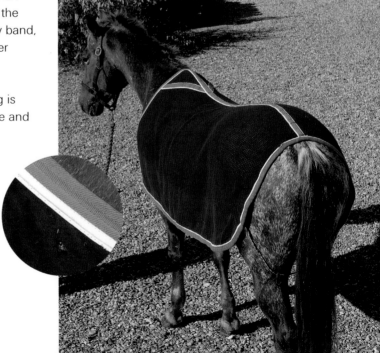

Here the horse is wearing a tight weave cotton sweat rug. The inset picture shows a cotton summer sheet, useful for keeping dust flies at bay in the summer. Opposite page, clockwise: horse in a slinky; one in a waterproof turnout rug; one wearing a quilted rug with ripstop exterior — excellent for warmth at night in winter; horse in a woolen day rug — also useful for traveling and cold days.

Coolers One of the greatest inventions! These rugs can be used after work or bathing and actively wick moisture away from the horse and onto the surface of the rug, while keeping the horse warm and preventing chills.

Fleece These smart rugs also wick moisture away, and are useful for traveling.

Slinky This is a tight-fitting nylon/lycra garment that covers the neck and head, and is useful for keeping braids tidy overnight, keeping the horse clean, and providing warmth in the winter. They are worn in conjunction with another rug and cut down on shoulder rubs. It is also possible to buy full-body slinkies.

Spring turnout These are lightweight, waterproof rugs for keeping the horse dry and warm during spring and summer rains.

Winter Rugs
New Zealand/turnout rug These tough rugs were originally made from waterproofed canvas, but now heavy-duty turnout rugs are mostly a combination of synthetic fibers with quilted inner

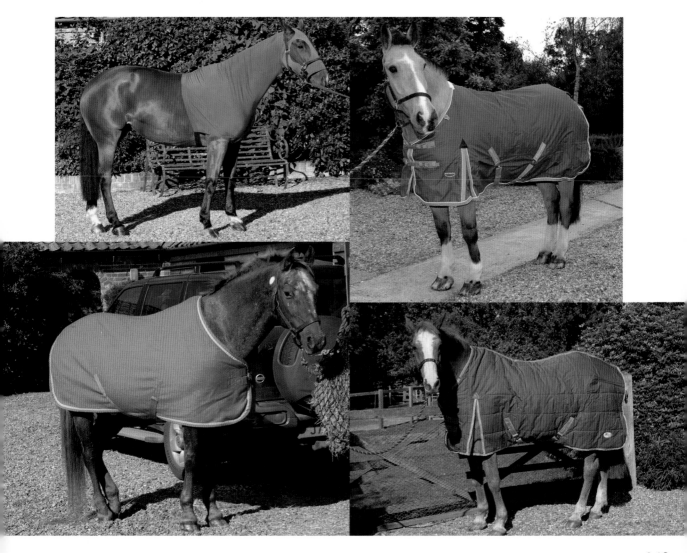

Horse in a fleece. In cold weather, when grooming, fold the rug back and groom the front half of the horse then swap and fold the rug forward, as seen here, to groom the quarters.

linings. These new fabrics are designed to be more waterproof, more durable, breathable and a better fit than canvas ones. I prefer turnout rugs with detachable neck covers and tail guards. If a horse is kept at grass and wears a turnout rug most of the time, ensure that the rug is removed and the horse is checked at least once a day. At the end of the winter, send turnout rugs off to be cleaned and reproofed if necessary.

Quilted night rug Traditionally the night rug was a jute rug over a layer or two of blankets, and held in place with a roller. Rollers are rarely seen now since cross straps and leg straps have all but replaced them. For extra warmth, you can use thin rugs under a night rug, or use a blanket providing it has been fitted with cross straps and front fasteners. Many quilted night rugs also come with detachable hoods and neck covers.

Day rug The smartest day rugs are the old-fashioned wool ones trimmed with colored bindings. They are designed to keep the horse warm and clean when stabled during the day, or for use when traveling. Now, day rugs are usually thinner versions of the quilted night rug, which work well and are washable.

Exercise rug/quarter sheet These are designed to sit under the saddle and cover the quarters and can be used when exercising during very cold weather. There are also waterproof quarter sheets for use in wet weather. When using quarter sheets, make sure they do not pull tight over the withers.

Problems with Rugging

For young horses or green horses, rugs can be pretty frightening things at first. If handling a horse you are not familiar with, always take precautions and approach rugging up as you would tacking up — i.e., quietly, calmly and slowly. Have the rug ready and lay it flat out on the ground. Starting from the back, fold the rug in about one-third of the way, then fold it over again. With the horse tied up, approach it and allow it to sniff the rug, which should now be draped over your arm. Standing with your back to the horse's head, gently place the folded rug over its withers. Be aware that as the horse feels the rug on its offside it may jump toward you. Now unfold the rug by the first third, holding it firmly in place. Allow the horse a minute to get used to the feel, and unfold the final third. Reassure and praise the horse and carefully fasten the rug at the front. Have a helper on the offside of the horse reach down and pass the cross straps to you — this prevents you placing yourself in danger by reaching under the horse to get the straps. Untie the horse and give it a haynet to take its mind off the rug.

If a rug is introduced in this manner the horse will rapidly come to see it as no big deal. The more familiar the horse becomes with a rug, the less time you need to take to put it on. Eventually, you should be able to throw a rug over the horse without a reaction. Do not fall into the trap of tiptoeing around the horse forever; your horse must learn to accept things flapping, banging and moving around.

If the Rug Rubs

Some horses are thin skinned and prone to rubbing, even when the rug is a very good fit. Horses that have particular problems are those with very high withers, which can become pressure points, or very muscular, round shoulders that rub on the inside of the rug.

- First of all check the rug is adjusted correctly.
- Buy sheepskin or synthetic sheepskin and stitch across the wither section of the rug.
- It is also possible to buy rugs that are cut back at the wither to relieve pressure.
- If the horse's shoulders are rubbing bald, it is possible to buy shoulder covers, which are similar to slinkies but just cover the base of the neck and shoulders. These covers should be worn underneath the rug, and are effective in cutting down on rubbing.

When the Horse Chews Its Rugs

Try to find out why: Does it irritate the skin? Is it too tight? Is it too hot? Is it a habit?

Unfortunately, rug chewing is habit-forming for some horses, and if this is the case with your horse, then try to rug the horse as little as possible. Very few horses chew their rugs when turned out, so keep your horse out as much as possible. Most habits form from boredom, so if the horse is stabled make sure it has ad lib hay. Use rugs that are made from as tough a material as possible, and spray the areas the horse chews with an offensive spray such as bitter apple. In the worst case scenario, the horse can be fitted with a plastic bib that attaches to the headcollar. These allow the horse to eat and drink, but prevent it from tearing its rugs.

It is essential that any rug in which a horse is turned out — whether that be a waterproof one or a flysheet — must fit correctly, and will stay secure and in place when the horse charges around, as seen here.

8

TRANSPORTING

It is essential that the horse owner has the equipment to transport his or her horse, if necessary. Trailers are an expensive but necessary evil. Even if you rarely transport your horse, in times of emergency you must be able to do so. If a horse is badly injured, with a severed artery, for example, and requires immediate intensive veterinary treatment, there is no time to track down a neighbor or friend and ask to borrow his or her vehicle. Vehicles should be well maintained and kept ready to go; keep the gas tank full and tires in good condition. Traveling equipment also should be kept clean and in good working order.

Vehicles

There are two types of trailers for transporting horses. One is the gooseneck, which hitches to a ball in the center of the back of a truck and the other is the bumper pull (also called a tagalong), which hitches to the back of the towing vehicle.

Gooseneck or Bumper Pull

Gooseneck trailers provide a very stable ride for the horse, and range in size from a small two-horse trailer right up to one that can carry eight horses. (There are even larger ones available, which require special towing vehicles and drivers' licenses.) These trailers can include living and tack accommodation, too. The disadvantages of a gooseneck trailer is that it has to be towed by a truck, is generally more expensive than a bumper pull and takes up more room. Bumper pulls tend to be more reasonable, are smaller and can be pulled by 4x4s and SUVs, providing the towing vehicle and hitch is suitable (see below). Bumper pulls can provide a less stable journey for the horse and tend not to track along behind the vehicle as smoothly as a gooseneck. If you are considering regularly transporting more than two horses, a gooseneck is the more appropriate.

Towing Vehicles

It is essential that your towing vehicle has the correct towing capacity for the size and weight of the loaded trailer, and this capacity will be found in the vehicle manufacturer's trailer towing guide. This will explain how the vehicle is rated to tow in terms of the G.V.W. (the gross vehicle weight) of the trailer when it is fully loaded. The easiest way to determine the weight of a loaded trailer is to load up the horse(s), tack, equipment, hay, etc., and take it to a truck scale to be weighed. Scales can be found at most truck stops or gravel yards.

The trailer will also come with a manufacturer's recommended maximum load weight, and it is both illegal and unsafe to exceed this.

Towing regulations vary from state to state; always err on the side of safety.

Trainer's Tip

If transporting one horse in a two-horse forward-facing partitioned trailer, the horse should always be on the side nearest the center of the road. That means that the single horse should travel on the left side. When traveling with two horses, the heavier horse should always be on the side nearest the center of the road

Understanding Hitches

The hitch, which is the ball attachment on the towing vehicle to which the trailer is connected must be of the appropriate strength for the weight of the trailer and its load. It is important to check this; don't assume that a vehicle that has a hitch on it will be suitable for pulling two or more horses.

The hitch for a bumper pull trailer should not be attached to the bumper directly (it will pull off) but to the vehicle frame, and these are referred to as frame-mounted receiver hitches. Every such hitch should have a sticker on it with two weights listed, those being the maximum weight carrying rate without weight distribution bars, and with weight distribution bars. As well as these ratings the hitches are also classed, with Class III or Class IV being suitable for horse trailers. Weight distribution bars are preferable and distribute the weight of the trailer and towing vehicle more evenly, preventing too much weight falling purely on the hitch and the towing vehicle's rear axle.

The hitch for a gooseneck will be positioned in the back of the truck bed, and should again be checked to make sure it is properly rated for the weight of the loaded trailer.

Trailer Brakes and Safety Chains

Trailer brakes are mandatory in most but not all states, and are strongly advised. They come in several different forms, although one of the best is

the electric brake. These are activated on the trailer when the brake is deployed in the towing vehicle. They come with a control box that attaches to the dashboard, which can be altered to change the level of braking in the trailer and also allows the driver to deploy the trailer brakes without depressing those of the the towing vehicle. Some trailers also come equipped with a breakaway brake, which is situated on the trailer coupler and will activate the trailer brakes if the trailer comes away from the towing vehicle.

Safety chains connect to either the frame of the towing vehicle (gooseneck) or the frame-mounted hitch (bumper pull) at one end and the trailer at the other, and are a safety device in case the trailer becomes unhitched. They are mandatory in 46 states and are strongly advised.

Commercial Driver's Licenses

If you are operating an equestrian business and hauling horses for money you are considered commercial by U.S.D.O.T. (United States Department of Transport). If traveling interstate with loads of a combined loaded weight (trailer and vehicle) exceeding 26,000 pounds (11,800 kg) you will be required to have a commercial driver's license and will have to comply with Federal Motor Carrier Safety Regulations. This includes carrying a logbook and medical card, having a federal

inspection sticker, ID number and sign on the vehicle, carrying certain safety items such as fire extinguishers and hazard triangles, and having certain safety features (trailer brakes, special lights, etc.) on the vehicles. Some states have additional or different requirements for commercial drivers with loads less than 26,000 pounds, so check with your local authorities.

What to Look For in a Trailer

There is a huge choice available, both in new and used trailers. First, determine your requirements, and choose a trailer that is large enough to easily accommodate the horse(s) both in width and height. As a rule a 16 h.h. horse will need a trailer that is at least 7 feet (2 m) high, and preferably

Left: A homemade tail guard; bandage a piece of thick foam over the top of the tailbone. Right: Putting on hind leg traveling boots.

basic traveling gear

Horses should always be transported wearing protective traveling gear – it is amazing how many injuries are sustained while horses are in transit, and the use of protective clothing greatly minimizes this risk.

- Padded headpiece for very large or tall horses that fits over the headcollar or halter.
- Leather headcollar or halter and soft cotton rope in good condition. (Leather headcollars, in the case of accidents and emergencies, can be cut off the horse if necessary, whereas nylon headcollars are much harder to cut.) Leather headcollars should always be used when shipping the horse on planes or boats.
- Appropriate traveling rug for the weather conditions. A breathable rug is always the best option, so that if the horse does sweat, the moisture is wicked away to the surface to dry.
- Leg protection. For long trips exercise bandages and pads provide the best support and minimize swelling that may occur through inertia, but be sure that the bandages are properly secured, and further secure with a strip of tape over the fastening. Bandages should run from below the knee or hock and over the pastern. Knee and hock boots can be used in conjunction with bandages. For shorter journeys, padded contoured leg protectors work well.
- Tail bandage and a tail guard. A good homemade tail guard is a piece of foam cut just longer than the tailbone. Bandage the tail as normal, then with a second bandage secure the foam so that it covers the base of the tail and the tailbone.

7.5 feet (2.2 m) wide. Don't cut the horse short on space in order to accommodate your own living or tack spaces! Trailers should have removable rubber mats over either a double wood or aluminum floor, and the mats should be regularly lifted so the floor underneath can be cleaned and checked for wear and tear. Trailers should have good ventilation. Many of them have side windows that open. These should also have grills across them so they can be opened if necessary during transit, but so the horse cannot stick its head out. *Never* travel a horse with its head poking out of the window. Trailers can come with ramps, or more commonly the horse is required to step up and into, or down and out of the vehicle. With this in mind, park in a low spot so the gradient is reduced. Do not encourage horses to "jump" into or out of trailers — this can lead to serious injuries for the horse (hitting its head on the door frame) and the handler (being squashed). If buying a secondhand trailer check it thoroughly to make sure the structure is safe and sound and that it complies with your vehicle's towing capacity.

The Journey

Before Heading Out

Quickly check your vehicle to ascertain that:

- Both indicators are working.
- Brake lights are working.
- The brakes work.
- The tire pressure is correct; add air, if necessary.
- The washer fluid is suffcient.
- There is enough oil; if going on a long trip have the oil changed before you leave.
- The gas tank is full.
- The floor beneath your mats is clean.
- There is a clean covering of dust-extracted shavings on the floor.
- You have water and buckets.
- The traveling first-aid kit is complete for both human and equine needs.
- You have sufficient feed and bedding.
- You have a shovel and a broom.

After loading the horse and driving down the driveway, stop, get out and check that all the ramps and doors are securely shut, and that everything appears to be in order. Make this a habit; it can help to prevent a silly accident.

Traveling can be stressful and exhausting for horses so try and make the journey as calm, quiet and stress-free as possible. It can take just one bad trip to sour a horse about loading, and once it has lost its nerve, it takes time to regain its confidence.

Traveling to competitions invariably involves staying overnight, so preparation must be made in advance. In rare instances, the journey may be relatively short, and you may be able to drive to a competition, compete and drive home in the day.

When traveling long distances with horses it is vital that frequent stops are made, and that you offer your horse a drink. If the facilities are safe and it is opportune to do so, also unload your horse and allow it to stretch its legs and urinate. If there is not a suitable area to unload, your horse is better left in the vehicle until you are able to stop for the night. *Never*, however, leave a horse in a vehicle overnight, and always make

Trainer's Tip

When feeding hay in horse trailers or trucks, make sure that the net is tied nice and high to prevent the danger of a horse catching its foot.

provisions in advance for somewhere suitable to stay with your horse. Nearly all towns have public "fairgrounds" and these are a good place to stop with your horse. Give a courtesy call to seek permission to stop there.

Proposed U.S. legislations for 2008 will make it illegal to travel with horses nonstop for longer than 10 hours. In view of this, many horse hotels are opening where both horse and owner can spend the night.

Documents and Paperwork

- Passport
- EIA (Equine Infectious Anemia) form
- Health papers
- Brand inspection

Horses traveling across state and occasionally county lines must travel with an EIA (coggins) form showing a negative blood result and health papers; some require a brand inspection. The health papers and required vaccinations will vary from state to state, so if planning a trip across several states, make sure your papers cover all the requirements. Some states require the EIA results to be within six months, while others will accept results within a year.

Plan ahead: the blood test for EIA can take a week to come back, and any required vaccinations should be done well in advance of traveling; some can make the horse feel off color for a few days and this can add to the stress of a journey. If you travel frequently with your horse, get a lifetime brand inspection done to save hassle and money, otherwise the brand inspector must be contacted and issue a certificate every time you travel.

The Traveling Environment

- It is important to keep the trailer well ventilated; a combination of roof vents and windows will generally keep the air circulating. Horses are more likely to get too hot than cold when traveling, so bear this in mind. If using a rug, choose one that wicks moisture to the surface to be dried. If the weather is very hot, try to travel at night or in the early morning.
- Cut down on dust by using dust-extracted bedding and either hay that has been soaked and drained or haylage. On short journeys, it is generally not necessary to provide the horse with hay. On longer journeys, hay should be provided; make sure you take enough hay to last the trip, the stay and the return journey — always overestimate.
- Never feed grain while on the road; stop and feed the horse, allowing at least an hour for it to digest the meal before continuing. When traveling long distances, treat the traveling day as a day off and adjust your horse's grain intake.
- Always take your own water in canisters and your own buckets. Dehydration (exacerbated by overheating) can lead to colic, which can be a problem when traveling. A horse prefers to drink its own water so get it used to drinking water flavored with Kool Aid or peppermint before leaving home and then add this to the water when traveling. *Never* allow your horse to drink from a communal tank away from home, or to share another horse's buckets.
- If staying overnight, make provisions ahead of time. Take your own bedding and mucking out equipment and, as with the hay, overestimate the amount you will need.
- When traveling long distances you must stop every couple of hours. Offer the horse a drink and, if possible, unload and walk or lunge it depending on the facilities. In the U.S., most towns have a "fairground" — a public arena that you will be allowed to use if you get permission.
- When towing or driving a horsebox, slow your speeds down, take corners slowly and avoid abrupt stops and accelerations.

TRAVEL CHECKLIST

- Horse (you'd be amazed!)
- Required health papers
- Tack
- Tack cleaning kit
- Lunging equipment
- Bandages and pads
- Brushing boots
- Overreach boots
- Rugs, including sweat rug and cooler
- Headcollar/halter and rope
- Hay
- Grain, if necessary
- Bedding
- Water jugs and buckets
- Electrolytes, Kool Aid or peppermint flavoring
- First-aid kit
- Stud kit
- Braiding kit
- Grooming kit and hoof polish
- Fly spray
- Spare rags and towels
- Shovel, broom and collapsible wheelbarrow
- Riding attire
- Show clothes
- Working clothes
- Spare show jodhpurs or jeans
- Hard hat or Western hat
- Hair net, if necessary
- Safety pins
- Sunblock
- Bottled water
- Electric fan and extension cord
- Old carpet square for doing feet

Loading

For many horses, loading poses no problems and they are more than happy to trundle up the ramp or step into the trailer. However, it is still a process that should be done correctly, and with the safety of the horse and handler in mind. It is when

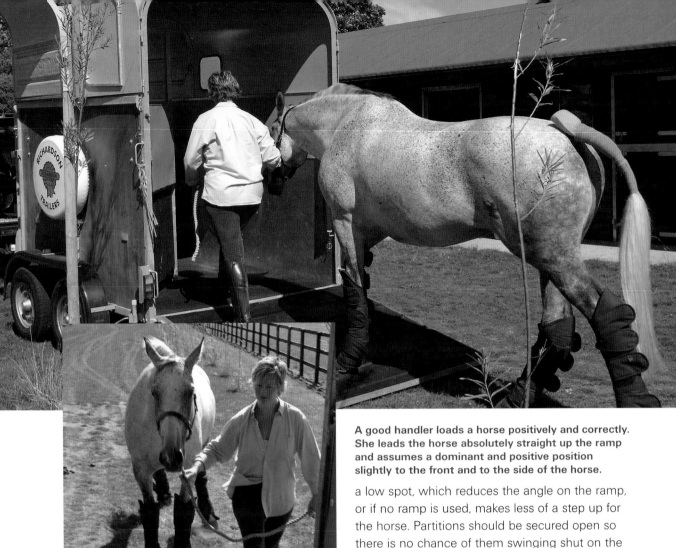

A good handler loads a horse positively and correctly. She leads the horse absolutely straight up the ramp and assumes a dominant and positive position slightly to the front and to the side of the horse.

a low spot, which reduces the angle on the ramp, or if no ramp is used, makes less of a step up for the horse. Partitions should be secured open so there is no chance of them swinging shut on the horse when it is halfway into the vehicle. The ramp gates, too, should also always be secured.

The Happy Loader

Using a correctly fitting halter and a soft cotton lead rope, lead the horse straight into the vehicle staying slightly in front of the horse, and with a little slack in the lead rope. Allow the horse a nice straight lead-in and walk it up the ramp or step and in; then tie up securely. The horse should be tied short enough that it cannot trap its head underneath the dividing partition or reach its neighbor, but should have enough room to move its head from side to side, lower it enough to cough or clear its nostrils, and be able to eat, etc.

Make sure to use a slip knot (quick-release knot) when tying the horse in the trailer and that the end of the lead is threaded back through the loop

shortcuts are taken with loading that accidents often occur.

Before loading the horse have everything ready. The vehicle should be packed and ready to go, last minute checks done, and paperwork in order. The horse should be wearing proper traveling equipment with all bandages securely taped up. Make sure that the vehicle is parked on a flat surface so that the ramp is flat and square to the ground. Also, where possible, try to park in so the horse can not untie itself. Always praise the horse when it has loaded, even if it is a seasoned traveler. Some horses are more than happy to "load themselves" i.e., they will jump into the trailer or go up the ramp while the handler stands and watches. This is something that should *never* be allowed to happen. The horse must always be directed and guided by the handler.

The Unhappy Loader

Some horses are extremely difficult to load, which is usually the result of poor traveling experiences, fear and insecurity. With difficult loaders and also young horses, it is advisable for the handler to wear a hard hat and gloves as safety precautions; nonslip footwear always should be worn, whether the horse is a happy or unhappy loader!

The absolute golden rule with a horse that is difficult to load is to allow yourself masses of time, and to work with the horse to resolve its problem well in advance of show day. There is no set procedure for curing the unhappy loader, but there are certainly procedures that will deter a horse even more from loading. Beating or pulling a horse into a vehicle will never result in a happy loader. The horse needs to learn that it is okay to load, and that loading and the vehicle can be a positive thing.

Some methods work with some horses and some on others, so it comes down to a question of common sense and devising the best plan to suit your horse. To begin with, use traveling bandages secured with tape, instead of boots. Traveling boots have a tendency to slip and even come undone, which can add to a difficult situation. Use a well-fitting halter with a soft cotton rope, and, in cases where the horse rears up or tries to bolt, also use a chifney.

Always approach loading with a positive attitude. Lead the horse in a straight line toward the vehicle, making sure you are in front of the horse and assuming the dominant role of "leader" of the herd. Never lose your cool; you may think the difficult loader is being stupid or stubborn but its reluctance will be based on fear and lack of

confidence, either in itself, the situation, the handler or all three. Loading the horse with a buddy can help. Load the buddy first and follow it with the difficult loader.

Parking the vehicle against a solid wall or the side of a building can help; it blocks off one escape route and the horse then can be more easily contained. However, with one escape route blocked, if the horse "throws a wobbly" and leaps around, the handler has less room.

Park the vehicle in a low spot so the gradient of the ramp or the height of the step in is diminished. Many horses are more worried about the ramp than the actual vehicle, and when the steepness is taken away they load more happily. Some horses are worried by the apparent lack of head room that a vehicle offers. Encouraging the horse to approach the vehicle with its head held low can help, and also allow the horse to smell the ramp, or floor of the trailer, and assess the situation for itself.

Give the horse a nice straight lead toward the vehicle, and have a helper on hand. If the horse puts its brakes on, have the helper give it a light tap with a long lunge stick to encourage it to move forward. This is not a reprimand, but should be used as an encouragement. Once the horse has come close to the vehicle, if it brakes, allow it time to assess the situation, but do not allow the horse to step backward. Vocally encourage the horse and reward it with a stroke as it moves forward. If the horse tries to back up, have the helper encourage it forward.

When walking toward the vehicle, the lead rope should have some slack in it, so that you are not pulling the horse. The horse needs to be encouraged to load without pressure. Use pressure on the lead rope as a deterrent; when the horse brakes and starts to back up, maintain pressure until it stops and steps forward a pace then allow a little slack back into the rope.

With a trailer, you can attach a lunge line to either side, and then have a helper on the end of each line. As the horse is led toward the trailer, the helpers cross over behind it, pulling the lunge

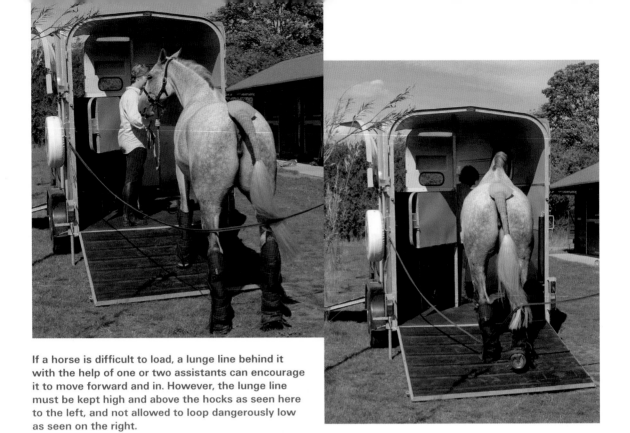

If a horse is difficult to load, a lunge line behind it with the help of one or two assistants can encourage it to move forward and in. However, the lunge line must be kept high and above the hocks as seen here to the left, and not allowed to loop dangerously low as seen on the right.

lines tight against the back of the horse to encourage it forward. Make sure the lunge lines are kept high enough and do not allow them to drop below the hocks. This approach can also be done using one line. Using lunge lines, however, can be frightening for the horse, and while they may overcome the initial problem of simply getting the horse into the trailer, they are unlikely to cure the underlying problem.

When using a front unload trailer, open up the front ramp, too, and practice leading the horse into, through and out of the trailer. By loading with the front ramp open the horse can feel less trapped and insecure.

Once an unhappy loader has been loaded, offer it a small feed, and then lead it back out again. Do this several times so that the horse anticipates loading as a positive experience. If feeding in the vehicle, suspend the bucket or the horse may throw up and bash its head on the partition or wall, further compounding its stress.

Try to keep as calm as possible, be encouraging and use lots of praise. Turn the event into a positive training session. Never try to load a difficult horse if you are running short of time — it is not a process that can or should be rushed.

Loading Young Horses

The ideal way to start a horse loading with confidence is to load it as a foal with its mother — providing she is a good loader! When loading foals, it is especially important to try and minimize the gradient of the ramp on a truck, and the height of the step up on a trailer. Once you have found a suitable place to park the vehicle, lead the brood mare in slowly allowing the foal the time to sniff the ramp and check out the new environment. This training session should only be done with the help of a second handler who is on standby to field the foal in the right direction and help out in case of any problems. If the foal is reluctant, then the helper can gently push it from behind. Never take the mare in so quickly that she becomes too far ahead of her foal; this will cause both to become distressed, and then the whole session becomes obsolete. Once the mare and foal are in the vehicle, give the mare a small treat, make a fuss of the foal, and then unload the pair. This needs to be done enough times until the foal is quite happy to load without any hesitation. If traveling with a mare and foal at foot, open up the internal partitions so that the pair have at least a double-sized area. Tie the mare and leave the foal loose, and make sure that the vehicle is well bedded down as the foal will probably lie down. Do not put traveling equipment on either one. There is a danger that the foal will remove, chew or untie bandages or leg protectors, which could lead to a more serious accident.

After foals have been weaned, and providing that they have been taught to stand tied up, they can be reintroduced to the trailer or truck. It is helpful to load a "nanny" horse first, and then the youngster. Leave both tied in the stationary vehicle with a haynet until settled. After the foal has learned to stand quietly in the vehicle, then start to take it with its nanny on short trips.

Loading chutes such as this are invaluable, particularly on stud farms and for training young horses and foals to load. The trailer or truck is backed up to the chute and the ramp lowered. The sides of the chute funnel the horse into the vehicle and prevent misbehaving or trying to sidestep the ramp.

Unloading

Horses must be taught to unload quietly and safely. Time and again you see horses launching themselves off the ramp, or out of the back of the trailer, which can be extremely dangerous, to the horse, handler and anyone else who happens to be in the vicinity. Young, nervous or overeager horses are the most likely to try and exit the vehicle with speed. Once you have untied the horse, turn it and lead it to the exit, and make it stand quietly. If the horse is particularly strong, make it back up a step and stand, then praise. Make the horse walk slowly down the ramp, or step off the trailer and then make it stand. Once it has cleared the vehicle, praise. If the horse is particularly unmanageable, slip a chifney on, or use a chain under the jaw as a last resort.

Some trailers do not have front or side ramps and so the horse is required to back out. This can be quite frightening for the horse because it cannot see directly behind it, so it is essentially being asked to step into the unknown. Position yourself to the front and side of the horse, so you

are not run over if it leaps forward. With a hand in the middle of its chest, quietly ask it to back up, allowing it to step one step at a time so that it feels the ramp sloping down behind it. It helps to park the trailer in a dip, which will then decrease the steepness of the ramp's angle.

A horse will learn quite quickly to trust the handler and to back out, but again, try to prevent it from rushing out backward. It can help to have a handler on the ground outside the trailer, who can put a reassuring hand on the horse's flank and encourage it to step back and down.

In cases where a horse flatly refuses to step back off the trailer, ask it to step forward toward you instead. Once it has taken a step forward, ask it to back up a step. Continue this process until it is stepping back happily. Once it steps a back foot down out of the vehicle, ask it to step up again, and continue to do this until the horse steps back and out of the trailer calmly.

Remember to always praise and encourage the horse; a little bit of praise goes a long way — both with the horse and the rider!

9

GROOMING

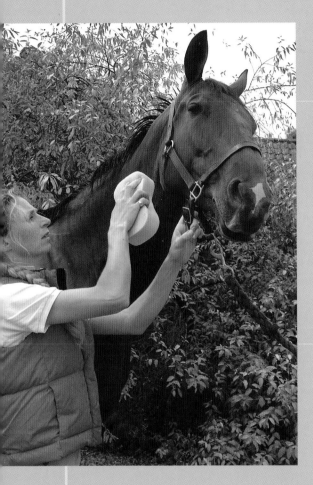

Your horse should always be tied up when being groomed (unless you are teaching it to ground-tie). This is especially relevant when working around an unfamiliar horse. It should be tied short enough so that it cannot reach around and snatch at you, and should never be tied below the level of the withers. Tying a horse with two ropes, or cross-tying, is highly recommended; however, only cross-tie a horse once it has first learned to be tied up conventionally to a ring. Then introduce it to cross-tying.

Ground-tying

This is when a horse has been taught to stand when the lead rope is dropped. This is a valuable lesson to teach a horse as once a horse has learned to stand on command with a dropped rope, it can be taught to stand anywhere. This basic groundwork is then used when teaching a horse to stand by the mounting block, stand on the lunge, stand to be shod, etc.

Begin by standing the horse in the middle of the stable with its halter (headcollar) and lead rope on. Tell it to "Stand" and step back from it. If your horse steps toward you, back it up to where it was and repeat the command.

Once your horse is standing, start to move slowly around it. Each time it moves, move it back to where it was, repeat the command,"Stand," and continue. When your horse stands without moving and allows you to move around it, step into its shoulder and praise it.

Horses will quickly learn this lesson, and it can be practiced while grooming.

Cross-tying

This is when the horse is tied by two ropes, one to each side of the halter, and then to rings high up on either side of the stable. This allows the horse to be secured in an open area, which makes working around it much easier.

Cross-ties can be bought pre-made with a snap at each end, but a cheaper method is to purchase a length of light chain, buy your own snaps, and attach them to either end. When measuring the length of the cross-tie allow enough for a slight bow, as can be seen in the picture below. Cross-ties that are too long are dangerous and allow the horse too much movement and the opportunity to catch a foot. Also avoid elastic cross-ties — some horses quickly learn that they stretch and will pull against them.

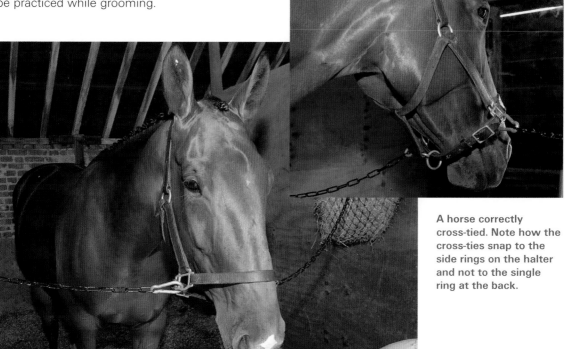

A horse correctly cross-tied. Note how the cross-ties snap to the side rings on the halter and not to the single ring at the back.

Procedures and Tools

Grooming routines are not set in concrete, but there are certain aspects that should be adhered to. Depending on the yard routine, it is a good idea to groom your horse in the morning, after breakfast and before riding.

Use a soft body brush and, every one or two strokes, clean the brush with the metal curry comb. The brush should be used hard enough so that the horse anticipates the contact and its muscles twitch. Sometimes, with horses that are nervous, a smaller body brush works well.

If it is warm, remove the rug and set it to one side. If it is cold, fold the front of the rug back so that the quarters are still covered and brush the front of the horse, then reverse the rug so the front end is covered and the quarters exposed to brush the back end.

Trainer's Tip

Use different colored face cloths for the eyes and nose and for the dock. Try to ensure that each horse on the yard has its own grooming tools and cloths/sponges. If this is not possible, then each should at least have its own cloths to prevent the spreading of contact diseases. Cloths should be washed regularly.

basic grooming routine

1 Tie up your horse, then begin brushing it using a soft body brush. Start at the poll and work down the neck in the direction of the hair, making short sweeps. Work down one side of the horse, including the legs, before moving to the other side and repeating the process.

2 Untie the rope and undo the halter and place it around the neck before brushing the face. Use a small body brush and take care when brushing the face not to spook the horse.

3 Using a soft damp cloth, wipe the eyes and nose. Take a different cloth and wipe the dock.

4 Using either a long-bristled water brush or, preferably, an old hairbrush, brush out the mane and lay it to the right side. Damp the mane down with water or with home-made hair conditioner. This conditioner (see box, right) can be used daily on the mane and tail.

Strapping

This is a further grooming process that helps to condition the muscles and improve circulation. Strapping should be carried out using a massage pad (or a wisp) and either a body brush or polishing cloth. Your horse will anticipate the sensation of the massage pad and will tense its muscles, causing them to contract. The body brush or polishing cloth relaxes the muscles. This process encourages the muscles to tighten.

Grooming the Grass-kept Horse

The grass-kept horse also needs grooming, but you must avoid removing the grease from its coat, as this is part of its insulation. Never use a body brush on a grass-kept horse as this has fine bristles set closely together, which are specifically designed to remove grease and dirt from the hair.

When strapping a horse, bring the massage pad down firmly over the muscle mass and follow with a polishing cloth/body brush stroke. It is important to establish a massage pad–body brush rhythm. When finished with one side, do the other.

Instead, groom gently with a dandy brush. These brushes are sold with different strengths of bristles: use a softer bristle for the summer coat and a tougher bristle for the winter coat. Rubber and plastic curry combs are useful tools for removing sweat stains, mud and loose hair, and can be used on either the stable-kept (if necessary) or the grass-kept horse.

After work, the horse should be sponged down to remove any trace of sweat. There are many products available. Lavender-based ones are good, especially for sensitive skin as well as being soothing. Mint or tea-tree oil products are effective for tired muscles. Whichever product you choose, make sure it is one that is for use in the rinse water and does not need to be rinsed off the horse after its application.

5 Detangle the tail with your fingers first and then brush through, being careful not to break or pull any of the hairs. It the tail is seriously knotted, there are a range of excellent products called "hair polishes" that help to detangle hair and prevent breakage. Never comb the tail unless absolutely necessary.

6 Pick the feet out into a garbage can. Check for any heat in the feet, and on the condition of the shoes. During the summer months when the feet are inclined to dry and crack, apply a hoof conditioner. Pay special attention to the area surrounding the clenches, and any cracks.

perfect hair conditioner

- Four squirts of baby oil.
- One capful of plain antiseptic mouthwash.
- Water.
- One spray bottle, labeled "Conditioner."

Put the first two ingredients in the bottle and fill with water. Shake well before each use. The mouthwash helps to kill any tiny bugs and cut down on irritation leading to scratching. The baby oil keeps the hair soft and supple.

the comprehensive grooming kit

- Body brush to remove grease and dust.
- Small body brush for the face.
- Dandy brush to remove mud and hair.
- Soft-bristle dandy brush for the sensitive grass-kept horse.
- Rubber and/or plastic curry comb to remove sweat, mud, and hair.
- Metal curry comb for cleaning body brush only; *never* use on a horse.
- Massage pad for strapping.
- Wisp for strapping (not seen so often now).
- Polishing cloths: have a good supply of soft, clean cloths for use during strapping, for final polish after grooming, and for applying baby oil, etc.
- Face cloths in two different colors — one for eyes and nose, one for dock.
- Sweat scraper for removing excess water after bathing or sponging.
- Sponges: have two differently colored ones, if possible. Keep one for soaping and one for rinsing.
- Old hairbrush (human) for mane and tail.
- Long-bristle water brush for mane and tail.
- Metal mane comb for pulling mane.
- Metal tail comb for tail, but avoid using too often.
- Painless plastic pulling comb with blade, used instead of pulling the mane.
- Short-bristle water brush for feet.
- Sanding block for smoothing feet before applying oil for the show ring. Use as infrequently as possible.
- Hoof pick for cleaning feet.
- Hoof oil — black for dark feet, clear for white feet.
- Rags for hoof oil spills, etc.
- Hoof conditioner — use in the summer.
- Baby oil for final show turnout.
- Vaseline is always useful.
- White chalk for final show cover up.
- Stain remover for last-minute disasters.
- Plastic razors for removing stubble on chins.
- Quarter markers for show turnout.
- Lavender wash for use after work.
- Buckets for rinsing.
- Vinegar for the rinse water.
- Shampoo.
- Homemade hair conditioner for daily conditioning.
- Hair polish for final show turnout.
- Olive oil for bathing before clipping.
- Blue bags for keeping gray horses gray.
- Lifesavers or carrots for outstandingly good behavior!
- Humane twitch for restraint if needed.

Bathing

Bathing removes the dirt, grease and dust from the coat, but should be kept to a minimum, especially for the grass-kept horse. This is because shampoos strip the horse's coat of its natural grease, which helps to act as an insulator for it.

You may have to bathe a grass-kept horse if preparing for a show, but this should be done as little as possible, and only on a really warm day. The mane and tail, however, can be thoroughly washed to remove any scurf, dander and tiny mites that will cause irritation, leading to rubbing and hair damage. Using a shampoo with mint, tea-tree oil, seaweed or kelp in the ingredients will help to soothe itchy skin.

A stable-kept horse can be bathed more regularly, but, again, only when needed. A horse should only be bathed when the weather is warm enough to ensure that it can be dried without chilling unless you have access to an indoor barn and wash facility with a heated drying bay.

Reasons for Bathing

1 Show preparation
2 Preparing the coat for clipping
3 To loosen the winter coat
4 Medical conditions requiring special bathing

If bathing to prepare the horse for a show, be sure to keep it rugged after it has dried or the chances are the horse will roll. It can be helpful to put on stable bandages to cut down on overnight leg stains, and a pull-on neck and head cover dependent on the temperature. If using a stretchy

Trainer's Tip

A good, hot bath in late spring when the coat is coming out really helps to loosen up the horse's winter hair and speeds up the shedding process, which can be useful.

Let the horse see and smell the hose before turning the water on. Once the water is on, start by hosing up the horse's leg to accustom it to the water's feel.

hood, make sure it fits and will not be pulled across an eye.

If bathing to prepare the horse for clipping, add half a cupful of olive oil to your rinse water, and do not wash out. The oil makes the hair much easier to clip and cuts down on "track" marks. Give the horse a bath the day before you plan to clip it, and keep it stabled and clean until you do.

What You Will Need

- Halter and rope.
- Hose hooked up to warm water, or several large buckets of warm water.
- Soap sponge and clean rinsing sponge.
- Small empty bucket.
- Shampoo and conditioner.
- Vinegar.
- Scrub brush for feet.
- Sweat scraper.
- Towels and sweat rug or cooler.
- Hair polish.

Where possible, use warm water for bathing; cold water is unpleasant for the horse unless the outside air temperature is very high and it is less effective in both the soaping and rinsing processes. Various attachments exist to connect a hose to a domestic faucet, so if there is a hot water faucet in the feed or tack room, it can be used for bathing. Alternatively, fill buckets with warm water.

Ideally, bathing should be done on a hard, non-slip surface that drains well toward a covered drain — a custom-built wash bay is ideal, although not many people have access to one!

Before bathing your horse, make sure that it is comfortable with the process — used to being sponged, hosed and washed. Don't leave it until the day before a show to teach your horse how to accept being bathed; this will make bathing a stressful situation.

Gray horses are notoriously difficult to keep clean. There are several equestrian products available to really brighten up their coats, which can be applied after or during shampooing. The traditional method was to use "blue bags" diluted in water; these were an old-fashioned whitening product for laundry, which are no longer available, but specific equestrian "bluing" products are available and effective.

The Reluctant Bather

Some horses hate being bathed and will throw a real tantrum as soon as the hose comes out. If your horse is one of these, it will have to learn to stand and tolerate bathing, even if you can't make it like it!

Have a helper hold the horse and, if possible, try to use a semi-enclosed area that is sufficiently roomy and easy to maneuver around (and get out of the way) but prevents the horse from being able to evade you. Make sure your helper stands on the same side as you so he or she can't be run

over. Throughout, vocally praise and encourage your horse.

Begin by getting your horse used to the hose without the water on, so that the hose itself is not frightening. Then, using a soaked sponge, get your horse used to the feel of water on its skin. Start with the sponge low on its shoulder in a quiet manner, and allow your horse to get used to it. Using warm water, allow the hose to trickle over the horse's fetlock, gradually working up its leg – the pressure needs to be enough so that it doesn't tickle and irritate, but not too much that it spooks the horse.

giving a bath

1 If the horse is used to being bathed, tie it up or else have a helper hold it for you. Check the temperature of the water to ensure it is sufficiently warm, and starting on a front leg, gradually soak your horse all over.

2 Add a little soap to the soap sponge and start to work the coat into a lather, starting up by the poll and working your way down the neck and toward the tail. Use a circular action to get all the dirt out of the hair. Be sure to get right down to the crest under the mane, and thoroughly wash the tail.

Gradually work the hose onto the shoulder and then the back. Take a sponge in one hand and massage the water into the hair. When your horse stands still and tolerates the water, praise it. Once one side is wet, turn your horse to face the opposite direction and repeat. If you are quiet but firm, and offer praise when it stands, your horse should learn to behave and tolerate its bath.

When washing its hindquarters and tail be sure to watch your horse's body language and stand to one side. If it so much as raises a hind leg, vocally reprimand it immediately and continue without a fuss. The less stressful and noisy the experience is, the more positively the horse will learn.

Trainer's Tip

When bathing your horse don't turn the hose on its head. First, there is a danger of water and/or soap running into its ears and eyes, and, second, it is unreasonable to expect your horse to tolerate this — use sponges instead. Keep your shampoo and conditioner bottles in a small empty bucket to prevent them getting knocked over and spilled.

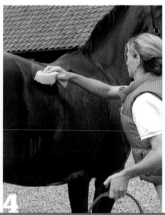

3 Using a small soap sponge with a tiny amount of soap, carefully wash the face, avoiding the eyes and ears. Scrub the hooves inside and out with water and a stiff scrub brush.

4 Rinse the mane and tail and add conditioner; work in thoroughly. Do not use conditioner on the body hair. Starting at the top of the neck, begin the rinsing process. It is important to get rid of all traces of soap, and rinsing will take some time. Take particular care around the head. Use the rinsing sponge.

5 For the final rinse, fill a bucket with warm water and add a cupful of white wine vinegar; this will remove any last traces of soap and leaves the coat wonderfully shiny. Using the sweat scraper, remove the excess water and, if required, apply hair polish, massaging it in. Never apply hair polish to the saddle area.

6 To dry off the horse, either use towels or rug it in a sweat rug (tight weave) or cooler. If there is access to a horse walker, 15 minutes of moderate walking is a good way to dry your horse without chilling it.

Mane and Tail

The mane and tail require constant attention to keep them looking healthy. Several factors contribute to the condition of the mane and tail.

Keeping the Mane and Tail in Good Condition

If your horse is on a balanced diet, its coat, including the mane and tail, and hoof quality should be good. A change in the condition of the coat is one of the first signs of a nutritional deficiency. Supplementing the diet with a combination of biotin, methionine and sulfur will improve the quality of the hoof wall and the hair, and adding linseed or cod liver oil to the feed will boost the condition and shine of the coat.

In very hot, dry climates with low humidity, the mane and tail will become brittle and dry, leading to the hair breaking off. Use a daily spray-on hair conditioner, avoid brushing out the tail where possible, and detangle using your fingers and lots of hair polish. Provide your horse with adequate fly sheets and spray to prevent unnecessary tail swishing, which will break off the hairs.

A horse will rub for a number of reasons: summer weather, worms and sweet itch (see page 240), for example. Irritation caused by scurf, dander, greasy hair, tiny mites and flies that infest the mane and tail; soap left in the hair after shampooing can cause itching. Mares will sometimes rub their tails when they are in heat. For some horses, rubbing becomes habit-forming. Once a horse starts to rub, the damage to the hair is enormous, and the hair can take months to grow back. Treat the causes where possible: keep the mane and tail free from scurf, use a daily hair conditioner, worm regularly and use fly sprays and sheets.

Pulling the Mane

Unless your horse is a specific breed that requires a long, free mane for showing — such as the Arabian, Quarter or Spanish horse, native pony breeds, or the Haflinger — the mane should be kept neatly pulled and trained to lie flat on the right side of the neck. Because it feels awkward, many horses object to having their manes pulled. To help the process, plan on pulling the mane after your horse has been worked. When a horse is hot, the hairs will come out more easily, and it will be slightly tired and relaxed. If your horse is very sensitive, there are a number of "painless" pulling combs on the market that incorporate a cutting edge and shorten the mane without any actual pulling involved — although generally the end result is not quite as good. A well-pulled mane should be 3–4½ inches (7–11 cm) long and completely even. Never use scissors because it

Metal mane comb and cutting comb.

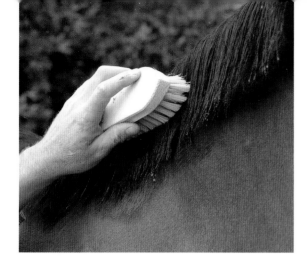

A well-pulled mane should be nice and even and lie on the right side of the neck. Train the mane to lie flat by wetting down with water daily.

is impossible to give the mane a natural look; it will look choppy and unattractive. If the mane is in particularly bad shape, plan on doing it in two halves over a couple of days.

Don't pull a mane the day before you plan on braiding it. The skin will remain sensitive and the horse will be expecting you to pull when you want to braid, and will fidget.

Hogging the Mane

Also called roaching, this is when the entire mane is shaved off. It can look very smart on a cob, but once done, it will require constant attention to keep the neat look. After hogging, allow at least three days before showing; this allows the hair to grow back just a fraction.

Starting at the withers, clip up the neck. Do a clipper run up the middle of the crest, and then

Trainer's Tip

Train the mane to lie flat on the right side of the neck by wetting it down after brushing every day. If it still persists in standing up or falling on the wrong side, braid the mane and leave for 24 hours, then wet it down. Never leave braids in for longer than this as the hair will break off.

pulling the mane

1 Tie up your horse nice and short and provide it with a hay-net. Comb through the mane and remove any knots or tangles.

2 Start by the poll and, using a metal mane comb, take a small section of hair and hold the bottom firmly with your left hand. With your right hand, backcomb the hair to the desired length, until a few strands remain in your left hand. Wrap these strands firmly around the comb once, and pull downward sharply.

3 Work your way down the neck, gradually thinning and shortening the mane as you go. The trick is not to try to pull too many hairs out at once, and to keep your pull short and sharp. Make sure you do not have to pull the same hairs twice.

one along each side of the crest. Look at the neck from both sides to ensure that the clip is even.

Braiding a Mane

This takes time, so it can be worth braiding the mane the night before. To keep the braids looking good overnight, use a nylon neck cover and hood. Failing that, cut the toe off a nylon stocking. Next, cut lengthwise up the stocking and lay it over the braids. Starting at the poll, secure the stocking to each braid with a rubber band.

Traditionally, horses were supposed to have seven or nine braids along the neck, with the forelock making an even number. However, the number of braids should be in relation to the horse's conformation. A big horse with a long

Trainer's Tip

To save time when braiding, thread all the needles before you start, and knot the ends. Then poke the needles through a piece of cardboard to keep them tidy until they are needed.

neck will need more braids than a pony with a short neck. If your horse has a weak top line, try to position the braids along the top of its neck; this will improve the look of the neck. Similarly, if your horse is heavily muscled through the top line, position the braids to the side of the neck.

braiding the mane

1 Comb through the mane and wet it down. Divide the mane into sections, securing each section with a rubber band. These will become your braids, so make sure the sections are even.

2 Starting with the section nearest the poll, divide into three equal portions and braid down to the end, pulling the braid as tightly as you can.

3 Stitch the end firmly, then either roll the braid up to the crest or fold it under once in half and then in half again. Take the thread, still attached to the end, and come up through the rolled braid, around the right side, up through from the bottom again and around the left side. Repeat until the braid feels secure.

4 Snip the thread off close to the braid, and move on to the next one. Braid down the neck, and then do the forelock last. Spray the braids with hairspray to keep them smooth and shiny.

the comprehensive braiding kit

Keep your braiding kit in a separate box from your grooming kit. That way you keep everything together and organized, and won't forget anything vital on show day.

- Strong thread in the color of your horse's mane and tail.
- Blunt-ended needles with large eyes; darning needles work the best.
- Braiding bands — black, brown or white.
- Mane comb and tail comb.
- Hairbrush.
- Clean cloth.
- Hair gel.

- Hairspray.
- Small pointed scissors.
- Large scissors.
- White tape or braid covers (dressage).
- Nylon stockings.
- Rubber thimbles x 2.
- 2 x 4 inch (5 x 10 cm) piece of strong cardboard.
- Baby safety pins.
- Portable step.

TAILS

Tails are even more vulnerable than manes, and the hairs are highly susceptible to breakage. Once damaged, a tail takes months to recover, and damage is virtually impossible to disguise. Some horses will chew another's tail, especially youngsters, so be warned.

Some people like a "natural" looking tail, and encourage it to grow as long as possible. This is particularly prevalent in the Arabian show world. In order to keep the length of the tails, which in some cases actually trail the ground, the tail must be kept in a soft cotton bag, or the bottom bandaged up to just below the tailbone. Take care when turning out a horse with a tail wrapped up like this. There must be nothing in the field on which the tail and its bandage can get caught.

Pulling the Tail

As with pulling the mane, this process is awkward, and many horses will not appreciate it. Again, plan on pulling the tail after a good workout when your horse is hot and tired. Pull a few hairs from each side of the tailbone at the

top, working your way down. The tail should be pulled to accentuate the hindquarters; as a guide, when standing behind your horse, pull down to the point where the bottom starts to curve away from you. Only pull hairs from the sides of the tail, and only a pull a few hairs at a time. Rubber thimbles can help to grip the hair. It will take a long time to pull a tail that has not been pulled before; it can take a month of pulling before it really starts to take shape. Once it has been pulled, maintain it weekly by pulling a few hairs as you need to. After pulling, dampen the hair and put a tail bandage on. Leave the bandage on for an hour, but no longer. Regularly bandaging the tail will help to keep it looking good.

Trainer's Tip
Provide your horse with a haynet to take its mind off the pulling.

1

2

3

banging the tail

1 Spray the tail with hair polish and, using your fingers, remove all tangles. Carefully brush out the ends.

2 This is best done with two people. Have an assistant place an arm under the tail to hold it at the level it is carried in during motion. Then run your left hand down the tail hairs pulling them tight.

3 With your right hand, cut the tail off absolutely straight, so that it hangs approximately 4 inches (10 cm) below the hocks.

Banging the Tail

In most show classes the tail should traditionally be "banged," that is trimmed straight across the bottom, and should hang to approximately 4 inches (10 cm) below the hocks when the horse is in motion. When banging a tail make sure your scissors are really sharp, or use a pair of clippers with sharp blades.

Braiding the Tail

This should only be done on the morning of a show as it will not survive a night!

Allow yourself plenty of time. Have all the required equipment on hand (see box page 175) as well as a damp cloth. Thread the needle and knot the end of the thread. Push the needle securely through the front of your jacket in order to keep it handy.

Make sure that your horse is securely tied up and standing still and patiently. If your horse is inclined to fuss, have a helper on standby.

The hardest part of braiding a tail is starting the braid off. It is helpful to be elevated so that you are looking down on the tail as you start. Use a step if your horse is taller than you are!

There are two methods of braiding a tail. The conventional overhand way results in a flat braid, or the braid can be done underhand, which gives a raised braid look. The underhand method looks stunning if well done, but is harder to do than the overhand way. Practice both before show day and decide which one you find easiest. Be sure to pad and bandage the tail for traveling.

Trainer's Tip

Standing on a step behind a horse can be alarming for it, so be sure to introduce the step slowly, and get the horse used to your standing on it.

Protecting Your Braid

Once you have made your braid, you'll want to keep it looking good. Nylon stockings are a great addition to any braiding kit. Before traveling to a show, cut the foot off a nylon stocking and thread it over the tail so that the top of the stocking is just above the bottom of the braid. Bandage the tail, and bandage over the top of the stocking to secure it. Tie a knot in the bottom of the stocking and you effectively have the tail in a nylon bag. Don't braid the bottom of the tail to travel to the show. Wavy tails are not considered proper etiquette in the show ring, and it takes a long time for the waves to fall out.

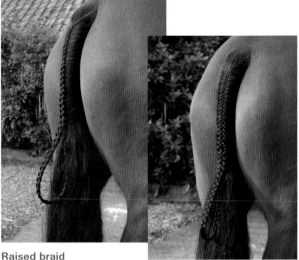

Raised braid
Raised braids are a bit harder to do than flat ones, so be sure to practice before show day!

Flat braid
Spraying hairspray onto the finished braid gives it a nice shine and helps to keep the short hairs lying flat.

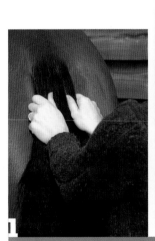  

1 **2** **3** **4**

braiding the tail

1 Dampen the top of the tail with water and a clean cloth or hair gel. Take three small portions of hair, one from each side of the tailbone at the top, and one from the middle.

2 Begin to braid, taking a small piece from each side of the tailbone as you work your way down. Continue to braid far enough down the tailbone taking small pieces from each side, to emphasize the line of the horse's quarters.

3 Finish the braid straight down without taking any from the sides. Stitch the end to secure, then loop the braid up behind itself and sew the end to the back of the bottom part of the braid, making a neat loop. Gently curve the horse's tailbone inward to match the line of the quarters.

4 After braiding the tail, spray with hairspray to help keep the hair lying flat and tidy until your class.

Clipping

Generally, if a horse is in work, it is clipped during the autumn and winter. At these times of year the coat is at its thickest, so when the horse is worked it will sweat profusely and take a long time to dry. By clipping part or all of the hair away, a horse becomes less hot during work, sweats less, loses less condition, dries more quickly and stands less chance of chilling. Do not clip a horse that is not in work. Horses that are clipped must be rugged to compensate for the loss of hair.

It can be helpful to clip horses during the summer if they sweat excessively when in hard and fast work. Any time a horse is sweating to a great degree it is losing valuable electrolytes, which can lead to dehydration and, eventually, a loss of condition.

Some horses are clipped for showing in the summer and in this case, all the body hair must be removed. The horse should be completely clipped no sooner than three to four days before a show to allow the coat a chance to "settle" and for any track marks to disappear. If a horse is clipped at the beginning of the summer and kept well rugged, it should not be necessary to reclip it, as the hair will grow back slowly.

Clippers and Blades

Clipping a horse well is a bit of an art, and a poorly clipped horse looks awful! Part of the trick is having super-sharp clipper blades, so be sure to have your blades sharpened annually, and more often if several horses are being clipped.

Clipper designs have greatly improved recently and in general have become quieter and lighter; electric clippers are the best. Most are handheld, although there are also overhead clippers that have their motors suspended from the ceiling and cables attached to the clipper heads. These are ideal for yards with lots of horses, but aren't necessary for the

A top-notch pair of clippers is usually lightweight, long lasting, and its blades remain sharper for longer; it also produces a much better overall end result. Heavy clippers can really make your arm ache.

clipping a horse

1 Bathe your horse the day before clipping, using olive oil in the rinse water. Then thoroughly groom directly before clipping.

2 Keep the tail and mane out of the way by braiding the end of the tail, folding it up toward the dock, and bandaging the entire tail; pull the mane into bunches and secure with bands. If your horse is used to being clipped and is good, then cross-tie so you can move around it; if not, tie up your horse to a ring. If your horse is young, nervous or does not like to be clipped, have a helper hold it.

Trainer's Tip

Clipped hair gets everywhere so wear a hat and tie long hair back. Coveralls or overalls and rubber soled boots are recommended.

private horse owner. Battery-run clippers are good for trimming, but tend not to hold a charge for long enough. There also are a number of small clippers called trimmers on the market. These are ideal for quick touch ups and are useful for trimming difficult areas like the ears and behind the jawbone.

Clipper blades come in different widths, ranging from coarse to fine. They should be kept clean and oiled. During clipping, spray the blades with oil and wipe clean to keep them working smoothly. It is ideal to have two or more sets of blades so that when one set becomes hot during clipping you can switch to another set. There are several blade-cooling products available also.

clipping essentials

- A tail bandage.
- Spare clipper blades.
- Cooling fluid.
- Oil and a rag.
- A long, soft-bristle brush.
- Chalk, saddle soap or a marker pen for drawing the clip outline.
- A helper should you need one.
- A traditional-style numnah for marking the saddle patch on a hunter clip.
- A rug for putting on the horse after clipping.
- A humane twitch in case of emergency.

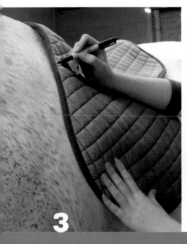 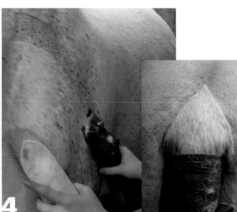 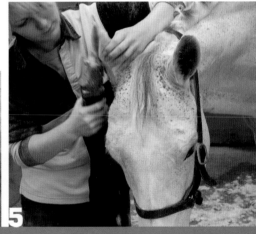

3 Using chalk, saddle soap or a washable marker pen, draw the outline of your intended clip onto the horse. For a hunter clip, lay the numnah where it would normally sit, and draw around it to get your saddle patch, or use your saddle.

4 Allow your horse to get used to the noise of the clippers, then start to clip on the flat shoulder area, which is easiest. Clip against the lie of the hair in short sweeps no longer than 12 inches (30 cm). After each clipper sweep, brush the hair away with the soft brush.

5 Clip the area you have marked, leaving a triangle shape above the base of the tail; *never* clip straight across here. Likewise, angle your line across the top of the legs. For the head and ears, ensure your blades are really cool.

6 When you have finished clipping, brush your horse thoroughly to remove any irritating loose hairs and put a rug on it. Clean and oil the clippers and blades.

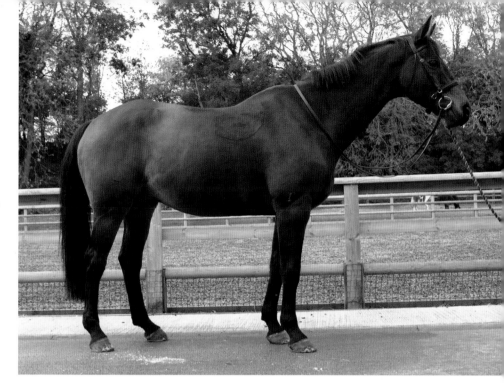

Left: A horse with a low chaser or Irish clip. This is a good clip for a horse that is in medium-to-light work; the legs are left on, and most of the body hair, with just the hair from the neck and belly being removed. Normally horses that are clipped would be rugged when turned out unless it is particularly warm.

Right: A horse with a hunter clip. Note that a saddle patch and the legs have been left on, and all the rest of the hair clipped off. This is a suitable clip for a horse in hard and fast work.

How to Clip

Clipping should be carried out in a large stable, or specific clipping box, preferably with rubber matting and with the bedding, buckets and manger removed. It is vital to have a good source of light, plenty of room to move around your horse and a convenient power source.

Some horses become highly agitated during clipping, so make sure you have a helper on hand.

Types of Clip

- **Full** All the body hair is removed apart from a triangle at the base of the tail.
- **Hunter** All the body hair is removed apart from the legs, a saddle patch and the triangle at the base of the tail.
- **Blanket** All the body hair is removed apart from the legs and a blanket shape covering the withers, back, loins and hindquarters.
- **Chaser** A line is drawn from the stifle to the poll. All the hair above the line is left on, and all the hair below the line, except for the front legs, is removed. The head is generally clipped, but does not need to be.
- **Trace** Similar to a chaser clip but less hair is removed.

- **Neck and belly** Only the hair on the underside of the neck and the belly is removed. Horses with this type of clip can live out providing they are rugged.

Perfecting Your Clip

Achieving the perfect clip is very hard to do, in particular creating smooth clip lines without joggles (the horse pictured on the opposite page has a slightly uneven clip line), and not getting track marks — lines of hair left by the clippers.

Track marks can be avoided by using good-quality clippers with sharp blades; making long sweeping motions with the clippers rather than short, jerky ones; overlapping each pass of the clips, and bathing the horse beforehand using olive oil in the rinse water. The cleaner the coat the better finish the clip will have.

Trainer's Tip
Always use a circuit breaker when using electrical equipment in the stable.

- Some horses become highly agitated during clipping and find it really stressful. If your horse is difficult to clip, be prepared to take all the time you need. Never approach a situation like this if you are yourself watching the clock and stressed. Make sure you are working in a safe environment with a good nonslip floor, and that you have a helper on hand. Depending on the facility, it can be a great help to have a nanny horse next to yours, provided there is enough room. It is also beneficial to allow your horse to watch another horse being clipped.

- Never tie up your horse, but have a helper hold it, and make sure that the helper and you stay on the same side of the horse at all times.
- Make sure that your blades are sharp so that they will not pull at the hair, and that your clippers are in good working order. Try to use the quietest, smallest clippers. At first, introduce your horse to battery-operated clippers. That way there are no cords for anyone to get tangled up in if the horse throws a fit.
- Without turning the clippers on, allow your horse to smell them and see them, then run them all over his body in the direction of the hair. Get your horse used to this feeling. When your horse relaxes, turn the clippers on using low speed, if possible. Allow your horse to become used to the noise before touching it with the clippers. When your horse relaxes, move the clippers across its shoulder in the direction of the hair. As soon as it allows you to do this, turn off the clippers and reward it. Continue doing this until you are able to move the clippers up your horse's neck and across its barrel, still in the direction of the hair. Once your horse has accepted this, start to clip the hair working from the shoulder.
- Lots of praise goes a long way. Never lose your cool, no matter how frustrating it is.

- Be aware of your horse's body language and reaction, and be prepared to spread the clipping over a couple of days. This is not ideal, but sometimes necessary. Most horses are difficult to clip because they fear the noise and the unusual sensation, but if they trust the handler, the stress of the process can be greatly diminished.
- Be careful when clipping under the belly, as most horses dislike this; it tickles and is irritating to them. Having someone pick up a front leg while clipping the belly can help.
- Some horses will not tolerate their ears being clipped. In these cases, using a humane twitch is effective. The twitch should not be on for longer than a few minutes.
- In rare instances a horse simply finds clipping too stressful to cope with. As a last resort, it is possible to have the horse sedated by a vet.
- Once your horse has settled and accepted being clipped, try to trim it up — bridle path, withers, whiskers — with the clippers as often as possible. The more you use them around your horse the less of an ordeal it becomes.

Tips for Looking Good

- Once a week clip the end of the mane from the bottom of the withers; this gives a cleaner outline and prevents the mane from becoming trapped under the front of the numnah. Also, clip the bridle path, allowing 1½ inches (4 cm) for English horses, 4 inches (10 cm) for Quarter Horses and 6–8 inches (15–20 cm) for Arabians.
- Trim under the jawline regularly, running the clippers in the direction of the hair.
- Trim whiskers for showing. Use clippers or wet shave with a disposable razor.
- Keep long hairs on the outside of the ears trimmed. Avoid taking too much hair from inside the ears as it provides natural protection against flies and dirt.
- Run clippers down the back of the legs in the direction of the hair to remove unsightly long hairs, especially from around the chestnuts.

Trainer's Tip

Some horses hate the noise of aerosols. Make sure your horse is used to, and prepared for, the hissing before diving in with the hairspray. Practice making a hissing noise first to see how your horse reacts. Calm and reassure your horse; talking to him can mask the noise.

- Following the direction of hair growth, trim the fetlocks with the clippers or scissors and comb.
- Trim the hair around the coronary band into a neat line using the clippers or scissors.
- Keep the end of the tail well banged.
- Before entering the show ring, wipe under the dock with a towel moistened with baby oil and darken the insides of the ears with the oil.

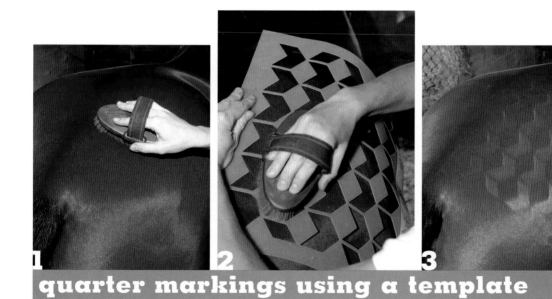

quarter markings using a template

1 Brush the hair thoroughly in the direction of the coat and place the template on the hind-quarters.

2 Lining the top edge of the template with the spine and holding it firmly in one hand, brush the hair downward with the other.

3 Remove the template and repeat on other side of horse, making sure you line the two markings up.

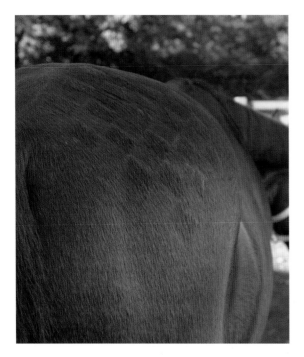

Quarter marking templates come in a variety of shapes; here the horse has squares. Do quarter markings right at the last minute before entering the show ring. Apply hair spray to the finished result to help fix the hair in place. Do not put a rug on the horse after doing the marks as they will rub out.

Turnout Details

It is the final grooming and turnout details that can make all the difference on show day, and it is worth taking the time to go that little extra distance. Marking the quarters of the horse with "buttock marks" and "sharks' teeth" can make a big difference to the appearance of the horse, and buttock marks in particular, if well done, can greatly enhance the look of the horse's conformation from behind. The horse has two large muscle masses that can be seen when standing behind it facing the tail, and these are what will be accentuated through buttock marking. Taking a body brush or a water brush, brush the hair in this area downward, then place the brush adjacent to the top of the tail and make a curving sweep downward following the muscle line. Do this on both sides.

Sharks' teeth are more complicated to do, so it is worth practicing first. These are made between the quarters and top of the thigh region. Brush the hair in the direction of growth then, starting approximately 4 inches (10 cm) below the hip bone, make a broad sweep diagonally upward toward the dock, then make a stroke diagonally downward the other way. Continue until you have made three good shark's teeth.

- Rub baby oil or Vaseline around the muzzle and over the nostrils and around the eye sockets to give the appearance of a big eye.
- Trim the long eyelashes below the eyes for the show ring.
- Use hair polish to give the coat sparkle, but do not apply to the saddle area.
- Sand the outside of the hooves with a sanding block before applying hoof oil.
- Choose a fast-drying hoof oil — it's worth it.
- Use white chalk to hide stains on the legs.
- Quarter markings, sharks teeth and buttock markings (see below) can improve the overall impression of the horse.

Trainer's Tip

It is possible to make quarter markings without a template. Take a body brush and brush hair in the direction of coat. Then make downward strokes with the brush tidying up the edges. Practice at home first!

Trainer's Tip

Take an old piece of short-pile carpet, or an old rubber car mat to shows and use under the feet when applying oil. Get your horse used to standing on this at home before you get to the show.

10

WORKING OUT

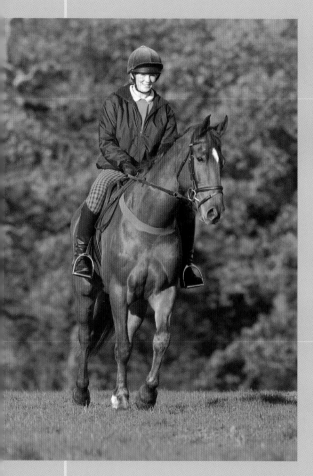

A fitness program is a vital part of the work routine for a horse that is expected to compete or perform in a long, hard or fast category. Many injuries, especially to the tendons, are caused by fatigued horses, which have not been properly prepared for the job they are asked to do. Unfortunately, similar to feeding, getting a horse fit is not an exact science. All horses vary; some are easier to get fit than others, and it is up to the individual to assess his or her horse and the degree of its fitness.

While undertaking a fitness program, feeding will have to be altered, and the fine balance of feed to work is one that must be continually considered. Every horse is different, and the process of getting it fit must be tailored to the horse, its age, disposition, prior history (with regard to injuries), how long it has been off work and the job for which it is being prepared to do. Alongside the physical aspects of getting a horse fit is the important process of preparing the horse mentally for competition.

Training Programs

Regardless of the job the horse will be asked to do, there is no diminishing the importance of the "walk" phase of the fitness program. This forms the basic building block of the horse's future fitness, muscle development and strengthening of its tendons and ligaments. Consistent, solid and purposeful walking has also been shown to improve the density and strength of the skeletal frame. Horses that are not started with a good walk phase to their programs are the ones that are more likely to sustain fatigue-related injuries.

As a rough guide, a horse that has come off grass (i.e., been out of work for a period of time) should be allowed between 12 to 14 weeks of fitness training in order to prepare it for an affiliated one-day event. If the horse has been in moderate work, such as regular hacking at least five times a week, this fitness program can be reduced to eight to 10 weeks, and if the horse has been in sustained hard, but not fast work, the program can again be reduced to approximately six weeks.

During interval training when cantering be sure to take your weight off the horse's back.

Vacation to One-day Event Fit

When planning a weekly work routine, the week is based on a six-day working week with one day off. During the horse's day off, it either can be walked in hand, or turned out for a period of time, but either way, must be allowed to freely move around. The following is a schedule for guidance only; every horse is different and it is up to the owner to take the basics and work with them to formulate the program that best suits his or her horse, circumstances and facilities.

Trainer's Tip
Invariably Thoroughbred and Arabian horses, i.e., "hotbloods," are easier to get fit, and tend to maintain their fitness levels better than "warmbloods" and "coldbloods."

Weeks one to four are the crucial "walk" weeks, the ones that will give the horse its solid fitness base. Some horses that are brought back into work can at first be difficult, excited and over-exuberant. In cases like this, try to "pony" (lead) the horse from another horse until it has been walked a few times. If possible, avoid lunging a horse that has been out of work. Lunging is excellent exercise for a horse in shape, but can put strain on the muscles of an unfit horse, especially if it is prone to tearing around.

Week 1 A half hour walking on a hard surface to be increased to 1 hour walking by the end of the week.

Week 2 One hour walking on a hard surface to be increased to 1½ hours walking by the end of the week.

Week 3 If possible, divide the work into two sessions, one in the a.m. and one in the p.m. If the facilities are available use a half hour smart walk on a treadmill or horsewalker as one session and build up a second session to 1½ hours walking on a hard surface.

Week 4 Still using two sessions, maintain the hour on the horsewalker and introduce some uphill work to the second walk session.

During these weeks of walking, the horse must be asked to walk forward in a positive and active manner and should be encouraged to walk forward into the bridle. It is important to keep the walk work primarily on a hard surface such as the road, and deep or heavy going should be avoided. By walking on the hard and flat, the horse's tendons and ligaments will begin to strengthen and its muscles will gradually start to build. By the end of week four, the horse should be striding uphill in an outline, and should be ready to begin the trot work.

Trainer's Tip

Horses that are being brought back into work after recovering from a leg injury can need up to six weeks of walk.

Trot Phase: Weeks 5 and 6

Depending on the horse, some trot may have been introduced at the end of Week 4, but if not, then by the start of Week 5 the horse should be in good shape to start really working. Aim to introduce trot work gradually, and as with the walk, the horse should be moving forward and into a contact. Avoid excessive trotting on the roads to reduce concussion; instead, start the trot work on tracks or around field edges as long as they are even and the going isn't too heavy.

Week 5 One hour of hacking including several short trots to be increased to 1½ hours hacking with increased trot work by the end of the week.

Week 6 A half hour flatwork in the arena including walk and trot and suppling exercises, followed by 1 hour hacking with increased trot work. By the end of the week, the flatwork can be increased to 40 minutes, and can be alternated with lunging sessions, followed by 1½ hours hacking including uphill trot work by the end of the week.

Canter Phase: Weeks 7 to 9

Canter should be introduced slowly and on the straight to begin with. As with the other phases, the horse should be asked to canter in an outline, and when out hacking should be asked to strike off on both leads.

Week 7 Forty minutes flatwork including trotting poles, followed by a half hour hacking to include several short canters on the flat. By the end of the week the canter spells should be increased.

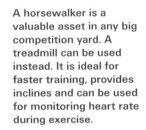

A horsewalker is a valuable asset in any big competition yard. A treadmill can be used instead. It is ideal for faster training, provides inclines and can be used for monitoring heart rate during exercise.

Lunging is a useful form of exercising the horse. Always lunge on both reins. Keep sessions to around 25 minutes and don't lunge more than a couple of times a week.

Week 8 One hour in the arena including a half hour of flatwork and a half hour of grid work, followed by 45 minutes hacking. Through the week, a second working session may be added, which can either be a half hour of short canter workouts (2–3 minutes) or a half hour on the lunge in walk, trot and canter.

Week 9 One hour in the arena including flatwork and jumping, both colored poles and natural fences. The horse should be ready for schooling around cross country courses, and is now ready to go out to dressage and show jumping competitions. A second working session per day of 1 to 1½ hours of hacking to include sustained canters, and pipe openers should now be introduced. The canter should be increased gradually from 3 minutes up to 10 minutes over the next two weeks.

Final Phase: Weeks 10 to 12
During the final phase of fitness the horse's stamina needs to be improved to prepare it for the rigors of the competition (two- and three- day eventing fitness programs will normally need to be 12 to 14 weeks and include greater stamina building work and longer sustained canter).

Week 10 Maintain a working routine based around 1 hour to 1½ hours of flatwork and jumping, interspersed with lunging, or half hour of jumping, or flatwork followed by 1½ hours hacking. Add to the working week several sessions of sustained canter. Do this at least every two or three days, and maintain a good hard canter for 10 minutes. Work in two gallops a week, and gradually increase the distance of the gallop from ¼–½ mile (400–800 m).

Weeks 11 and 12 Keep the horse in the same amount of work, and try to keep the program interesting by swapping flatwork sessions for cross country-schooling sessions; use lunging and

---

PONYING

This is a useful exercise that involves leading one horse while riding another. Always have the led horse on the side furthest from the traffic and make sure that both horses have brushing boots on all four legs. The horse that is being led should be wearing a bridle with either the reins threaded through the bit ring nearest the lead horse, or a lead rope threaded through the nearest bit ring and snapped onto the other bit ring. If the horse that is being led is particularly difficult, it is a good idea to use a surcingle with breastplate (to prevent slipping) and loose side reins.

INTERVAL TRAINING PLAN

This plan is based on a horse that has been in relatively hard work, and would be at around Week 8 of its traditional fitness program. If the horse has not been in such hard work then the canter sessions should be moderated, shortened or alternated with trot.

MONTH ONE

C = CANTER T = TROT W = WALK

WEDNESDAY	CANTER SPEEDS OF 1,300 FEET (400 M)/MINUTE		
	3 min C	1 min T	2 min W
	3 min C	1 min T	2 min W
	3 min C	1 min T and W cooling down time (10 min)	

MONDAY	CANTER SPEEDS OF 1,300 FEET (400 M)/MINUTE		
	4 min C	1 min T	2 min W
	4 min C	1 min T	2 min W
	4 min C	2 min T and W cooling down time (10 min)	

WEDNESDAY	CANTER SPEEDS OF 1,300 FEET (400 M)/MINUTE		
	5 min C	1 min T	2 min W
	5 min C	1 min T	2 min W
	5 min C	1 min T and W cooling down time (10 min)	

MONDAY	CANTER SPEEDS OF 1,300 FEET (400 M)/MINUTE		
	6 min C	1 min T	2 min W
	6 min C	1 min T	2 min W
	6 min C	1 min T and W cooling down time (10 min)	

WEDNESDAY	CANTER SPEEDS OF 1,300 FEET (400 M)/MINUTE		
	6 min C	1 min T	2 min W
	6 min C	1 min T	2 min W
	6 min C	1 min T and W cooling down time (10 min)	

MONDAY	CANTER SPEEDS OF 1,500 FEET (450 M)/MINUTE		
	7 min C	1 min T	2 min W
	7 min C	1 min T	2 min W
	7 min C	1 min T and W cooling down time (10 min)	

WEDNESDAY	CANTER SPEEDS OF 1,500 FEET (450 M)/MINUTE		
	7 min C	1 min T	2 min W
	7 min C	1 min T	2 min W
	7 min C	1 min T and W cooling down time (10 min)	

MONTH TWO

WEDNESDAY	CANTER SPEEDS OF 1,500 FEET (450 M)/MINUTE

7 min C	1 min T	1.5 min W

8 min canter uphill with two short gallops, 1 minute trot, walk and cool off

WEDNESDAY	CANTER SPEEDS OF 1,650 FEET (500 M)/MINUTE

7 min C	1 min T	1.5 min W

8 min canter uphill with three short gallops, 1 minute trot, walk and cool off

WEDNESDAY	CANTER SPEEDS OF 1,650 FEET (500 M)/MINUTE

7 min C	1 min T	1.5 min W

7 min canter, one minute gallop on the flat, 1 minute trot, walk and cool off

WEDNESDAY	CANTER SPEEDS OF 1,700 FEET (520 M)/MINUTE

7 min C	1 min T	1.5 min W

9 min canter uphill with four short gallops, 1 min trot, walk and cool off

When cantering during interval training, take the weight off the horse's back and maintain a good, steady rhythm at the correct speed your program dictates.

At the end of a session of interval training it is essential to walk your horse for at least 10 to 20 minutes to allow it to cool off and relax.

while increasing the hacking. Keep an open mind, and above all keep the horse interested and happy in its job.

Interval Training

This is a useful, and "scientific" approach to fitness training that some people prefer to use. With interval training, as with any fast exercise session, the horse must be thoroughly warmed up before the session begins.

Interval training is based on a series of short workouts with a period of rest in between, every three to four days. The break in between the sessions of interval training allows the horse to recover fully from the rigors of the session, before subjecting it to the strenuous workout again. In this way, the horse's muscles are able to recover and then build with each session.

The longer the time lapse between the sessions, the more time the horse's muscles have to soften, so if a horse is becoming very fit very quickly, the interval training can be reduced to once every five or six days, which will, in turn, slow down the rate of achieving fitness.

During the interval training session, the horse is cantered three times with a period of rest in between. As the horse becomes fitter, the session may include two longer canters with a period of rest in between. The rest period allows the horse to partially recover before being asked to work again. By partially recovering, and then continuing work, the horse's body is encouraged to meet the stress of the workout and the heart and lung capacity is improved, hence enhancing its stamina. The horse's pulse and respiration rate should have returned to its normal level after being cooled down, by 10 minutes of walk after the final canter phase of the training session. If the horse is not recovering sufficiently, then it is

hacking to keep up the work levels and maintain the twice-weekly canter and gallop sessions. For the last few weeks, the horse should be taken out and about to small competitions to prepare it for the "big day" — both mentally and physically.

Read your horse and suit your fitness program to its needs. Some horses become increasingly wound up the more they are taken out, while others respond well to the excitement of competition days. If your horse falls into the former category, keep training sessions low key.

Once the eventing season has kicked off, the horse should maintain its level of fitness quite easily, with each competition helping. It might be that once the horse has reached an optimum level of fitness, you are able to ease back on the canter/gallop sessions to once a week instead of twice, and reduce the amount of schooling work being pushed too hard and the length of the training sessions need to be reduced until the level of fitness has improved.

Warming Up and Cooling Down

Before the horse begins any strenuous working session, no matter what that might be, it is essential to warm it up properly, and to allow the muscles to start working without any strain. If there is access to a horsewalker or treadmill, these are both useful tools for warming up a horse. The horse can be put onto the walker for 15 minutes before the working session starts and walked at a good pace to loosen up and prepare for work. If walkers or treadmills are not available, then the horse must be walked, then trotted on a light contact for around 10 minutes before he goes to work. Warming up is particularly important in the winter when the horse is cold, its muscles are stiff and cold, and it is tight through its back. It can be advisable to start the warming-up process with a quarter sheet on if the weather is truly terrible!

Cooling down is just as vital, and at least 10 to 20 minutes must be allocated at the end of a working session to walk the horse and cool it off. A hot, sweaty horse that is chucked back into the stable, or turned out, will stiffen up and can become chilled down. The horse must be walked until it has dried off and relaxed from its working session. Alternatively, in the summer when it is hot, the horse may be sponged down then walked to dry off, or rugged with a sweat sheet or cooler. The addition of either lavender, menthol or witch hazel washes to the water can have a soothing effect on tired muscles and help to remove stubborn traces of sweat.

Roughing Off and Turning Away

Horses need to have downtime, either when their workloads are greatly reduced at the end of the eventing or hunting season, for example, or when they are actually given a period of rest and turned out. Turning a horse out requires some planning, and is not something that can just happen! Before

Trainer's Tip

Deworm your horse before turning it away, and consider pulling off its shoes to allow the hoof wall a chance to grow and regenerate.

the horse is turned away, it must be roughed off, i.e., toughened up to cope with life outside.

Generally it takes two to four weeks to prepare a horse for being turned out depending, obviously, on the time of year. First, as soon as its workload is lessened, a horse's feeding must be altered accordingly with concentrates being cut down and roughage increased. Some horses need to remain on a level of concentrates and will lose weight if weaned off them completely, but many horses, providing the grass is good, can be put on to a diet of just roughage.

Rather than abruptly stopping the horse's working sessions (if it has been in hard fitness work), gradually reduce the work from strenuous sessions to gentle hacking, cutting out the interval training and canter work completely. Gradually reduce the amount of rugs the horse is wearing, and, at the same time, decrease the amount of grooming with a body brush (which removes grease, the natural insulation from the coat).

It may be that the horse will need to be turned out in a waterproof rug if it is not particularly hardy, and if this is the case, then make sure that the rug is checked twice daily and removed so that the horse can be checked underneath it. Increase the period of time each day that the horse is out at grass, and then finally, try to pick a nice warm day to turn the horse out for its vacation. Be warned that some horses simply don't rough off very well and will not grow sufficient coat to stay warm. In cases such as this, the horse will either have to be rugged, brought in at night or given supplementary feeds.

11

BREEDING AND FOALING

Deciding to breed from a mare is not something that should be undertaken lightly, and there are a number of factors that must be considered before the decision to breed is made. The biggest question to ask is, "Why am I breeding from this mare?" If the answer is, "Because I can't do anything else with her," then she should not be being bred from, *unless* the mare has proved her value and merit in some capacity other than eating carrots! All too often a sub-standard mare is bred from when it becomes unsound because the owner either doesn't want to part with it, or feels that the horse somehow needs to appear to be useful. It is extremely important to remain objective and to very carefully assess the mare for her merits — conformation, temperament and performance — before deciding to breed from her.

Deciding to Breed

First and foremost the mare must be considered, and this will be further covered in the next section.

Decide why you are breeding a foal — is it with a view to sell, and, if so, at what age — weaning, yearling, 2-year-old, etc. — or is it because you wish to try and breed a horse for yourself.

Try to evaluate the logistics. Breeding a foal to sell is a risky business for the individual single horse owner. First comes the emotional attachment, whereby it can be very difficult to sell a youngster that you have raised. Second, a foal starts to cost money from the minute you decide to breed the mare, until the minute it walks up the ramp of its new owner's trailer and leaves your establishment. Roughly work out the cost of your covering fees, vet's fees, stud fees – if the mare is to be sent away, feed for the mare and foal, and vaccinations up to weaning. Get a ballpark figure then double it, and you might come close to the cost, and this is *only* if nothing goes wrong, and you sell the foal at weaning. It is not rocket science to work out that unless the foal sells for considerable money you will be out of pocket. While the eventual sale price will go up the longer the youngster is kept and the more training it receives, so also does the cost of keeping it and the potential for problems — unforeseen colic, a punctured sole, etc.

Breeding a horse for yourself can be both the most rewarding and the most devastating thing to do. It is a long-term commitment; you are looking at between three to four years before the horse is being ridden, and a further year before it is competing at any significant level. Within that time frame you can rest assured that the apple of your eye will be on self-destruct in every conceivable way, and sadly, there is also no guarantee that breeding a great mare with a great stallion will produce a great offspring — the chances are more likely, but it is not a sure thing.

Another consideration is your facility. This must be a safe environment for a foal. The fences must be stud mesh, post and rail/hedge, or synthetic. Smooth wire is not suitable and barbed wire should never be used for any kind of horse fencing. You will need a stable large enough to house the mare and foal; even if they are primarily kept out, you must be able to stable them, if necessary. And if you decide to foal the mare at home, you must have a suitable foaling stall.

Finally, do you have the experience and confidence to deal with youngsters?

Assessing the Mare

What is important is that the basic good qualities are there; if the mare does have a fault, make sure it is one that is minor, or can with luck be improved on by breeding to a stallion who

Embryo transfers, whereby a 6–8-day-old embryo is transferred to a recipient mare allows, for example, a competition mare to carry on competing. Here, a matronly mare is seen with a "super foal" that she has raised, but which is clearly not related to her!

compensates for the mare in the areas that she is weak. There are three main considerations when assessing the breeding viability of the mare:
• Conformation
• Temperament
• Performance

The mare should score an excellent on all three of these, the only exception being where a lovely filly suffers an accident that renders her unsound and therefore unable to perform. Providing she qualifies in both other areas, and has good performance in her bloodlines, then there is no reason not to use her for breeding purposes.

Another consideration is the mare's age. The prime reproductive window is between 3 and 12 years. That is not to say that an older mare can not be reproductive, but her chances of conceiving will be reduced, and the older she gets, the more draining a pregnancy is to her. A filly younger than 3 will herself still be growing and developing, and so the added burden of pregnancy can be detrimental.

Some mares have poor conformation under the tail, whereby the vulva is long and sloping and appears sunken beneath the anus. This can be a problem and lead to infection due to fecal contamination through the vulva. A Caslick operation is a simple procedure during which the top part of the mare's vulva is stitched up after she has been covered, leaving a small opening at the bottom. It is vital that if the mare has had a Caslick operation she is unstitched before foaling. Also, if you have bought a mare and are unsure of her history, check to see that she is not stitched before she is covered.

Assessing the Stallion

First, you must decide what type of foal you are trying to breed and what job it is hopefully destined for! Second, keep in mind any faults that your mare may have, and make sure that when you are selecting a stallion, he excels in the areas in which she is weak. For example, if the mare is slightly upright in the shoulder and so lacks an expressive stride, be sure to select a stallion with

a particularly free-flowing stride. Third, it is wise to choose the best stallion you can afford. Set yourself a budget and do not look at anything over that.

The stallion must also be judged on his conformation, temperament and performance. Always research the stallion's bloodlines and any progeny that he may already have bred to see how well they are doing. If choosing a young stallion, make sure that he has good, sound bloodlines and a performance track record.

Where possible try to view the stallion; ask to see him in the stable and also moving. Make sure that his movement is correct and straight, and evaluate his temperament to the best of your ability; the eye is a great window on the soul!

Breed societies set a standard for stallions, and in the warmblood breed societies, the stallion is required to pass rigorous performance testing (conformation, pedigree and attitude are also considered) and is then graded on his merits, so you know that the stallion is of a high standard.

There are certain genetic defects that some stallions will pass on to their offspring, so be very careful to thoroughly research the stallion. A common such defect is Hyperkalemic Periodic Paralysis (HYPP), which is a form of muscle disorder that manifests itself as periodic tremors, collapse, labored breathing and occasionally sudden death following an attack. The condition is seen in some Quarter Horses, some Paints and some Appaloosas, and is thought to have originated with the champion halter stallion.

Breeding Methods

Artificial Insemination

Semen is mechanically collected from the stallion and then transferred to the mare via a syringe on the end of an insemination pipette. This procedure can be done immediately after the stallion's semen has been collected, or the semen can be frozen. If the latter, the semen can then be shipped over great distances (worldwide) to the mare, and the mare then inseminated with it. This process, which has become increasingly popular, has many advantages: the risk of injury to the stallion from the mare is removed; the mare does not need to be sent away from home; the mare can be bred to a stallion who is based in a foreign country; semen frozen from a dead stallion can be used; the semen can be extended, i.e., one ejaculation can be divided and used to inseminate several mares; the choice of stallions is huge; the risk of infection from mare to stallion or vice versa is reduced, and it is a safer option when breeding a mare with a foal at foot. In many

Trainer's Tip
The Thoroughbred breed does not permit artificial insemination.

cases, even when a mare is sent away to stud to be bred, the stud will collect from their stallion, and artifically inseminate the mare with fresh semen to prevent the stallion from being injured.

The main disadvantages with artificial insemination are veterinary costs, which can escalate, the difficulty of organizing the shipping of the semen to arrive close to when the mare ovulates, and the fragility of the semen.

Hand Breeding

This is the traditional breeding method, used by the thoroughbred industry. It involves allowing the mare and stallion to breed naturally in a controlled environment. Usually, the mare is sent to the stud where the stallion is standing, She will be bred several times during her heat cycle.

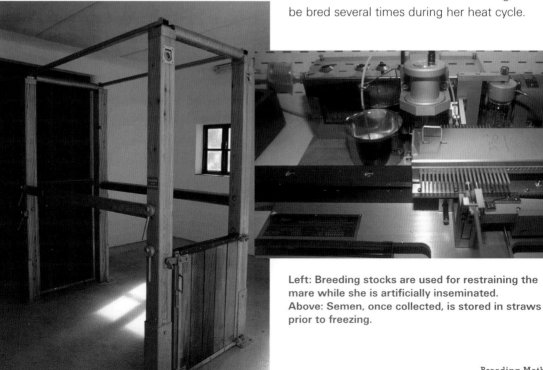

Left: Breeding stocks are used for restraining the mare while she is artificially inseminated.
Above: Semen, once collected, is stored in straws prior to freezing.

This is an example of herd breeding where the horses are allowed to breed naturally. First the stallion approaches the mare to court her and to make sure she is receptive. Next he starts to mount her; finally he breeds her.

Herd Breeding

This is rarely done now due to the value of the stallions and the potential for injury to the stallion, and the mare. It is, however, the most natural way for the horse to breed! The stallion is allowed to run with a group of mares throughout the breeding season, and the breeding itself takes place in a natural environment without the benefit of any human direction.

Heat Cycles

Every mare will cycle slightly differently, but the average cycle for a mare lasts between 21 and 23 days. This period is split in two. The estrus is when the mare is "in heat" or "in season" and lasts for approximately seven days. The diestrus, that portion of the mare's cycle when she is not in heat and therefore not receptive to the stallion, lasts for approximately 14 days.

Mares start to come into heat in the spring when the days are lighter and warmer, and will continue to cycle through to September or October. During the winter they tend not to come into heat, and are described as being "in anestrus," although some studs will encourage mares to start cycling early by keeping them under heat lamps.

While the mare is in heat, follicles grow rapidly in the ovaries, and as she nears the end of her heat, one of the follicles ruptures releasing a mature egg, which is ready to be fertilized. The rupturing of the follicle is referred to as ovulation, and generally occurs one to two days before the end of the heat cycle. The mature egg will only survive for approximately 12 hours, so the timing of breeding is crucial.

When hand breeding a mare, she may be bred several times — often every other day from around day three of her heat cycle — until she no longer accepts the stallion. However, when artificially inseminating a mare with chilled or frozen semen, there is often only enough semen available for one or two inseminations, so the timing is absolutely crucial. The veterinarian will determine how the mare's heat cycle is progressing through the use of ultrasound scans and is generally able to predict fairly accurately when she will ovulate.

Going Away to Stud

Sending a mare away to a stud farm to be bred is in many cases the easiest option. The stud takes responsibility for the management of the mare, monitors her heat cycles, breeds her in a controlled environment and has the equipment and veterinary backup to determine the progress of her and her conception. Many studs will then take the mare back when she is due to foal, and oversee the foaling, and the rebreeding of the mare if the owner wishes.

Before sending your mare to a stud, find out what requirements the stud has. A good stud should want to see a record of your mare's vaccination and worming program, and will re-worm her on arrival. Although the United States and Canada have remained relatively clear of CEM (contagious equine metritis) since the late 1970s, some studs may require that the mare has had a clitoral swab to check for it. This swab can be taken at any time during her cycle, and the results will take roughly a week to come back. The stud also will generally take a cervical swab, which can only be taken when the mare is in heat, to determine whether she has an infection.

Trainer's Tip

Most studs use breeding stocks for examining the mare. These stocks keep the mare still and are designed with the safety of the vet, the handler and the mare in mind.

Mares seem to conceive more readily if they are in good shape, being neither too fat or too thin, so bear this in mind when preparing to send your mare off. Make sure she has had her feet trimmed, shoes pulled off and is roughed off sufficiently to live out. Most studs keep mares at grass. It is possible to have them stabled, but this pushes the costs up, and is not generally needed. Before sending her away, try to have a rough idea about your mare's cycles, and plan on sending her about a week before she is due to come back into heat. The stress of moving the mare often can disrupt her cycle so waiting until she is actually in heat is not always the best idea.

Once the mare arrives at the stud farm, the staff will watch her closely to try and determine

her heat cycles. She will be "teased" every other day by a teaser stallion. This involves the mare being introduced to a stallion over a special heavy-duty teasing wall. If the mare is not in heat, she will clearly reject the stallion, lay her ears back, attempt to kick or squeal and clamp her tail. As she comes in to season, however, she will become more receptive to the stallion, whose job it is basically to sweet talk her. As she comes into season she will start to lift her tail and be less aggressive; once in full heat, she will start to crouch slightly, lift her tail and "wink," straddle her hind legs and urinate.

The teaser stallion is not used for covering the mares, although he might be given one or two mares at the end of the season; his main role is to reduce unnecessary stress on the breeding stallion by flirting with the mares in his place.

Each stud will have slightly different procedures, but once the mare is in heat, the stud veterinary surgeon will probably take a cervical swab to make sure that the mare is free from infection. The results of the swab can be obtained quickly, and if the mare is clean, she can be bred. If she has an infection, a course of treatment might be prescribed.

The veterinarian will determine how the mare's heat cycle is progressing through the use of ultrasound scans and is generally able to predict fairly accurately when she will ovulate. It is not unusual for a veterinarian to inject the mare with HCG (human chorionic gonadotropin), a hormone that stimulates ovulation usually within 48 hours.

The Breeding

Once it has been determined that the mare is ready to be bred, she either will be haltered or bridled, and will then have her tail bandaged up to prevent any hairs wrapping around the stallion's penis and causing damage, and to keep the genital area as clean as possible. Next she will have her vulva and surrounding area thoroughly washed with warm water, and then carefully dried. The stallion also will have his sheath and penis cleaned with water and

dried. Water can kill sperm so the latter is very important.

If the mare is particularly "difficult," she may be twitched or have breeding hobbles or soft "kicking" boots put on. All of these are done with safety in mind, to protect the stallion, the mare and the handlers. In some cases, the mare may have a thick leather blanket put on; this is to protect her from an overly zealous stallion who might bite or damage her back with his hooves. Studs will have their own preferred places to breed. Some favor a round pen — the mare is situated and the stallion brought in. There will be a brief courtship during which time the stallion

may exhibit *flehmen* — curling his top lip back in response to the smell of the mare in season — nickering and snorting, and might chew at the mare's neck, back and quarters. When he is ready, they will copulate, which will take up only a few minutes or less. Once he has finished and dismounted, the mare handler must turn the mare away from him so that she is not able to kick, and the stallion is led away. Occasionally, the stallion might breed her again immediately, if he failed to do so properly the first time.

Other studs prefer to use a solid fence against which the mare can brace herself. The handler stands on the opposite side of the fence and the stallion is brought up to the mare.

Often the stud staff will collect a sample of the stallion's semen on a microscope slide as he dismounts the mare, and then check the quality of the semen under the microscope. In cases where the mare has been bred using artificial insemination, it is very important that the semen sample is examined under the microscope to ensure that it is viable.

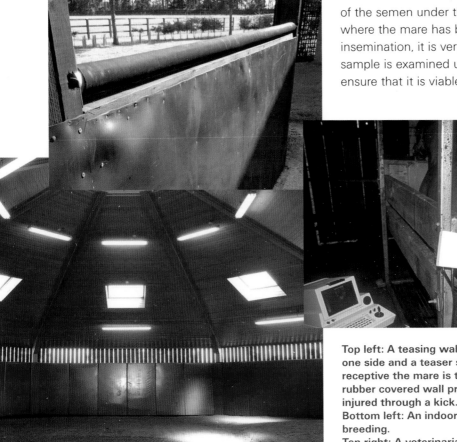

Top left: A teasing wall. The mare will be led along one side and a teaser stallion the other to test how receptive the mare is to being bred. The heavy-duty, rubber covered wall prevents either party from being injured through a kick.
Bottom left: An indoor breeding facility for hand breeding.
Top right: A veterinarian scanning a mare with an ultrasound machine to check for pregnancy.

Pregnancy and Foaling

Detecting Pregnancy

Today, ultrasound scanning is the most common method of detecting pregnancy in mares. The vet inserts the ultrasound probe into the mare's rectum, where the machine will read through the rectum wall and produce a picture of the uterus by way of high-frequency sound pulses.

Generally, if the mare has remained at the stud, she will be teased when she would next expect to be coming into season following the breeding. The mare's reaction will then give some idea as to whether or not she is pregnant — if she is, she would normally violently reject the teaser stallion's advances. She would then have an ultrasound scan at around 21 days, at which point a pregnancy should be clearly visible. It is advisable that the mare have a further ultrasound at around 35 days to check that she is still in foal, and by this point the heartbeat should show up.

Manual detection of pregnancy used to be the norm, and is still used in cases where the fetus is more than 45 days old. By this point, the fetus is so big that ultrasound is not able to be accurate. To manually detect pregnancy, the vet inserts his or her gloved arm into the rectum, and then palpates through the rectum wall to the uterus.

There is also a blood test available that determines pregnancy based on the levels of equine chorionic gonadotropin (eCG) produced as a result of pregnancy. The test is not 100 percent accurate; some mares produce false negatives, and a false positive result can occur if the fetus dies, because eCG still continues to be produced. This test is not carried out until the fetus is between 40 and 60 days old.

Care of the Pregnant Mare

Once your mare has been declared pregnant, you can then work out her due date. The gestation period for a horse is approximately 11 months, or 340 days. A mare can safely give birth up to two weeks early or late, but any greater deviation than this time frame should be cause for concern.

The first two months of pregnancy are the most critical; it is during this time that the mare stands the most chance of losing the pregnancy. With this in mind, keep the pregnant mare in quiet surroundings. Where possible, avoid any stressful situations and make no sudden changes to her routine. If necessary, due to weight problems, the pregnant mare can be kept in light work for the first five months of the pregnancy, but light means light, and no charging around!

Feeding the broodmare, as with all feeding, is a matter of common sense. During the early stages of pregnancy, a grass diet should be sufficient, providing the quality of the grass is good. However, the pregnant mare should have her diet supplemented with vitamins and minerals, and generally the easiest and most accurate way to ensure the mare is receiving these, is to give them to her in a small feed. As her pregnancy progresses, and certainly by her last four months, her diet will need to be bolstered by hay and

TWINS

Unlike most other animals, horses are not designed to carry twins. The presence of twins can be detected in early ultrasound scans at around 18 to 21 days, and at this point, the vet may decide to either "pinch off" one of the twins, or abort both. There are instances when the mare will reabsorb the smaller twin in these early stages, so some vets may wait until 35 days and then redo the scan to check.

If twins are not detected until after 40 days, there is a very high risk of the mare aborting, and then, due to the hormone upset this causes, she will be difficult to rebreed for some months. If the mare manages to carry both twins full term, which is unusual, and they survive the birth, it is common for either one or both of the twins to be very poor.

concentrates. There are a number of complete feeds available that are specifically for the pregnant mare, and these, fed in the correct quantities, will provide the mare with the extra protein and nutrients that she needs. Most importantly remember to feed the mare "little and often," and break her rations into two or three meals a day. As she nears her due date, decrease her roughage, and maintain her concentrates according to the manufacturer's guidelines. It is essential that the protein levels of her diet remain high — approximately 16 percent. If you are able to accurately predict your mare's foaling, then the day before she does so, feed her a bran mash and a low-energy feed.

Throughout the pregnancy continue the mare's worming schedule as normal, and keep her feet trimmed and in good condition. In the last month of pregnancy, reworm her.

Pregnant mares should be vaccinated against equine rhinopneumonitis in the fifth, seventh and ninth months of pregnancy. Also referred to as equine herpes, one strain of this virus can cause abortion. The mare should then be given booster shots of her normal vaccinations in the last month of pregnancy. Consult with a vet as to which vaccinations she might need. These will vary from country to country, but in the United States and Canada, these will certainly include tetanus, flu,

Trainer's Tip
The majority of mares foal between midnight and 4 a.m.

and eastern and western encephaloymyelitis. If the mare is to be sent to stud to foal, then be sure to do this in plenty of time — at least one month prior to her foaling date. This will allow her to settle in to her new environment; she will have time to build up antibodies in relation to the new surroundings and it is less stressful than transporting near her due date.

Trainer's Tip
There are several different types of foaling alarms. Some are activated when the mare lies down, which is not very effective if the mare is prone to lying down, and others react to an increase in body temperature

Signs of Foaling

- The mare's udders gradually increase in size and fill out, but in the days prior to foaling, they will become noticeably larger, tighter and shinier — known as "bagging up."
- The mare's belly will appear to have dropped.
- Approximately two to three days prior to foaling, tiny waxy droplets appear on her nipples; this is called waxing. Be warned, though, some mares wax for several days and some mares don't wax at all. The only certainty with mares foaling is that they rarely do it by the book! If in any doubt, have the mare checked over by your vet.
- Usually the day or so before foaling the mare will start to become restless, possibly change her pattern of routine, and often go off her food.
- In that same time frame, the muscles around the pelvic bones appear relaxed and "wobbly," and the muscles around the vulva relax so that it has the appearance of "slackening" and lengthening.
- As the mare approaches labor, she will become increasingly restless. She may sweat, roll, kick at her belly or keep turning to look at her belly — all signs also associated with colic.

Be Prepared!

You should be set up and ready for foaling at least a month before the mare is due, just in case she delivers early.

The foaling box, which should be at least 16 x 16 feet (5 x 5 m) must be well bedded down with straw or paper *not* shavings, and should have been thoroughly cleaned. Any protruding objects such as mangers should be removed and haynets should not be used. Feed hay on the ground instead and hang up water buckets; there is a risk with water buckets on the ground that the foal might drown at birth, or they will get knocked over during labor.

Start bringing the mare in at night around a week before she foals; this will allow her to settle into the routine and become familiar with the foaling box. If using a foal alarm or CCTV get it organized early.

Foaling
Stage One: Labor

With the onset of labor, the mare will become very restless. If she is out at pasture, she will go away on her own. She will get up and lie down and exhibit colic like symptoms of sweating, kicking at her belly, etc., caused by the discomfort of her contractions. At this point, put on the halter and bandage up her tail to keep it out of the way and to cut down on contamination. If you have arranged to have a vet present, now is the time to call him or her.

Stage Two: Birth

The mare's contractions will come faster and will be increasingly painful. Her waters will burst and then a whitish blue membrane (the amniotic membrane) will appear at the opening of her vulva. If more than 7 to 10 minutes pass after her waters break and she continues to strain with no membrane appearing, call the vet immediately.

If the birth is progressing normally, the first foot will appear, followed quickly by the second, and then the foal's nose. If the foal does not appear like this, then it is presenting wrongly and you must call the vet right away. The shoulders of the foal are the hardest part to expel, and it may be that you need to gently assist the mare if she is continually straining and unable to push the foal out. However, only pull on the foal when the mare has a contraction and is also pushing, otherwise the birth canal may be damaged, and only pull above the fetlock joints. The bag (amniotic membrane) should now have split, and you need to gently make sure it is completely clear of the foal's nose and mouth.

The mare may rest before expelling the rest of the foal, so remain unobtrusive. Once the foal has been born, it will still be attached to the umbilical cord. Do not wade in and cut the cord; the foal will still be receiving oxygen through it. Let it

Trainer's Tip

Be discreet and, if possible, monitor the mare without her knowing you are there. Mares are more comfortable foaling in the quiet and seclusion of night, and even can be put off foaling if they are continually disturbed.

The hippomane is a brown, liverlike object passed with the placenta. It is thought to be the accumulation of debris from the foal during gestation.

Suckling for the foal, as demonstrated by this older one and its mother, should be one of the most natural things in the world, but it is surprising how many newborn foals struggle to find the teat.

break naturally as the mare or foal stands up, and once it has broken, immediately treat the foal's umbilical stump with betadine or iodine solution to prevent infection.

Towel the foal down to stimulate its circulation and warm it up, and tie up the afterbirth to prevent the mare standing on it and tearing it as it needs to be examined intact (see below).

Offer the mare a warm bran mash and add clean bedding to the stall, then allow the mare and foal some quiet time to bond. After 30 minutes or so, go back and check on the mare and foal. Ideally by now the foal should be standing and trying to suckle — or at least thinking about it!

Stage Three: The Afterbirth

From the moment the mare's waters break to the actual birth of the foal should take no longer than 30 to 40 minutes, and can be as quick as 10 minutes. If the process is taking longer, there is a problem and the vet must be called immediately. The third stage of foaling, which is the expulsion of the placenta, generally occurs quickly, normally within an hour after the foal is born. It may take

quick reference

Foaling – When to Call the Vet

- If the waters have broken, the mare is straining and nothing has appeared after 10 minutes.
- If the foal is not presented normally, i.e., the nose appears first and no feet; one foot and the nose but not the other foot; more than two feet appear together; a foot appears with the sole pointing upward — this indicates that it is a back foot and that the foal is presented backward.
- If the mare is having contractions but nothing is happening, and the foal is not coming any further.
- If the first and second stages of foaling have gone on longer than 40 minutes.
- If the mare stops having contractions and appears to have given up.
- If the placenta comes out before the foal — if you see a mass of red membrane preceding the foal instead of the blue/white membrane of the amnion (birth sac).
- If the placenta, when expelled, is any other color than a normal bright red.
- If the placenta is not expelled within four hours.
- If you suspect the placenta is torn.
- If the mare's vulva is torn and she requires sutures.
- If the mare suffers a uterine prolapse, i.e., the uterus follows the foal out. This condition can be fatal, the mare must be restrained and the weight of the uterus held by an assistant until the vet arrives. If the weight of the uterus breaks any of the major blood vessels the mare will die from hemorrhaging.
- If the mare remains excessively weak after foaling and reluctant to move. There is always a possibility of a torn uterus internally and internal bleeding. Call the vet immediately.
- If you are ever in any doubt, call the vet.

some mares longer than this, but if the placenta has not been delivered by four hours after foaling, then veterinary advice must be sought. During the expulsion of the afterbirth, the mare will again show colicky symptoms due to the abdominal pain caused by the contractions. Once the afterbirth has been delivered, immediately collect it in a sack and lay it out on the floor where it can be thoroughly examined. If any of the placenta remains inside the mare it will cause severe infection, so when checking the placenta make sure that it is intact. There should be one tear it in where the foal came through, and the rest of the placenta should be complete and a healthy red color. If you are in any doubt about the placenta, then keep it in a sack for the vet to have a look at.

Sometimes the ground is just such a long way away!

The Very Young Foal

The foal should be standing and suckling within 30 minutes. The first drink that the foal has is very important because it contains the colostrum. This is a potent cocktail of antibodies to protect the foal from its new, and unsterile world. The colostrum also has a mild laxative effect, which encourages the foal to pass meconium — the buildup of feces that has collected in the foal's bowel while it was in the uterus. This should be passed within the first five hours and is usually dark in color. If the meconium has not been passed after six hours or if the foal is straining but not passing anything it should be given an enema.

The importance of the colostrum to the young foal cannot be stressed enough. The foal must be seen to have drunk well otherwise his chance of infection increases by almost 50 percent. The mare's production of colostrum will tail off quite quickly (usually 24 hours) after foaling so the foal must drink well as quickly as possible. If after several hours the foal has still not suckled properly, then you must milk the mare's colostrum (or already have some frozen and thawed on hand) and feed the foal using a bottle. If possible, hold the bottle up under the mare's teat to try and encourage the foal to figure it all out. However, try not to interfere unless there is an obvious problem. Let nature take its course; the foal should find the teat on its own, and learn to stand by trial and error. If the foal is really struggling to suckle then you can gently guide it toward the teat.

It is beneficial to handle the young foal (or imprint it), but never do this until the foal has bonded with its mother, had a good suckle and preferably passed the meconium. The foal and mare must be allowed to bond before you intervene, and this process takes several hours. Early imprinting sessions should be kept short and objective. Aim to handle the foal's entire body, both sides, under the tail, in the ears, and nose and feet. Gradually increase the sessions over a period of weeks to include putting on and taking off a foal slip, leading, picking up feet,

being rubbed with towels and plastic, and the noise of spray bottles and clippers. One of the disadvantages of sending a mare to a stud to foal is that studs do not normally have the time to handle the foals. Without doubt, the younger the foal becomes accustomed to being handled, the easier life becomes for the handler and the foal.

If the foal was born in a stall, and providing both foal and mare are healthy, then turn them out the following day in a small, safe pasture. The routine of bringing the pair in at night and turning them out during the day is a useful one to establish. The foal becomes used to being handled, and to being in both environments. Once the foal is a few weeks old, it is good to turn it and its mother out with other mares and foals so that the youngsters learn to act and interact with each other, and grow up being "horses."

12

HEALTH AND FIRST AID

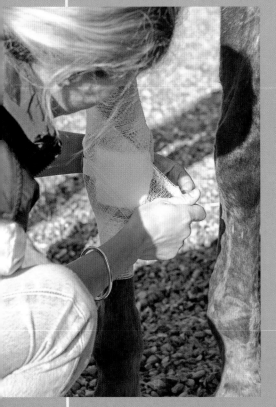

Sickness and injuries are always alarming, especially in the case of extensive blood loss, or if the horse is extremely agitated. It is important to remain calm and quiet, and to act quickly and efficiently.

Injuries and lameness are generally apparent, but symptoms of ill health may come on over a period of time. It is important to know your horse's normal behavior, so that you realize there may be a problem as soon as your horse deviates from this. Any change in pattern, such as a gradual decrease or increase in the number of droppings done overnight or water intake, for example, should be a warning sign. Similarly, the horse should be thoroughly checked all over (this can be done while grooming) daily, and any unusual swellings, bumps, lumps, areas of pain or other abnormalities should be noted and addressed.

Establish a habit of making a mental checklist so that assessing your horse becomes automatic. Always be aware of the way your horse moves – in the stable or field, as he is led and under saddle. Being able to detect lameness quickly is vital.

When to Call the Vet

Deciding on when to call the veterinary surgeon is a matter of common sense, but the golden rule is always to err on the side of caution. If in doubt, call the vet. Often an early diagnosis will improve the extent of recovery. There is specific advice throughout the chapter.

First-aid Kit

Every yard or individual horse owner should have a comprehensive first-aid kit that is labeled and accessible (see page 213). A secondary first-aid kit should be kept in either the horse truck or trailer, to be taken whenever traveling.

Next to the first-aid kit — and also taped to the telephone — should be the phone number of your vet.

Don't forget to replace anything that is used from the first-aid kit, so that it is always full.

Assessing Health

All horses are different; some, for example, will typically produce more droppings than others; some will always lie down for periods at night, while others rarely do. Water consumption will vary from horse to horse. However, there are basic guidelines to assess the healthy horse, and it is up to you to take stock of the horses in your care and become familiar with their particular biorhythms.

The first check in the morning is the most important because your horse will have been unsupervised for a long period of time during the night. If possible, your horse should be checked last thing at night as well — this certainly applies to the stabled horse, but it is also good to check the horse at grass. This final evening check is a chance to straighten rugs and top up water, if necessary, as well as making sure that the horse is behaving normally.

The Healthy Horse
- It should exhibit its normal behavior and characteristics.
- It should be alert, bright-eyed, interested in what's going on.

Take a horse's temperature with a plasic digital thermometer

- Its eyes should be clear, open and free of discharge.
- Its coat should be shiny and smooth, and its skin elastic.
- It should be passing normal fecal balls — these should be green or brown (depending on what it is eating), firm and should break on impact with the ground. The horse should have passed its normal amount during the course of the night.
- It should have drunk its normal amount of water.
- The urine should be normal, i.e., virtually colorless, without strong odor and in a normal quantity.
- There should be no discharge around the horse's nostrils.
- Its breathing should be regular and even.
- Its mucous membranes should be salmon-pink.
- It should be able to take weight evenly on all four legs.
- There should be no signs of excessive disturbance in the stable, which would suggest it had been thrashing around.
- There should be no indication that the horse has sweated profusely during the night.

- Its appetite should be normal.
- It should be its normal weight and should not appear to have lost or gained weight.
- Its breath should smell normal with no strong odor.
- Its temperature and pulse should be normal (see box, below).
- The horse should be able and willing to move normally.

Any deviation from the above would indicate a problem of some degree. An elevated pulse rate and respiration suggests the horse is in pain. The respiration will also increase if the horse has a temperature. A horse will develop a temperature for a number of reasons, but primarily it indicates an infection.

Trainer's Tip
Never leave a thermometer in the rectum without either holding it, or securing it to the tail — do this by looping a piece of string through the end of the thermometer and attaching it to a hair clip. The clip can then be fastened onto the tail.

VITAL SIGNS
- **Temperature 100–101°F (38°C)**
- **Pulse 32–42 beats per minute**
- **Respiration 8–14 breaths per minute**
- **All horses' vital statistics vary, and it is worth recording your horse's over the course of a week to ascertain its normal level so you have an accurate figure to compare with in case of suspected illness.**

Taking a Horse's Temperature

Stand to the side and back of the horse, and make sure that the horse is either tied up or being held by a handler. It helps to put a small dab of Vaseline or KY Jelly on the end of the thermometer before insertion. Raise the tail with one hand and gently insert the thermometer into the rectum with the other. Once it is in place, turn the thermometer on and wait for it to read the temperature. Most thermometers indicate when they have finished by beeping. Make a note of the reading, and thoroughly clean the thermometer before putting it away – wiping it with alcohol works well.

Taking a Horse's Pulse

There are several areas where the pulse can be felt relatively easily; one of the most accessible being just behind the jawbone. Always use three fingers to feel a pulse, and never use your thumb, which has its own pulse.

Run your fingers down the inside of the cheekbone on the left side until they rest just above where the cheekbone curves

(roughly where the halter would sit). The artery will be felt as a slightly raised "cord." Apply the most pressure in your finger furthest from the heart, and the least in your finger nearest the heart; this helps to amplify the pulse, making it easier to count.

The pulse also can be taken just above the sesamoid bones on the front and hind legs (see page 233) and is then referred to as a "digital pulse." One of the classic symptoms of laminitis (see page 232) is an increase in this pulse.

The pulse rate in foals and young horses is different from that in the mature horse. Foals will have a pulse rate of 70–120 beats per minute; yearlings 45–60 beats and 2-year-olds 40–50 beats.

Counting Respirations

Watch the rise and fall of the ribcage, and count one inhale and one exhale as one breath. The inhalation and exhalation should be of equal length, and in a healthy horse the actual movement of the ribcage should not be exaggerated. The rate of respiration will increase with work and in very hot weather, or can be an indicator of pain

Adding a powdered flavor such as apple or orange to the water can encourage a dehydrated horse to drink.

and/or a temperature. The horse at rest should never have obvious labored breathing.

Dehydration Test

A healthy horse should drink at least 5 gallons (19 l) of water a day, and if not, dehydration will quickly occur. You must monitor how much your horse is drinking, so you should fit automatic waterers with quantity gauges.

To test if your horse is dehydrated, pinch a small amount of skin on the neck between your thumb and forefinger then let go; in a healthy horse the skin should immediately flatten back into place, but if the horse is dehydrated, the skin will slowly recoil and appear wrinkled.

Capillary Refill Test

This is a simple test that allows you to assess the horse's blood

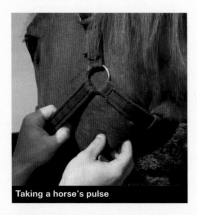
Taking a horse's pulse

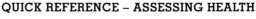
QUICK REFERENCE – ASSESSING HEALTH
- **Always look for any deviation from normal**
- **If in doubt call the vet**
- **Vital statistics — temperature 100–101°F (38°C) , pulse 32–42 beats per minute, respiration 8–14 breaths per minute**
- **Capillary refill test checks the blood circulation**
- **Test for dehydration by pinching the skin on the neck**
- **Healthy horses have gut sounds**

circulation. Lift the horse's top lip and firmly press your thumb or finger against its gum for two seconds until the area has turned white. Release your finger, and the white tissue should immediately fill back up with blood and return to its normal color — this should happen in one to two seconds. If the blood is slow in returning to the white area then there is a problem with the horse's blood circulation. Slow capillary refill will often occur in horses suffering from shock.

Mucous membranes are normally salmon-pink and are an indicator of blood's circulation; so any deviation from normal should be cause for immediate concern.

Listening for Gut Sounds

The healthy horse's gut should exhibit audible rumblings, which are a sign that the digestive system is working properly. When the gut is silent there is cause for concern. Listen for gut sounds by pressing your ear against the barrel just behind the last rib. Check both sides of your horse, and if it is difficult to hear gut sounds, try using a stethoscope.

Listening for gut sounds

The Comprehensive First-aid Kit

- Plastic digital thermometer
- 4 tubes sterile KY Jelly
- 1 jar of Vaseline
- 6 conforming bandages (Vetrap)
- 2 rolls of adhesive bandage i.e., Elasticon or Equiplast
- 4 rolls of brown/white gauze
- 4 rolls of gamgee
- 4 rolls of cotton wool
- 10 nonstick sterile wound dressings
- 10 poultice dressings i.e., Animalintex
- 1 tub of kaolin paste
- Selection of bandages including elastic support bandages and woolen stable bandages
- 2 tubigrip bandages
- 4 ice packs kept ready in freezer (these can be bought in several different forms, or kaolin paste can be smoothed between two plastic bags and frozen, or prepared Animalintex can be frozen)
- 1 roll of electrical tape
- 1 roll of wide packaging tape (i.e., duct tape)
- 2 cartons of Epsom salts
- Antibacterial skin wash
- 1 bottle of Betadine (iodine-povidone solution)
- 2 bags of sterile saline solution
- 1 bottle of witch hazel
- 1 bottle of surgical alcohol
- 1 bottle of hydrogen peroxide
- 2 tubes of triple antibiotic cream
- 1 bottle of wound powder
- 1 can of gentian violet and antibiotic spray
- 1 gallon of distilled water
- 1 spray bottle
- 1 gallon of PSS/Bet (see box, page 219)
- 1 metal bowl
- 1 galvanized pail
- 2 scrub brushes
- 2 clean towels
- 2 clean washcloths
- 1 pair of tweezers

- 4 babyproof safety pins
- 1 stethoscope
- 1 tourniquet
- 1 humane twitch
- 1 hoof pick
- 1 pair of half-curved blunt-ended scissors
- 1 pair of straight blunt-ended scissors
- 2 tubes of phenylbutazone paste or equivalent in powder
- 4 60-cc catheter tip syringes
- 2 packs of disposable gloves
- notebook and pencil

The traveling first-aid kit should be a pared down version of this, and should provide enough material to administer immediate first aid and bandaging.

Wounds and Open Injuries

The faster an injury is addressed the greater will be the chance for a full recovery. Once an injury has been located the following steps should be taken:

1 Stem the flow of the blood.
2 Rapidly assess the severity of injury; if necessary, call the vet.
3 Clean the wound and reduce the risk of infection.
4 Dress the wound.
5 Apply post-injury recuperative treatment.

Shock and Handling the Injured Horse

It is very important to remain absolutely calm in a first-aid situation — with you thinking clearly and acting sensibly, the horse stands a much better chance of recovery. Also, be aware that although horses are not affected by the sight of their own blood, they are susceptible to shock. Symptoms of shock are shaking, elevated respiration with shallow breaths, pale mucous membranes, a slow pulse due to low blood pressure, a fall in temperature and a cold sweat. If your horse is exhibiting signs of shock, call the vet at once. Horses naturally have a fairly high pain tolerance, and if it is exhibiting signs of shock, your horse is likely to be suffering severe pain, has lost a large amount of blood and is seriously injured. Keep the shocked horse quiet and warm until the arrival of the vet, and try to move it as little as possible.

When a horse is in pain and agitated from the perpetrator of the injury, its behavior will change, so always take care when handling an injured horse. Make sure that your horse is held securely by the reins or lead rope and, if possible, have a helper with you to hold the horse while you assess the injury. You and your helper should stay on the same side of the horse at all times.

Be aware that any animal in pain can become aggressive, and this can be heightened with a horse because you are restricting its natural flight instinct by holding it still, which can make the fight instinct kick in. Calm and reassure your horse and, if necessary, use a chifney bit or a humane twitch to restrain it enough to allow you to stem the blood flow and prepare the wound for the vet.

Stemming Blood Flow

If your horse appears to be bleeding profusely, don't panic! A horse can lose a lot of blood before it becomes life threatening, and a pool of blood on the ground always appears more than it actually is. Blood loss from minor wounds is generally minimal and will cease of its own accord due to clotting. More severe blood loss indicates damage to a large vein or artery, and must be controlled as quickly as possible. Arterial blood will appear bright red and will "pulse" from a wound, while venous blood will flow in a steady stream.

Pressure is the key to stemming blood loss, but bear in mind the wound needs to be kept as clean as possible to prevent infection, so if you are able, wash your hands first, and gather together clean bandage material. Before applying

> Always keep your horse's tetanus shots up to date.

WHEN TO CALL THE VET

- If the horse is bleeding profusely
- If a foreign object is suspected
- If any of the vital organs or major muscle masses have been damaged, or appear vulnerable
- If the horse is suffering from shock
- If the injury requires suturing
- If the injury is excessively dirty and contaminated
- If the injury is a puncture wound
- If the injury is to the eye
- If you are not confident that you can treat the horse yourself

Superficial cuts can be treated at home by the individual, but be vigilant for the onset of infection.

---

pressure to the wound itself make sure there are no foreign objects present, otherwise applying pressure will further damage the tissue. If the wound is on the body of the horse, or in an area where it is hard to apply a bandage, apply direct pressure with a nonstick sterile wound dressing and a gamgee pad; hold the pad in place firmly and wait for the vet to arrive.

If the blood loss is from the leg and appears to be arterial, then apply pressure approximately 1 inch (2.5 cm) above the wound and on the artery. If the bleeding is severe, then apply a tourniquet. This can be a single piece of material (a tie for instance) that is applied above the wound. Insert a pencil beneath the tourniquet, which can be twisted to increase the pressure until the blood stops. Once the blood flow has been controlled, apply a pressure bandage to the wound itself. A pressure bandage must include a large gamgee pad. Put the bandage on tightly and do not remove until the vet arrives. If the horse is continuing to bleed through the bandage, apply another bandage on top.

A tourniquet must be loosened every 10 minutes or so to allow blood flow to the lower limb. Keep the tourniquet loose for one to two minutes, then tighten again.

If your horse has damaged a major vein, then applying pressure approximately 1 inch (2.5 cm) below the injury can help to stem the blood flow. Veins carry the blood back to the heart, so applying pressure below the injury

on the leg will stop the blood being pushed back up the leg toward the heart. Then apply your pressure bandage as above.

Suturing Versus Open Wound Healing

Suturing greatly increases the speed with which a wound heals, and will decrease the chance of scarring. Some wounds obviously require suturing due to their severity, but often smaller flesh wounds, which would heal naturally, can be candidates for suturing. One great advantage of suturing a wound is that it cuts out on the development of proud flesh. Proud flesh involves the formation of grayish yellow granulation tissue that protrudes from the wound and, if unmanaged, will retard healing, increase scarring and can affect the nerve endings in the pastern area, resulting in lameness. Granulation tissue must be reduced, and this will be at the direction of the vet.

A wound cannot be sutured if:
- There is insufficient skin to draw the wound together.
- The wound is more than 12 hours old.
- The skin flap has died through loss of circulation.
- The wound is infected.

If a wound has been sutured, antibiotic creams or Vaseline should not be applied; these substances will break down the sutures.

Sutures are generally removed after 10 days, by which point the wound should have healed. Sutures will break down if the wound is

infected or the skin loses its integrity. Some vets favor metal staples over sutures in some circumstances. These are quick and easy to apply but are often more expensive.

Cleaning the Wound and Reducing the Risk of Infection

To properly clean and treat a wound, your horse needs to be in a clean, well lit area. If the injury occurs at a distance from home, then be aware of the contaminative effects of straw and woodchips in a trailer, for example, and, if possible, put a light, loose bandage on the horse until you can get it home and clean the wound properly.

One of the biggest problems with treating wounds is contamination leading to infection. Bear in mind that the skin and hair surrounding the wound will be dirty and will need to be cleaned thoroughly.

If your horse is in great pain and the vet has been called, stem the blood flow, keep the horse warm and reassured, and wait until the vet arrives. If, however, you are treating the wound yourself, wash your hands and prepare what you will need to clean the wound. Place all the items ready on hand on a small portable table or chair, or on a towel.

You will need:
- A clean bucket of boiled and cooled water, or saline solution, or PSS/Bet;
- A roll of guaze or a packet of gauze squares;

- A dry wound dressing and tape;
- Antiseptic solution, i.e., Hibiscrub, Pevidine or Betadine solution;
- Clippers with surgical blades, or blunt-ended scissors;
- KY Jelly;
- Disposable gloves;
- Tweezers (for a suspected foreign body; it is advisable to call the vet if there is one);
- 60-cc syringe;
- Clean towel.

First, using a cotton ball or gauze squares soaked in saline solution or boiled and cooled water, gently remove the worst of the dirt and contamination from the wound

When using a syringe to irrigate a wound be careful that the stream is not too strong, otherwise the force of liquid can damage the tissue and drive the dirt deeper rather than removing it.

itself. Use new cotton or gauze for each dab; work from the center of the wound outward. This will allow the wound to be properly assessed.

Next, squeeze sterile KY Jelly into the wound, being sure to get in under any flaps of skin. Now hold a dry wound dressing over the wound to protect it, and then start to clean the skin and hair surrounding the injury.

Hose away mud and dirt, running the flow of water down and away from the injury. Using a mild antiseptic solution, start to scrub clean the area around the injury. Once this is completely clean and toweled dry, clip the hair away, leaving a good 2-inch (5 cm) margin all the way around the edge of the wound. Remove the dressing and clip the hair up to the edge of

   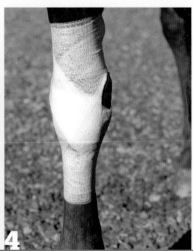

1 2 3 4

bandaging the knee

1 The main thing to avoid is bandage pressure over the bony prominence at the back of the knee. Cover the wound with a dressing and hold it in place with a "figure-eight" wrap using light gauze.

2 Start below the knee and make two passes before bringing the gauze up and diagonally across the front of the knee, around and back down to form a figure-eight.

3 This wrap is intended only to hold the dressing in place and so is of light gauze, which will eventually be covered by padding and self-adhesive bandage material.

4 The bony prominence is clear and free from pressure. The bandage is smoothly applied and can be seen to be holding the dressing secure.

the skin flap, or use blunt-ended scissors to remove any long hairs.

Now the wound can be cleaned thoroughly. Put on disposable gloves and gently start to clean the KY Jelly and any dirt from the wound using a new cotton ball with each dab. Clean from the middle of the wound to the outside, being sure to get in under any skin flaps. If you have difficulty getting under the skin flaps, irrigate using a spray bottle (on mist) or a syringe-full of PSS/Bet, or a weak Hibiscrub solution.

By thoroughly cleaning the wound and with proper aftercare,

the risk of infection is greatly reduced. However, if the wound is particularly dirty or deep, then the horse should be seen by a vet and prescribed a course of antibiotics.

Dressing the Wound

The primary reason for dressing a wound is to prevent contamination. Before dressing the wound, have everything you will need ready.

You will need:

- A wound dressing such as Animalintex or a gauze square impregnated with antibiotic cream;

- A pair of blunt-ended scissors;
- A roll of brown gauze;
- A precut length of gamgee, or a roll of cotton gauze;
- A roll of conforming bandage, i.e., Vetrap;
- A roll of adhesive bandage, i.e., Elasticon or Equiplast;
- A support bandage and padding for the opposite leg;
- Wool stable bandages (if winter).

What to do

Apply the wound dressing and hold in place with a single wrap of brown gauze. Next, apply either the gamgee pad or cotton and place a

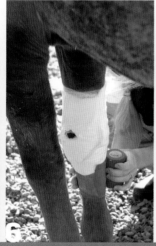

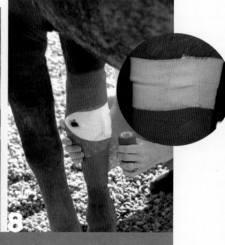

5 Layer a double thickness of gamgee or sterile cotton wool padding around the knee; remember to leave the bony prominence free from pressure.

6 To secure the padding, apply a single-layer gauze figure-eight bandage or the conforming bandage. Begin below the knee and make a pass with the bandage before starting a figure-eight configuration as described in Step 2.

7 Having passed the conforming bandage diagonally over the knee make a single pass above the knee. Be careful to achieve the right tension. The bandage must be tight and secure, but not excessively tight. Conforming bandage sticks to itself and molds to any contour.

8 Make one or two more diagonal passes with the conforming bandage before finishing. Then apply a single pass of sticky Elasticon or Elastoplast around the top of the bandage partially on the horse's coat (see inset). This will help to keep the bandage up and in place.

Types of Bandages

SURGICAL BANDAGES
A dressing held in place with brown gauze, a layer of gamgee or cotton, a layer of brown gauze, a conforming bandage and a wrap of adhesive bandage at the top and bottom.

PRESSURE BANDAGES
A dry dressing, a large pad of gamgee, a layer of brown gauze and a conforming bandage applied tightly. Pressure bandages should not be left on for longer than 20 minutes at a time.

SUPPORT BANDAGES
These are elastic bandages. Tail or exercise bandages work well, and should be applied over either a specific bandage pad or a precut piece of gamgee. Generally, support bandages run from below the knee or hock to just above the fetlock, and they should be applied firmly and evenly but not tightly. If extra support is needed, the bandage can be extended down to the coronary band, providing the padding also extends beyond the perimeter of the bandage.

TRAVELING BANDAGES
These provide protection and support to the horse while traveling. Although purpose-built boots that self-fasten have now largely replaced the traveling bandage, if taking the horse on a long trip, bandages should be used as they provide the horse with extra support and help to minimize any filling in the legs due to confinement. Elastic bandages such as exercise bandage may be used; the bandage should extend from below the knee or hock to above the coronary band, and a thick layer of padding or gamgee should be used beneath the bandage. Traveling bandages should have a single wrap of adhesive tape placed over their fastening to ensure that the bandage cannot come undone and cause an accident.

STABLE BANDAGES
These are wide, thick bandages made of wool or brushed cotton. They can be applied without a pad, although it always is preferable to use pads or gamgee under a bandage. Stable bandages provide warmth, help prevent the legs from filling with fluid when the horse is stabled or keep it clean before a show. They extend from below the knee or hock to above the coronary band.

EXERCISE BANDAGES
Of the same material as a support bandage, they provide support to the tendons while the horse is being worked and prevent any interfering injuries. They should be applied over a pad and run from below the knee or hock to above the fetlock. There are many excellent boots on the market now, which have in great part replaced the need for exercise bandages.

TAIL BANDAGES
These are elastic bandages that help keep the shape of a pulled tail and protect the tail during traveling. The bandage should start at the top of the tail, go down to just below the end of the tail bone, and back up to finish in the middle of the tail bone. Tail bandages should not be left on for longer than an hour at a time. They should be fastened with a double bow and the knot should be made to the side of the tailbone.

single layer of brown gauze over this to hold it in place. Then take the conforming bandage and start to bandage from below the wound down the leg, and back up over the wound. Keep pressure on the bandage material firm, but not excessively tight, and be sure to maintain the same pressure throughout the bandage. Seal and hold the bandage in place using a single wrap of Elasticon or Elastoplast tape around the top and bottom of the bandage.

Put a support bandage on the opposite leg, which will be taking more weight than usual, and, if cold, put stable bandages on the remaining two legs.

Bandages should be changed once or twice daily depending on the severity of the wound and the progress of healing.

Wounds That Cannot Be Dressed

Sometimes wounds occur in places that make it impossible to dress them successfully. It is vital to keep these wounds as clean as possible. Keep the horse on paper bedding and away from mud or dust. Irrigate the wound twice daily with either PSS/Bet or a weak antiseptic solution such as Hibiscrub, or plain saline. Excessive use of wound powders and creams can inhibit the natural healing process, so keep these to a minimum. It may be necessary to use an antibiotic powder or cream for the first few days, and these will also help to prevent flies. Keep the horse well sprayed with fly spray (taking care not to get any in the wound).

Knee and Hock Injuries

If your horse has injured its knee or hock area, it should be seen by the vet. Healing here is difficult due to the constant movement, and any injury near to a joint and the joint capsule should be thoroughly checked out. Bandaging the knee and hock area is difficult and requires practice.

A tubular bandage works well, although it can slip. Ease the bandage up over the injury and then roll it down to cover the injury and the dressing. A single wrap of adhesive bandage around the top of the tubular bandage can help to prevent slippage.

Bandaging the Hock

Use a double layer of gamgee in a similar figure-eight pattern to that on the knee; cut out a hole for the point of hock to prevent pressure. Take another small piece of gamgee or of cast felt and make an extra pad to lie across the tendon at the back of the hock. Make sure

to watch out for and avoid:
- Pressure on the Achilles tendon at the back of the hock;
- Pressure on the point of hock;
- Pressure on the bony prominence on the inside of the hock joint.

Recuperative Treatment

In the case of anything other than a minor flesh wound, your horse should be seen by your vet, who will recommend post-injury treatment. In the case of serious wounds, the horse should be given a tetanus booster and prescribed a course of antibiotics. Depending on the injury, the vet may suggest administering pain control, normally in the form of the nonsteroidal anti-inflammatory drug, phenylbutazone ("bute"). This effective pain-relief agent is given orally and can be added to the feed in powdered form, or can be given as a paste.

There are different legislations surrounding the availability of equine drugs, and it is possible for you to buy some drugs without a

veterinary prescription. Only treat a horse yourself if you are confident in what you are doing, and if in any doubt, seek the advice of a vet.

Phenylbutazone should not be given to foals (unless in exceptional circumstances and under the supervision of a vet), and care should be taken when administering it to very elderly horses. It has been known to trigger side effects, and overuse of "bute" has been connected to gastric ulcers.

In the case of small flesh wounds that you have treated, your horse should be able to be turned out as usual, providing the turnout area is free from mud. If it is not possible to turn your horse out in an area that is clean, keep it in and give it gentle hand exercise, or lead it from another horse. Post-injury treatment must be based on common sense, and it is up to you to evaluate the seriousness of the condition. If you are in any doubt, call the vet.

Dressings should be changed twice daily, and after three days use dry dressings without antibiotic cream. Once the wound has started to heal over, the bandage and dressing should be removed to allow air to it.

Dealing with Box Rest

In the case of severe injury, the vet will require your horse to be box rested for a period of time. This can be extremely frustrating to the horse, especially if it is used to being turned out. The diet must be altered — concentrates reduced to a minimum and forage increased.

Hay should be fed ad lib.

Try to keep your horse in a box where it can see or be near other horses at all times, and never remove all the horses from the yard except the one on box rest. Providing a radio may or may not entertain your horse, but is unlikely to upset it. Look out for inflammation in the lower legs due to lack of movement. It can be helpful to massage the lower legs and to keep them bandaged — although the bandages should be removed and replaced twice a day.

Make sure your horse is kept warm, and continue its daily grooming routine to help its circulation. Be aware when handling a horse on box rest that it may be wound up and lively. Take particular care when removing your horse from the box and when turning it out for the first time. After a period of box rest, your horse

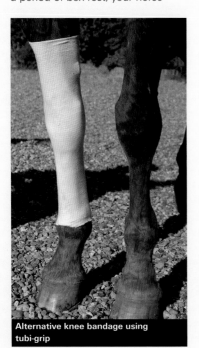
Alternative knee bandage using tubi-grip

BANDAGE KNOW-HOW

- Bandages should be applied over a pad, gamgee, or cotton padding
- The pressure should be even throughout the bandage
- Do not to bandage too tightly; this can result in serious damage to the tissue and skin
- Bandages should be changed regularly or at the suggestion of the vet
- Surgical bandages should start below the injury; all other bandages should start below the knee. Work down the leg and back up.
- To start a bandage off, make one wrap and turn a corner over so that it is caught in the second wrap — this helps keep the bandage up and secure.
- Iron the ties on your bandages to keep them flat.
- Always fasten bandages in the middle of the cannon on the outside; never have the knot at the back or inside of the leg.
- A single piece of adhesive tape can be placed over the fastening on the bandage to further secure it.

should be turned out in a small area where it is not able to charge around, and should be turned out with a quiet buddy.

Types of Wounds

There are four main types of flesh wound:

Laceration – This is a "tear" wound caused by the skin catching and ripping on a foreign object such as a nail, barbed wire fencing, a

An alternative way to hold a knee dressing in place is by using an elasticated support bandage manufactured for people. The bandage should be rolled up above the dressing site, and then folded down over the dressing to keep it in place. Make sure the bandage is not too tight. The top and bottom of the bandage can be held in place by a single layer of adhesive tape, and a light bandage put on over the top.

broken plank of wood, etc. These are often "dirty" wounds because the object that causes them is invariably highly contaminated. Lacerations, however, tend to heal well and relatively quickly if they are treated properly and kept clean.

Incision – This is a clean-edged wound caused by a sharp protuberance such as a piece of tin, glass or sheet metal, etc. Incisions can be very deep wounds, which can make them difficult to clean. They can be slow healing, but if sutured tend to heal much more quickly.

Contusion – This is a bruising injury that can be caused by the horse running into something at speed, or being kicked. The skin is not broken, but the blood vessels below the skin are damaged causing blood to leak out and

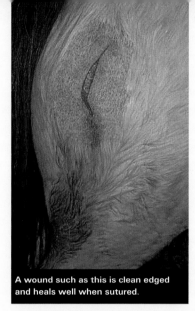

A wound such as this is clean edged and heals well when sutured.

collect as a soft swelling beneath the skin. Generally, these heal well, and the blood gradually dissipates. If the wound does not appear to be healing, your horse should be seen by the vet.

Puncture – This is one of the most dangerous wounds. It most often occurs on the foot, caused by stepping on a nail or other narrow sharp object, but can occur anywhere. The wound can be very deep, but narrow, making cleaning difficult. It is vital that puncture wounds are kept open to heal from the inside out. They are extremely dangerous, and should always be seen by a vet.

- Puncture wounds often have a small entry hole that is sometimes not detected immediately.
- They can be very deep, and can penetrate underlying organs and muscle masses.
- They are extremely difficult to clean thoroughly, so the risk of infection is great.
- Due to their narrow entry holes, puncture wounds have a

tendency to heal over at the surface, instead of healing from the inside out. When they heal at the surface the rate of infection is very high and the healing time is greatly increased.
- When a horse steps on a nail there is a chance of the nail penetrating the internal structures such as the coffin joint, which can cause serious problems.

If the foreign object is still protruding from the wound, it is best to leave it in place until the vet arrives. If it is a nail in the foot, and it appears that the horse could cause further damage to itself by leaving the nail in, then carefully extract the nail. Make sure to remember the exact angle that the nail went into the foot, and keep the nail to show the vet. This will help to determine the extent of internal damage.

Once the nail has been removed, scrub the foot thoroughly with antiseptic solution and soak the foot in Epsom salts for 20 minutes, then put on a light, clean dressing and wait for the vet.

Trainer's Tip

An Epsom salt (magnesium sulfate) solution for hot tubbing must be saturated to work. Keep adding Epsom salts to the water until the water is unable to absorb any more – this is a saturated solution

Hot Tubbing the Foot

This is a good preliminary treatment for a puncture wound, a bruised sole or an abscess. Fill a clean bucket with enough warm water to just cover the foot but not the coronary band. Add a generous amount of Epsom salts and stir until it has dissolved. After scrubbing the foot clean, soak it in Epsom salts for 20 minutes twice a day. Keep adding hot water to keep the temperature warm.

Soak Boot

An alternative to "tubbing" the foot is to make your own "soak boot." Before putting a soak boot on, grease the horse's heels well with Vaseline. Wrap the foot in a generous double layer of cotton making sure the whole foot, including the sole and up to the coronary band, is covered. Bandage over the cotton with brown gauze to hold it in place, and over this apply a layer of conforming bandage. Next, take packing or duct tape and cover the entire bandage with tape, adding extra layers at the toe. Be sure not to make the bandage too tight around the coronary band.

Mix up the Epsom salt solution and, using a 60-cc syringe, start to fill the bandage with the liquid.

Put the bandage on in the morning and add the Epsom salts; leave the bandage on until the evening, add more Epsom salts, and remove and change the bandage the following morning.

1   **2**   **3**

how to poultice a foot

1 Thoroughly clean the entire foot and hot tub if necessary. Dry the foot.

2 Apply the prepared poultice (see below). Wrap the foot in a plastic bag, which helps to keep in the heat of the poultice, then cover with padding and bandage in place using a conforming bandage.

3 Finally, cover the entire foot with waterproof packing tape or an equiboot to strengthen the bandage and keep the foot clean. Keep the horse stabled and on clean bedding.

Hot Fomentation

Also known as hot compressing, this is a process that produces a similar effect to hot tubbing, but can be used on parts of the body that cannot be tubbed or poulticed. Fill a bucket with hand-hot water and take two folded hand towels. Immerse each towel in turn and hold one towel onto the affected area for a couple of minutes, or until the towel begins to lose its heat. By using each towel in turn, the horse always has one hot treatment in application. Continue for 20 minutes.

Cold Hosing

One of the most effective forms of treatment for a painful injury or inflammation is a combination of hot and cold therapy. Heat encourages healing by increasing the blood flow to the injured area.

Conversely, cold helps to reduce inflammation and pain, although also slows down healing.

Cold hosing, which involves running a steady stream of cold water from above the site of injury downward is an old-fashioned, simple treatment that is highly effective, especially for strains and damage to the tendons and ligaments, and bruising. Cold hosing should be carried out three times a day for 20 minutes at a time, and should be followed by heat therapy.

POULTICES

Poultices are useful dressings that come in several different forms and can be used hot or cold. Hot poultices act as drawing agents and encourage the removal of dirt and small foreign bodies from a wound, while also providing heat, which aids healing by increasing

the blood supply to the injury site.

A hot poultice should be changed twice daily; it should not be so hot as to cause a burn. The poultice should be applied to the injury and covered with a layer of plastic then a layer of gamgee or padding followed by a bandage.

A cold poultice is used to reduce swelling and inflammation and is a good immediate first-aid step in the case of pulled, strained or damaged tendons or ligaments.

For foot injuries, it is advisable to first hot tub the foot, and follow this by applying a hot poultice.

Types of Poultices

Animalintex – A good mess-free poultice that comes as a long length of padding that can be cut to size. This is impregnated with bassorin and boric acid, and one side is covered in a layer of plastic.

To prepare Animalintex:

- Cut it to size and place in a shallow dish, then saturate it with water that has been boiled and allowed to cool slightly.
- Allow to steep for one minute and then drain. The best way to do this is by pressing the poultice between two small plates.
- Make sure the temperature is acceptable; apply to the injury with the plastic side facing out.
- Take a plastic bag, and further wrap the leg with this before applying the gamgee and outer bandage.

Kaolin – This is a useful poultice that can be used hot or cold.

- It generally comes in a can or a tub. Remove the lid and stand in a bucket of very hot water.
- Allow to warm through; check the temperature carefully before applying.
- Tear an old pillowcase, bed sheet or similar piece of cotton into two equal sizes — large enough to cover the injury.
- Spread the paste evenly onto the cotton and place the second piece of cotton on top.

- After again checking the temperature, mold the cotton to the leg or foot, and wrap with a plastic bag, followed by gamgee and a bandage.

To use cold, follow the above instructions then take the cotton poultice "sandwich" and place in the freezer. Keep frozen until required. The poultice will keep cold for approximately 15 minutes after it has been applied.

Bran – This is an old-fashioned poultice that can be good on feet, but has the distinct disadvantage of being edible, which may encourage the horse to tear at its bandages.

- Fill a clean bucket with approximately one-quarter bran.
- Add Epsom salts or linseed oil.
- Add enough boiling water to make the bran consistency damp and flaky.
- Allow to cool slightly so that the mixture is still warm but not overly hot.
- Empty the mixture into either a strong plastic bag or the corner of a nylon feed bag.

- Put the horse's foot into the bag so that the bran covers the sole and part way up the wall.
- Secure the neck of the bag around the pastern with packing tape, apply a layer of gamgee or padding, and bandage. Bolster the toe using several layers of packing tape.

Self-adhesive diapers make excellent padding for foot injuries.

Equiboots or Easy Boots

These rubber boots are useful for keeping dry dressings in place on the sole of the foot.

First you need to apply the dressing and hold it in place with a single piece of adhesive tape. Pad the sole with a piece of gamgee cut to size. Take a second strip of gamgee and run it from the toe across the sole and out over the back of the boot at the heels. Slip the horse's foot into the boot and secure.

- There must be padding between the back of the boot and the horse's heels
- The boot must fit correctly or else it will rub or be discarded
- A single wrap of adhesive tape across the top of the boot, taking care to avoid the coronary band, can help to keep the boot in place.

Eye Problems

Any injury directly to the eye, or in the eye area, should be seen right away by your vet. While waiting for the vet to arrive, keep your horse quiet and calm and, if possible, in the dark. Try not to let it rub the injured eye as this may cause more damage. If necessary, keep hold of your horse's headcollar or halter until the vet arrives. Also, be aware that if the horse's sight has been affected, it may be particularly jumpy or nervous, so try to stay on its good side where it can easily see you. If the eye is partially or fully closed, do not attempt to force it open to assess it – forcing it open may cause more damage to the tissues. Wait for the vet who will then administer a local anesthetic to the eye, which will enable it to be examined painlessly.

After assessing the injury the vet may prescribe a course of eye drops or ointment — these can be notoriously difficult to get into a horse's eye.

Administering Eye Medication

- Always have the horse in a stable, preferably with the light off, and out of direct sunlight.
- If necessary, have a helper hold your horse and stand the horse against one wall with its bottom in the corner.
- Quietly and calmly, hold the bottom eyelid down with your thumb, while pushing the top eyelid up with your forefinger.
- With your other hand, holding the tube horizontally, lay a ribbon of medication across the eyeball, starting at the corner and working to the outside.

TIPS FOR SUCCESS
- Warm the medication in your hand or pocket before administering it.
- Some horses become intimidated by two people descending on them. If this is the case, stand the horse in the corner of the stable, and if treating the left eye, slide your left hand under the check piece of the halter and open the eye as described above. By having your hand under the halter it allows you to steady the head by bracing against the head and the halter. Reverse for the right eye.
- Sanitary napkins make very good dressings for covering the eye; attach using tape. Alternatively, if the eye needs to be covered, a dry dressing can be held in place by using a pair of nylon pantyhose. Cut both legs off to form one large hole. Just below the waistband, cut out two holes for the ears, and then a further hole for the good eye. Roll the pantyhose over the horse's head, waistband first, and cut a notch out if necessary beneath the throatlatch (gullet). Hold in place with the headcollar.

Horse with conjunctivitis; note the weeping eye and crusty discharge

CONJUNCTIVITIS

This is one of the most common eye problems, especially in dry and dusty climates. Conjunctivitis is inflammation of the pink membrane that lines the eyelids (the conjunctiva). Symptoms usually include excessive watering of the eyes combined with the horse keeping them squeezed half closed. The eyes might appear red and swollen and are generally painful, which can lead the horse to try and rub them, shake its head and show signs of distress and irritability. In severe cases and where there is a secondary bacterial infection there may be a discharge of pus.

Conjunctivitis can be caused by a number of irritants, including dust and wind, a foreign body, a blow to the eye area, an allergy, severe fly irritation or as a secondary symptom of a respiratory viral infection. Generally both eyes are affected, unless the cause is trauma or a foreign body.

Conjunctivitis can usually be quickly and effectively dealt with. The horse must be seen at once by a vet who, confirming a diagnosis, will prescribe a course of antibiotic and corticosteroid eye drops or ointments. These are applied to the inside rim of the eyelid three times a day and will clear up the infection and reduce the inflammation. However, in cases where there is an actual injury to the cornea, such as a scratch or trauma injury, then steroids must not be used because they delay the healing process. Although conjunctivitis is easily treated, it is important to ascertain the cause of the condition, such as bedding dust, pollen, flies, etc., and remove it so that the conjunctivitis does not recur repeatedly.

CATARACTS

These are opaque areas that appear on the lens of the eye, and can be very tiny and undetected. In this case, they may only become apparent during the vetting of a sale animal when the eyes are examined with an ophthalmoscope. Although this may affect the sale of the horse, tiny cataracts generally cause no problems.

There are two types of cataracts, progressive and nonprogressive. Progressive cataracts, as their name implies, increase in size over time,

Horse with a cataract

and this will eventually lead to vision problems, which can cause the horse to stumble, spook suddenly, bump into things and suffer facial injuries. The only treatment available for cataracts is surgery, which, is a very difficult procedure in horses and should only be carried out if the rest of the eye is in perfect order. Even with surgery the horse is unlikely to have full vision restored. Cataracts can be hereditary, but they also can develop as part of the natural aging process or following an injury or disease of the eye.

RECURRENT UVEITIS OR MOON BLINDNESS

This is a serious eye disease in horses and is the biggest cause of equine blindness. It affects the uveal tract, which is made up of the iris, the ciliary body and the choroids, and causes inflammation and pain. It can occur in one or both eyes, and is a recurrent disease, with each onset causing more damage to the eye, which can eventually result in blindness. The causes are largely unknown, although injury and trauma to the eye can lead to the development of the disease; other factors can be eye infections, viral agents, bacterial organisms or parasites.

The length of time between recurrences ranges from weeks to years, while an attack normally lasts between one to two weeks. Once the vet has made a diagnosis. generally the horse will be treated with antibiotic and corticosteroid drops as well as systemic non-steroidal anti-inflammatory drugs.

Tendon and Ligament Injuries

Tendons are long bundles of fibrous tissue that, in simple terms, join muscle to bone. The fibrous tissue is made up of collagen fibrils, which are closely grouped and lie parallel to one another longitudinally.

Tendons are very strong and have a small degree of elasticity, which helps to deal with concussion and stress during movement. Gradual and extended fitness programs for horses will increase their elasticity to a maximum effect, which is why unfit horses that are asked to perform excessive work will invariably suffer tendon injury. It can't be overly stressed how important a fitness regime is to a horse that has to undertake hard and fast work.

Despite their strength and marginal elasticity, tendons are still one of a horse's "weak" points, and tendon injuries are common. Proper care and management can help to prevent them; catching the warning signs early can certainly help to increase the chance of recovery.

The most common site of tendon injury is in the foreleg, midway down the cannon bone. This is where the superficial flexor tendon is at its narrowest, and therefore comes under the greatest stress. Strains of the deep digital flexor tendon are less common.

TENDONITIS

Any strain injury that results in inflammation of the tendon can be described as tendonitis, and tendonitis can range from mild to severe. Indications of a mild strain will be some inflammation along the tendon and some degree of heat in the leg, although the horse may not necessarily be lame. Inflammation will appear as a "thickening" in the tissue running down the back of the cannon bone.

It is very important to catch tendon strain early; if it is not noticed and the horse continues to work, then the injury will quickly become extremely serious.

As the severity of the injury increases, the symptoms compound. There will be greater swelling along the tendon and obvious heat in the leg; the horse will be lame and, in some cases, virtually non-weightbearing. The fetlock will appear to be closer to the ground than normal and the tendon will be painful to the touch.

The most serious tendon injury is a rupture and the term "bowed

The bowed appearance to the back of this horse's leg is due to a severe strain of the superficial digital flexor tendon

tendons" is often used to describe it because inflammation is extensive and the back of the leg appears to bow outward.

Depending on the site of injury, the bow either can be high, where the inflammation is centered just below the back of the knee, middle (the most frequent) or low, where the inflammation is most pronounced just above the back of the fetlock joint.

Causes
- Poor conformation (see pages 32–33).
- Excessive jarring on uneven and hard ground.
- Fatigue in a horse that is being worked beyond its fitness level.
- Sudden dramatic impact.

First Aid

Specific equine ice packs, boots, bandages or gel can be bought, and should be kept ready and available in the freezer. Otherwise make up frozen kaolin packs (see page 223).

- Immediate cold therapy by either cold hosing for 15 minutes (see page 222), or applying an ice pack.
- Dry the leg and apply a firm bandage over padding, using even pressure throughout. Bandage from the coronary band up to below the knee.
- Bandage the other leg with a support bandage.
- Repeat the cold therapy every two hours and reapply the bandage.

- Confine the horse to a clean stable.
- Wait for the vet to arrive.

Ongoing Treatment

- The horse should be prescribed a course of painkillers, normally phenylbutazone, which also acts as an anti-inflammatory.
- The cold therapy will be alternated with heat therapy in the form of poulticing to stimulate healing.
- The vet may advise applying DMSO (see box) topically under the bandage for seven days.
- The horse will be confined to box rest for a period of time. This will depend on the severity of the injury, and will range from two to 12 weeks.
- There are a number of therapies that can also be used, such as hydromassage, physiotherapy, laser, ultrasound treatments or carbon-fiber implants.
- After the initial box rest, your horse will need a period of controlled exercise in hand at walk, before being turned away to rest in the field.

QUICK REFERENCE – TENDONS AND LIGAMENTS

- **Tendons join muscle to bone.**
- **The most common site of tendon injury is in the forelegs, halfway down the cannon where the superficial flexor tendon is at its most narrow.**
- **Tendonitis is inflammation of the tendons.**
- **Phenylbutazone is a nonsteroidal anti-inflammatory analgesic.**
- **Tendons heal slowly.**
- **Ligaments connect bones or cartilage together.**
- **Ligaments have a poor blood supply and heal slowly.**

- Tendons are notoriously slow healers, and the recovery time in a serious injury can take up to 14 months. Even after this period, the tendon will not regain its initial strength, and although the horse may be sound to undertake light work, it may not be able to resume hard and fast work again.
- Even tendons that are "successfully" recovered will invariably suffer a relapse at some stage.

LIGAMENT INJURIES

Ligaments are strong bands of fibrous tissue that connect bones or cartilage together, and also support internal organs. Ligaments support joints and act to prevent joints from overextending. They have a poor blood supply, and take a long time to heal post-injury. The most common ligaments to sustain injury are the suspensory and check.

Most suspensory strains occur in the foreleg where the ligament runs from the bottom of the knee down the back of the cannon bone to just above the fetlock where it branches into two. The branches run on either side of the fetlock, attach to the sesamoid bones, and run across the long pastern to connect to the common digital extensor tendon.

Inflammation of the suspensory ligament is referred to as "desmitis," and most frequently occurs in horses in hard and fast work, racehorses, eventers and the Standardbred breed. Causes include poor conformation – broken hoof/pastern angle, long toes, toed in or toed out conformation, back at the knee conformation (see pages 32–33); stress and fatigue and working on uneven ground.

The most common site of a suspensory strain is just above the fetlock where the ligament branches. Signs of ligament damage include inflammation, lameness and pain on palpation.

The inferior check ligament is found at the back and just below the knee and blends with the deep digital flexor tendon as it runs down the back of the leg. Symptoms of check ligament strain are the same as those for a suspensory ligament strain, and treatment will be similar and at the direction of the vet.

The plantar ligament is found on the hind leg, just below the point of hock, and runs from its point of attachment on the calcaneus down to the top of the lateral splint bone. Strain of the plantar ligament is commonly referred to as a "curb," and is generally not serious. Curbs are primarily caused by defects in conformation such as sickle hocks and cow hocks (see pages 32–33), both of which place added stress on the ligament. They also may be caused by repeated trauma such as when a horse habitually kicks the stable walls or trailer when

A curb is a strain to the plantar ligament and can be seen as a bowed area below the hock

traveling. A small, soft swelling becomes apparent below the hock and at the top of the cannon, and tends not to cause any problems other than cosmetic ones. Once formed, a curb is permanent. In acute cases, there may be heat and some lameness, and this should be treated with immediate cold therapy followed by rest, painkillers and anti-inflammatory drugs, and topical applications of DMSO.

First Aid

Immediate first aid should include cold therapy and bandaging as

A strain is an injury to the soft tissues. A sprain is an injury to a joint.

with a tendon injury. The horse should definitely be seen by the vet, and follow-up treatment will consist of pain therapy, continued cold treatment for three days before starting alternating hot and cold therapy, box rest, support bandaging and possibly the use of laser or ultrasound therapy.

Depending on the severity of the injury, the horse will need to be on box rest for approximately eight weeks. As the inflammation goes down, it should be given short gentle walks in hand, which should be gradually increased to two sessions daily of half an hour each. After box rest, the horse will be turned away for a period of months on the advice of the vet.

Soft Swellings – Bursal Enlargements

These soft, fluid-filled swellings appear when the synovial membrane surrounding a joint or tendon sheath is damaged. As a consequence an excess of synovial

Whenever there is heat and swelling in the leg it should be cause for concern.

fluid is produced. Synovial fluid is the body's natural lubricant, which protects and aids the movement of joints and tendons.

These swellings typically do not cause lameness, although in severe cases they might, and they are not painful to the touch.

WINDGALLS

Articular windgalls are relatively common in horses that jump or

engage in frequent hard and fast work, but rarely cause problems.

After a particularly hard session of work however, 20 minutes of cold hosing will be therapeutic.

Articular windgalls can be seen at the top and to the sides of the fetlock joint, and are an enlargement of the synovial membrane of the fetlock joint. They may increase or decrease depending on work.

Windgalls

QUICK REFERENCE – SOFT SWELLINGS –
BURSAL ENLARGEMENTS
• When a synovial membrane makes an excess of synovial fluid, a soft
  swelling appears.
• Articular windgalls are inflammations of the fetlock joint capsule.
• Tendinous windgalls are inflammations of the tendon sheath enclosing
  the flexor tendon.
• Bog spavins are unsightly but rarely cause lameness.
• Thoroughpins sometimes dissipate.
• Help to avoid capped knees and hocks by providing a deep, thick bed
  and protection when traveling.

Tendinous windgalls are an enlargement of the tendon sheath enclosing the flexor tendon, and will be seen at the top and to the sides of the fetlock joint, between the suspensory ligament and the flexor tendon. Like articular windgalls, these do not generally cause a problem, and do not require treatment.

BOG SPAVIN

These are swellings of the hock joint and appear as two soft enlargements – one on the front of the hock toward the inside, and the other marginally higher on the outside of the joint. Bog spavins may occur in one or both hocks, and are associated with poor hind leg conformation such as cow hocks, sickle hocks and straight hocks (see pages 32–33). Although unsightly, they rarely

Bog spavin

cause lameness and no treatment is required.

THOROUGHPIN

These are also found on the hock, and are the result of an enlargement of the tendon sheath enclosing the deep digital flexor tendon as it passes over the hock. The swelling can be seen just above the point of hock, and may appear on either the inside or

outside of the hock, or on both sides. Thoroughpins will occasionally go down, and this can be helped by topical application of DMSO (see page 227). Otherwise no treatment is necessary.

CAPPED HOCK and KNEE

Both the hock and the knee will develop fluid-filled bursae as a result of repeated trauma. Both incidents are associated with lack of bedding, a blow or banging on the stable wall or door. Fluid collects on the point of hock or on the flat front surface of the knee. Neither condition causes lameness or problems, unless they are associated with bruising or other effects of the initial trauma injury. Providing ample bedding and protection, such as knee or hock boots during traveling, will help to prevent these problems.

Lameness

Unless your horse is obviously lame, i.e., three-legged and unwilling to put any weight on one foot, it can be hard to detect lameness. Some lameness is harder to see than others. For example:

- When a horse is lame in both front or both hind legs
- Hind-leg lameness
- Marginal lameness
- Intermittent lameness

Any lameness, no matter how slight, should be investigated. It is up to you to be aware of your horse's normal gait and attitude. If your horse is experiencing pain in both front or hind legs, it will become reluctant to move, or will move with a shorter and uneven stride. Any deviation from normal should alert you to a potential problem. Often, problems caught early can be greatly helped.

FRONT LEG LAMENESS

If your horse is resting a front leg or stands with one front leg pointed in front of the other, it should be an immediate cause for concern. Other signs of lameness are stumbling and a reluctance to move forward. The horse may feel pottery (taking short, hesitant steps), or uneven in its strides when ridden. It may be reluctant to turn a particular way, or may feel worse on one rein.

With more pronounced lameness, the horse will bob its head; as its lame leg hits the ground its head will come up, and as the sound leg hits the ground, its head will drop down.

Turning the horse in a circle will amplify the lameness. If the horse is lame in the left fore, for example, and is circled on a small circle to the left, its lameness will be emphasized; by turning the horse this way it is forced to carry more weight on the sore leg. If it is then circled to the right, the lameness will be less obvious as it carries more weight on its sound leg.

HIND LEG LAMENESS

Your horse may be reluctant to canter on one rein, or may develop a lumpy trot, which throws its rider onto a particular diagonal. The same principle is applied here as to front leg lameness – the horse will try to alleviate pressure from its sore leg. When seen from behind the hips might appear uneven, with the hip held higher on the side of the lame leg.

FOOT PROBLEMS

Signs of trouble include:
- Your horse is lame.
- There is heat in the foot.

- There is an increased digital pulse (see page 233).
- Your horse has heel pain.
- Your horse has toe pain.
- There is obvious trauma to the foot.
- The hoof wall is of particularly poor quality, split, cracked or crumbling.
- The frog is black and mushy with a foul smell.

NAIL PRICK and NAIL BLIND

These are similar and are a direct result of a visit from the farrier!

A nail prick is when a horseshoe nail has been driven into the sensitive tissue of the foot. The horse will immediately react and the nail must be withdrawn. The horse will be lame and the injury must be attended to at once to prevent infection.

Nail bind occurs when a nail is driven too close to the sensitive laminae without actually puncturing it. The horse may not be lame immediately but will gradually become worse over a period of several days as pressure increases on the laminae. The offending nail should be removed, and the foot should be soaked and poulticed for three days.

Treatment
- Using a syringe, flush the nail hole with antiseptic solution.
- Apply a poultice (Animalintex) and bandage, and keep the horse stabled.
- Change the poultice twice daily

for three days, and soak the foot in Epsom salts for 20 minutes each time the poultice is changed.

- Make sure the horse is up to date on its tetanus shots.
- If lameness persists call the vet; an abscess may have formed and will need to be opened.

THRUSH

This is an anaerobic bacteria that causes an infection of the tissue of the frog. Black, foul-smelling material forms around the frog, and if left untreated, the infection can cause lameness.

Thrush, however, is easily avoided by proper stable management. Keeping the bedding clean and the horse's feet picked will prevent its onset.

Treatment

- Thoroughly clean the foot using water with an antiseptic solution (Pevadine, Hibiscrub or Betadine). Scrub all the cracks and crevices using a hard-bristled brush.
- The farrier should trim away any dead frog material.
- Apply daily a mixture of 10 percent formalin and iodine (obtained from the vet), or Gentian Violet spray, or sugardine.
- Keep the foot clean and dry.
- Keep the bedding clean and dry.

> Sugardine is a "home remedy" that is very effective for a number of problems. It promotes healing, reduces swelling and acts to fight infection.

- Mix Betadine (or povidone-iodine) with sugar or honey to create a thick paste.
- Apply liberally to the frog area and cover with a bandage.
- Use every day for five days, or until the thrush has gone.

SEEDY TOE

This condition results in the separation of the sensitive and insensitive laminae of the foot at the toe, leading to the horn decaying and a cavity forming. The condition is seen at the toe of the foot and can be caused by foreign matter trapped between the shoe and foot causing irritation, by poor shoeing or as a sequel to laminitis. It also can be caused by very wet ground conditions where the foot is permanently soft and therefore more susceptible to damage from hard foreign objects (grit, stones, etc.). Often, a secondary infection festers in the decaying laminae.

Treatment

- The farrier should remove the decayed horn and clean out the cavity.
- The foot should be soaked in Epsom salts to further draw out any foreign matter.
- The cavity can be packed with Stockholm Tar.
- Shoe with a wide-webbed shoe.
- If the cavity is deep and secondary infection present, the

vet will advise hot tubbing and poulticing.
- In some cases, your vet may recommend applying Keratex and formalin to harden the hoof wall.
- Move the animal to a dry area.

CORNS

These are bruises that develop in the area of the hoof called the "seat of corn," which is in the angle between the wall and bars of the foot. Corns can be caused by poor shoeing; fitting shoes that are too small, which creates pressure on the seat of corn area; leaving shoes on for too long so that the heels of the shoe are pressing on the seat of corn area; grit trapped between the heel of the shoe and the foot, and poor foot conformation (long toes, low heels and flat feet).

Treatment

- The farrier should remove the shoe and pare away the sole to the level of the bruise to relieve the pressure.
- Hot tub the foot and apply a poultice twice daily for a week, or until the horse is sound.
- When the horse is sound, reshoe and be vigilant about reshoeing frequently.
- Some corns become infected, in which case the pus must be allowed to drain and the foot thoroughly cleaned with an antiseptic solution. The area should be flushed with a weak antiseptic solution and tubbed and poulticed twice daily until sound. The foot should be kept clean and bandaged until the corn has healed over.

SAND and GRASS CRACKS

Sand cracks arise in the coronary band and travel down the foot vertically; they vary in their severity, depending on whether the crack is superficial or extends through to the sensitive structures. Grass cracks are those that extend from the ground surface vertically up the hoof wall. Both types are described according to their location, i.e., toe, quarter or heel cracks.

Sand cracks are often the result of a direct trauma to the coronary band, which stimulates the hoof to grow abnormally. Grass cracks can be caused by poor hoof care and quality (brittle and dry feet), poor conformation (long toes, low heels) or trauma.

Deep cracks can become infected, in which case call the vet and treat as for a puncture wound (see page 221), hot tubbing, poulticing, flushing the crack and keeping the horse stabled and the foot clean. If the crack is not infected, call the farrier. In the case of a sand crack, he or she will

Trainer's Tip

Adding a supplement of biotin and methionine to the diet can help to improve the hoof quality and decrease the chance of grass cracks.

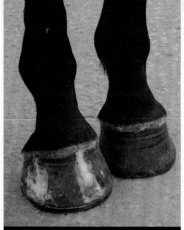

Severe sand cracks, cleaned out and filled with equithane

stabilize the crack by cutting two grooves in the hoof wall diagonally from the tip of the crack back to below the coronary band to form a triangle. Alternatively, the farrier might use a shoe with clips positioned either side of the crack to hold the fissure together, or use a hoof staple to bind the two edges of the crack. If superficial, the crack will eventually grow out.

With a grass crack the farrier will again position clips on either side of the crack, and will cut either a straight horizontal groove at the top of the crack, or a horizontal groove with an upside-down triangle above it. Both of these methods should prevent the crack from extending up the hoof capsule.

LAMINITIS

Also known as founder, laminitis is a devastating disease that can be managed but is rarely overcome. The disease causes inflammation of the sensitive laminae in the feet, which become engorged with blood. The circulation within the feet is compromised and the pressure of fluid buildup causes intense pain. If the condition is not addressed, the sensitive laminae

will start to die, and once this starts, the horse is in serious trouble. The sensitive laminae support the pedal bone within the hoof capsule, and as they weaken and die, the pedal bone starts to rotate downward and sinks toward the sole. In extreme cases, the pedal bone will penetrate the sole just in front of the point of frog.

There are a number of factors that may trigger laminitis, but the exact nature of the disease is still

Heart bar shoes are sometimes used on horses or ponies with laminitis

the subject of ongoing scientific research. Possible causes include:

- Age and weight. Ponies are at greater risk than horses, and overweight animals are at greater risk than those in working condition.
- Lush grass, especially in the spring, or grass that has recently been fertilized.
- Pasture with a high percentage of clover.
- Excessive feed for the individual pony or horse and its workload.
- Excessive intake of starch-rich food.
- Quantities of inappropriate feed.

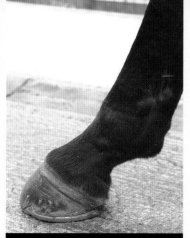

Serious ridges in the foot can indicate prior problems such as laminitis

- Concussion through hammering on hard ground, excessive work, jumping and athletic performances on uneven and unforgiving ground.
- Poorly balanced feet.
- Excessive weight carrying on one leg due to injury in the other.
- Toxemia due to bacterial toxins being absorbed, i.e., retained placenta, colic, strangles, etc.
- Stress in the form of chronic fatigue, electrolyte imbalance or heat exhaustion.

Horses developing laminitis adopt the classic "laminitic stance"; that is, leaning backward to take weight on their quarters and off their front ends. The front legs will be set marginally forward and the animal will appear to be rocked back on its heels. The horse will be reluctant to move and will take small pottery steps. There will be an increased digital pulse and often heat in the feet. The horse may have a temperature and high respiration rate due to pain. It will show pain when hoof testers are applied to the area in front of the frog.

Treatment

If you suspect laminitis, call your vet immediately. The sooner that your horse is seen, the greater its chances of recovery will be. While waiting for the vet, apply frog supports to both front feet. These can be in the form of a piece of rubber folded into a 4 x 2 x1 inch (10 x 5 x 2.5 cm) pad, or a 4-inch (10 cm) section of polystyrene or similar material, or a 4-inch (10 cm) roll of open weave bandage taped to each frog, Keep your horse in a well-bedded stable and do not move it until the vet has arrived.

Treatment

This will vary depending on the initial cause of the laminitis. In all cases, one of the priorities will be managing the pain with analgesics and anti-inflammatory drugs. Other treatments may include the sedative ACP to calm the horse and lower blood pressure, vasodilators such as Isoxuprine to help circulation in the foot, antibiotics in the case of toxemia, and remedial shoeing, often in the form of a heart bar shoe.

AZOTURIA

This is also sometimes referred to as "Monday Morning Sickness," "set fast," "tying up" and, more scientifically, as Equine rhabdomyolysis! The exact causes of azoturia are not clear. The traditionally accepted theory of carbohydrate overloading is now under review. The theory is that the horse that is given full rations on its day off builds up an excess of glycogen (carbohydrate) in its muscles. When the horse is then worked, the glycogen breaks down and produces excessive lactic acid, which damages the muscle fibers and causes the release of the pigment myoglobin from the damaged tissue (myoglobin accounts for the discolored urine

A grass guard cuts in half the amount of grass a pony can eat and is good to use with overweight ponies that might be at risk of laminitis

that is one of the symptoms). The condition is related to a lack of blood supply to the muscles, which means the buildup of lactic acid is not dispersed. However, this is a greatly simplified explanation of the syndrome, which is now believed to be caused by a series of factors.

Symptoms

- Generally, symptoms occur in the horse that is worked after a day off. They begin to show about 10 minutes into the work session.
- The muscles of the hindquarters appear to seize up; they become hard and painful to the touch.
- The gait becomes increasingly stiff behind and the horse is reluctant to move.
- It might break out in a sweat and exhibit colic-like symptoms.
- Temperature, pulse and respiration increase.
- The horse will attempt to urinate, and if successful, the urine can be reddish brown to dark brown.

Treatment

- Dismount immediately and do not move the horse.

- Cover its hindquarters with a coat to keep the muscles warm.
- Arrange for transportation back to the stables.
- Call the vet, who will suggest treatment that might include any of the following: nonsteroidal anti-inflammatory drugs and analgesics; sedatives to calm the horse and relax the muscles; electrolytes to restore fluid balances; diagnostic testing to determine the extent of muscle damage; thiamine, vitamin E and selenium.

- The horse should be box rested until the muscles have recovered with gentle walking in hand after two to three days.
- For horses that are prone to the syndrome, preventative measures should be taken. Reduce the amount of soluble starches and sugars and reduce rations overall the night before a day off; try to turn out every day, especially on a day off; always warm the horse up before hard and fast work and use a program of gradual fittening.

QUICK REFERENCE – LAMENESS

- **Lameness occurs to a greater extent in the front legs rather than the hind legs; a horse carries approximately 65 percent of its weight on its front end.**
- **Indications of lameness or pain associated with movement are stumbling, shortened strides, change in attitude and a reluctance to move forward.**
- **With front leg lameness, the head comes up as the sore limb hits the ground, and drops as the sound leg hits the ground.**
- **With hind leg lameness, the hip on the lame side will be carried above that on the other side.**
- **Problems in the foot can be indicated by lameness, heat, increased digital pulse or obvious trauma.**
- **Thrush can be avoided by good stable management practices.**
- **Seedy toe is a separation of the sensitive and insensitive laminae, often with a secondary infection.**
- **Corns can be the result of poor or infrequent shoeing or poor conformation.**
- **Sand cracks travel from the coronary band down the hoof.**
- **Grass cracks travel up the hoof from the bottom.**
- **Laminitis is seen more often in ponies than horses, and is an inflammation of the sensitive laminae of the foot.**
- **Horses with navicular disease exhibit heel pain.**
- **Pedal ostitis is inflammation of the pedal bone.**
- **Azoturia and lymphangitis both fall into the "Monday Morning" group of disorders because typically they occur after a day off work.**

LYMPHANGITIS

This is inflammation of the lymph vessels generally caused by an infection from a minor injury, but can be the result of the horse being fed normal rations without being exercised. As such, it falls into the "Monday Morning" group of disorders because symptoms generally occur after a day off work.

Symptoms

- The leg appears very swollen; sometimes both front or both hind legs will be affected.
- The horse is in considerable pain and very lame.
- The skin might ooze yellow serum.

Treatment

Call the vet, who will generally prescribe the following treatments:

- Antibiotics to treat the infection.
- Diuretics to remove the excess fluid.
- Analgesics for the pain.
- Gentle walking in hand to reduce inflammation and improve the circulation.
- Feeding a low-protein diet.

> ### WHEN TO CALL THE VET
> - **If your horse is reluctant to move or is lame.**
> - **If it is behaving erratically, wobbles, has weakness in the hindquarters, circles or shows any other unusual behavior.**

Bone Problems

The majority of bone disorders occur in a horse's lower leg bones, joints and stifle.

Poor conformation can play a major part in the likelihood of a horse developing bone-related problems. Other contributing factors include nutrition (especially relevant in foals and youngsters), concussion, excessive fast work on hard ground, and working young horses still in their "growth" phase too hard.

NAVICULAR DISEASE

This is a degeneration of the navicular bone in the foot and usually occurs in one, or both front feet. Horses with particularly "boxy" feet or with one foot that is significantly smaller than the other appear to be more prone to this devastating disease.

The exact causes of the disease, however, are not certain, although it is linked to a reduction in the blood supply to the foot, which causes the navicular bone to undergo structural changes. The roughening of the exterior surface of the navicular bone damages the deep digital flexor tendon, which moves across it, and causes progressive pain due to the trauma of the tendon and the elevated blood pressure within the damaged bone.

The disease can manifest itself in all types of horses, though is rarely seen in ponies. It can progress slowly, and at the first onset there may not be lameness. Early-warning signs include

> **Trainer's Tip**
> Brushing boots should always be worn when the horse is in work, and it is a good idea to turn out in boots, too.

stumbling, a gradual shortening of the stride and standing with one toe in front of the other or "pointing." This posture relieves heel pressure, which in turn takes the pressure off the deep digital flexor tendon.

Treatment

Navicular disease is treatable, and the sooner it is detected, the greater chance your horse has of returning to work. There are various different treatments available, with the emphasis on corrective farriery as a necessity.

Anti-coagulant drugs such as Isoxuprine have proved very successful in improving the blood flow to the foot, and anti-inflammatory drugs will help with the pain but not the disease.

Permanent nerve blocking is an option although this can have complications, and a procedure called navicular suspensory desmotomy is available. This involves cutting the suspensory ligaments that join the navicular bone to the long pastern bone in order to relieve pressure and stress on the navicular bone. The disease is not curable, but is manageable although the long-term prognosis is rarely good.

PEDAL OSTITIS

This is inflammation of the pedal bone and is usually caused by concussion. It most often arises in horses with particularly thin soles. It can also develop as a secondary condition in horses with laminitis, or be a result of a direct injury to the foot. It often manifests in both front feet, making an initial diagnosis difficult.

In a similar way to a horse suffering from navicular disease, an affected horse will start to shorten its stride, and will be worse when working on hard, uneven ground. There is no cure for the disease, but an initial period of rest followed by shoeing with a wide-web shoe to cut down on concussion may help.

SPLINTS

On either side of the cannon bone is found a splint bone attached to it by a strong ligament. "Splints" or fibrous tissue, which eventually ossifies and forms new bone, generally only form on the inside and appear when the ligament is damaged. They are commonly seen in young horses starting work, but also can form in response to a direct injury to the splint bone and as a result of poor conformation.

While the splint is forming, the horse may become lame, and there can be heat, swelling and pain down the inside of the cannon bone. At this time, anti-inflammatory painkillers will help,

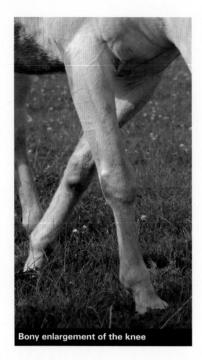
Bony enlargement of the knee

and cold therapy with support bandages should be used. The horse should be box rested with limited walking in hand until the splints have resolved themselves. Once they have formed they tend not to cause any problems unless they are so severe that they affect the knee joint, or unless they are excessively pronounced, in which case they may be knocked by the opposite leg during movement.

SESAMOIDITIS

The sesamoid bones, of which there are two on each leg located to the back and side of the fetlock, become inflamed. Symptoms can appear similar to those for navicular disease: the horse moves in a "pottery" manner, stumbles and becomes lame, especially on uneven or hard ground.

Sesamoiditis can be caused by a direct blow, or be the result of poor

shoeing (long toes), or due to damage to the suspensory ligaments. Depending on the severity of the case, treatment can involve box rest and cold therapy initially followed by a period of some months off work.

BONE SPAVIN

This is a degenerative disease of the hock joint, which manifests itself as a bony enlargement on the inside of the hock. Horses with cow hock or sickle hock conformation are particularly susceptible to the condition, although it is also related to stress and concussion, so jumping horses also can be prone.

Bone spavins can occur in one or both hind legs. Initial signs are a decrease in the length and elevation of stride, dragging the toe, stiffness and a reluctance to work. Once the spavin has formed, the horse may become sound again, although in severe cases, the prognosis is not good and the horse is unlikely to return to work.

RINGBONE

Another degenerative joint disease that can affect any of the limbs, ringbone is most often seen in the forelimbs. There are four types.

High articular ringbone - A degeneration of the pastern joint, the joint capsule becomes inflamed and the articular cartilage within the joint degenerates. New bone is laid down and movement within the joint may be compromised.

Low articular ringbone - A degeneration of the coffin joint, which is affected the same way as high articular ringbone.

High non-articular ringbone – New bone is laid down around the bottom end of the long pastern bone and/or the top end of the short pastern, but the joint is not affected.

Low non-articular ringbone – As above except new bone is laid around the ends of the coffin bone and the short pastern bone. Ringbone can be caused by a direct trauma such as a blow to the joint, or an invasive injury like a puncture wound. Certain conformation such as base wide or base narrow horses are predisposed to the condition, as are horses that jump or are in hard and fast work associated with sharp turning and sudden stops.

Signs of ringbone are hard lumps forming around the pastern area, heat, pain and lameness. If the joint is affected, the prognosis is not good and movement will be restricted. However, for non-articular cases, after the initial formation of new bone the horse may become sound enough to resume work. There is little treatment available for this condition other than anti-inflammatory drugs and analgesics.

SIDEBONE

A relatively common condition, sidebone results in the ossification of the lateral cartilages that hold the pedal bone in place. It is usually seen in the front legs, and normally occurs in older horses.

Sidebone can be linked to concussion, working on uneven ground, poor shoeing, poor conformation (base narrow and base wide) or direct trauma to the foot. There may be slight lameness during the onset of sidebone, but once the cartilages have ossified, the horse will generally become sound and require no treatment.

INTERMITTENT UPWARD FIXATION OF THE PATELLA

This condition is often referred to as a "locking stifle." The stifle joint in the horse has a similar structure to the knee joint in humans, and is made up of three bones, the femur, tibia and patella (the kneecap), which together form two joints. The bones are held in place by strong ligaments, which also serve to prevent the joint from overextending in any direction.

The patella has three ligaments that hold it in place, and which also allow the horse to lock its leg while standing — which is why horses can sleep standing up.

Sometimes, however, the stifle locks and the horse is unable to "unlock" it. This can be seen in varying degrees from the horse walking with a slightly stiff walk and dragging the toe, to being completely unable to bring its leg forward. This is generally seen in horses that are weak in the hindquarters, unfit or particularly straight through the back legs.

The immediate problem of a locked stifle can usually be overcome by backing the horse up or making it jump forward. Long term, the horse should be put on a fitness program to build up muscle, including hill work, which will generally help to overcome the problem.

QUICK REFERENCE – BONES

- Avoid working horses excessively on hard and uneven ground.
- Avoid starting horses too young, and working young horses too hard.
- Splints are relatively common; they may cause lameness while forming, but once formed rarely cause further problems.
- There are two sesamoid bones at the back and to the sides of the fetlock. Symptoms of sesamoiditis are similar to those for navicular disease.
- Bone spavins are the result of degenerative joint disease of the hock.
- Ringbone can be articular, which is when it affects the pastern or coffin joint, or non-articular, which is when the joint is not affected.
- Sidebone is ossification of the lateral cartilages.
- The horse's stifle joint is the equivalent to the human knee joint.

Skin Conditions

A horse's skin can be divided into two layers: the outer epidermis, which is mostly covered by hair (the coat), and the inner dermis. The quality of your horse's coat reflects, in great part, its overall health and condition. It is cause for concern whenever its hair appears dry, dull, excessively greasy, scurfy, staring or starts to fall out.

SUNBURN

Any horse with particularly pink or light skin pigment is at risk of sunburn in hot climates, and equally in the winter when bright sunshine is reflected off snow. Sunburn in horses happens quickly and can be extremely painful. Generally, it occurs around the muzzle, although it can also affect the eye area, especially in Appaloosas, Palominos, Paints and colored horses.

Prevent sunburn by keeping your horse in during the day and turning it out at night, or by using protective sunscreen (waterproof sunscreen for babies is the best), or by turning it out in a protective mask that covers the nose.

The coat also will be affected by the sun, and the ends of the hair will become bleached. Turn out in a protective anti-UV fly sheet and use fly spray with added sunblock. A bad case of sunburn can become infected, so treat with an antibacterial cream and keep the horse out of the sun until the burn has healed.

PHOTOSENSITIZATION

This condition should not to be confused with sunburn, although the symptoms can look similiar. It occurs when the horse eats a toxic plant, such as St. John's wort, which contains chemicals that sensitize the skin to the sun. Photo-dynamic agents in the plant are absorbed through the digestive tract and travel to the skin. They absorb energy from the sun, which damages the surrounding skin.

Photosensitization also can be a sign of liver disease; when the liver is not working properly, it fails to remove the normal breakdown products of chlorophyll found in green plants. These products remain in circulation and on reaching the skin cause photosensitization. The pink pigmented areas of the horse on the face and lower legs become swollen and itchy, the area can become infected and the skin eventually dies and sloughs off.

Treatment
- Remove the cause if a toxic plant.
- Keep the horse in until it has healed.
- Run a blood test to check for liver disease.
- Clean the affected area with warm water and antibacterial solution.
- Apply antibiotic cream.

RAIN SCALD

This is a skin infection that thrives in persistent wet conditions and is caused by the organism

Rain scald

Dermatophilus congolensis. This actinomycete (which behaves like both bacteria and fungi) lives on the horse in the coat in a semi-dormant state, but with prolonged exposure to the wet, it is able to penetrate the skin and cause a rapid inflammatory response.

Horses that live out with no protection are the most at risk, and symptoms are most often seen along the back and quarters since the horse turns its back into driving rain. The affected skin oozes a discharge that mats into the hair, forming clumps of crusty coat that will eventually come away leaving a bald area. There is a risk of secondary infection with this condition.

Treatment
- Good stable management and preventative action is essential. Always provide shelter and/or clean, dry turnout rugs.
- Keep the horse stabled until the condition has resolved.
- Gently remove the scabs and treat the underlying area by

washing with an antibacterial solution, being sure to gently dry the area afterward.

- Antibiotics may be necessary at the discretion of the vet.

MUD FEVER

This is caused by the same actinomycete as rain scald and affects horses that are kept in very muddy conditions. Mud fever typically occurs on the lower legs, but in severe cases will be seen down the back of the legs and across the underside of the belly.

Wet and muddy conditions allow the actinomycete *Dermatophilus congolensis* to invade the skin, causing a painful inflammatory response. Pale pigmented areas are particularly at risk. Typically, scabs form, normally starting at the heels and the back of the pastern; these may exude serum. The skin becomes sore, the hair mats and the legs may swell. In severe cases, the horse will become lame.

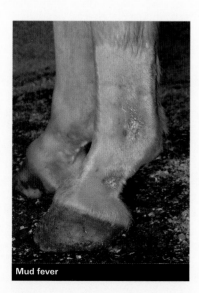

Mud fever

Treatment

- Keep the horse stabled and out of mud.
- Trim as much hair away from the site of infection as possible.
- Wash with antibacterial soap to remove dirt and dry gently with a towel, or a hair dryer on low if the horse will tolerate it.
- Gently try to remove the scabs. This will hurt so be careful.
- Apply a soothing antibiotic cream to the entire affected area then cover with a dressing and stable bandages.
- In severe cases, poultice the legs first before removing the scabs. Be careful that the poultice is only just warm, not hot.

SCRATCHES (Cracked Heels)

This condition is similar in appearance, cause and prevention to mud fever, although with cracked heels only the back of the pastern and heels are affected. The skin becomes extremely sore and cracks open horizontally, causing great discomfort, and often lameness. There is a risk of secondary infection.

Treatment

- The horse should be kept clean and dry and out of the mud.
- Clean and dry the area and apply antibiotic cream.
- Bandage with stable bandages and a light dressing to allow the cream to be absorbed.
- When riding or turning out cover the area with a thick layer of grease.

RINGWORM

This fungal skin infection is very distinctive and easily recognized. Small circular lesions will appear on the coat. At first the hair will appear tufty, then a scab will form, and the lesion will fall away, leaving a scaly round spot. In some cases, the lesion will first exude a sticky serum before drying up and becoming scaly. Hair will regrow in four to six weeks. Generally, lesions first appear on the neck or head, and can spread rapidly across the horse's body.

Ringworm is highly contagious both to people and other horses, and isolation procedures should be carried out immediately to help prevent it spreading through your yard. If left untreated, ringworm will eventually clear up on its own, but this should not be considered as an option.

Treatment

- Isolate the horse and all its tack, rugs, brushes, etc.
- All equipment should be disinfected.
- If lesions appear in the saddle, girth or bridle area, stop exercising the horse until the condition has cleared up.
- Wear overalls and an old pair of boots when handling the horse and its stable. Remove the overalls and boots before approaching another horse or stable.
- Use gloves when handling the horse and its treatments.
- Ringworm will live in the stable environment, so after the horse has healed and been moved from

the isolation box, the stable must be completely disinfected from top to bottom.

- There are a number of topical and systemic treatments available that the vet will prescribe.

LICE

There are two types of lice that affect horses: those that live on blood and tissue, which are generally found at the base of the tail and along the crest, and those that live on scurf, which are generally found on the lower parts of the body. Lice tend to infest horses that are in poor condition and their effects are worse during the winter when the horse's coat is long. Lice cause extreme itching leading to rubbed bald patches, which can become sore, and in severe cases there will be an overall loss of body condition.

Prevent infestation by proper care and management.

Treatment

- A liberal dose of louse powder or dousing with antiparasitic washes.
- Retreat after 14 days to kill any lice that might have hatched.
- A few drops of witch hazel concentrate diluted in water can

Trainer's Tip
Feeding garlic as a supplement can help to alleviate itchiness.

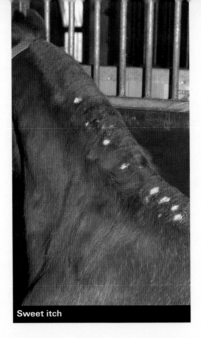
Sweet itch

be sprayed onto the itchy area providing the skin is not broken to help reduce itching.

SWEET ITCH

This is a devastating condition seen in horses and ponies that are allergic to a protein in the saliva of a biting midge (the *Culicoides*). The midge bites primarily along the crest and the dock, which causes intense itching. The animal can rub itself bald and cause open sores in an effort to alleviate the itching, and will invariably become miserable and bad tempered as a side effect.

Ponies are more commonly affected than horses, and are typically only affected during the summer months, although in severe cases, the symptoms will persist through the winter. Sweet itch is hereditary and mares with the condition should not be used for breeding purposes.

Treatment

- Try to remove the cause – the midge breeds in stagnant water

and feeds at dawn and dusk.

- Keep the animal stabled during these times of the day and provide fly sheets, neck covers and a hood.
- Remove any water barrels, full buckets or other sources of still water from the vicinity of the horse.
- Put screens over the stable door and windows.
- Use fly spray liberally.
- Use a soothing lotion on the affected areas.
- Shampoo every week.
- In severe cases, steroids may be prescribed, but these can have side effects such as laminitis.

URTICARIA

This is also sometimes called "nettle rash" or "hives" and can be caused by a number of different things, such as a contact irritant, an allergic reaction to barley, a reaction to some medications or a sudden change in diet.

A series of small bumps appear under the skin, usually concentrated in one area that tends to be either the flanks or shoulders. The bumps are not painful but can be itchy. In severe cases, bumps will appear all over the horse and may exude serum, and occasionally the horse will become highly distressed. Usually the bumps appear rapidly and then disappear within 12 hours.

Treatment

- If the horse is distressed, the bumps are causing swelling or they do not disappear within 24 hours, call your vet.

MITES

Chorioptic mange is caused by mites (*Chorioptes bovis*); an affected horse experiences intense itching and discomfort. The symptoms of mite infestation — inflamed skin, itching, scabs, crusty discharge and inflammation — are similar to those for mud fever and sometimes the two conditions are confused, although treatment is different.

- If the horse develops bumps after starting on a course of drugs, stop administering the drug and call the vet.
- Stop feeding barley products and other concentrate feeds; feed a bran mash with Epsom salts until the bumps have disappeared.

GIRTH GALLS and SADDLE SORES

These are lesions that appear either in the region of the girth or under the saddle. Early indication of a sore spot developing is the hair appearing roughed up. Then the areas become sore, the skin becomes inflamed, a lump may form and, eventually, the skin will crack open and weep.

Both these conditions are the result of poor fitting and dirty tack,

and will be avoided by good stable management. Make sure the saddle is fitted correctly by a saddler, keep tack clean, use a numnah and avoid nylon or string girths.

Horses that have been off work for a period of time are particularly

Trainer's Tip

Avoid nylon or rope girths or cinches, which have a tendency to chafe. Use leather or a good quality synthetic such as neoprene. Leather must be kept softened and in good condition through cleaning and leather creams.

at risk when brought back into work because their skins will have softened. To help harden up the skin, apply surgical spirit topically to the girth and saddle area for one week prior to starting work.

Treatment

- Stop work immediately — the horse will have to be off work until the lesions have completely healed.
- Keep the area clean and dry; wash with a mild antiseptic solution and pat dry with a clean towel.
- Apply antibiotic cream until the wound has healed.
- Once the wound has healed, apply surgical spirits to the area once a day for a week.

Digestive Problems

The horse has a very large and delicately balanced digestive tract. Horses evolved as trickle eaters, eating small amounts of grasses and legumes almost constantly, so modern stable management practices (though necessary with competition horses) of restricting grazing and offering several feeds of concentrates daily, is totally divergent from the natural workings of their digestive tracts. Safeguard your horse's digestive tract by:

- Turning out – Turnout is vital to the horse both mentally and physically. If your horse is overweight or in hard and fast work, turn out in a horse-poor pasture so that it is still able to move freely and forage for food.
- Providing roughage – The digestive tract is designed for roughage (hay or grass). Horses in hard and fast work must have their fiber content reduced, but try to find the right balance.
- Feeding concentrates in small quantities spread over three to four meals a day.

The horse has a limited capacity to vomit and rarely does unless intense pressure has built up in the stomach. The strong sphincter muscle between the top of the stomach and the bottom of the esophagus stops food being regurgitated.

COLIC

Colic is an umbrella name for abdominal pain, which can be caused by any number of different things from toxic feed, sudden changes in diet, an excessive worm burden, gas in the intestines from fermented substances (grass clippings especially), stress and blockages in the intestine, etc. Colic can range from mild to severe, and in some cases, euthanasia is the only humane option. The most important thing with colic is recognizing the signs early and acting on them immediately – swift diagnosis will greatly improve the horse's chance of recovery.

Types of Colic

There are five different types:

Impaction – Caused by food piling up in the intestine, normally at the pelvic flexure where the intestines narrow and turn.

Spasmodic – A result of the peristaltic movements of the intestine becoming spasmodic. The spasms are acutely painful but the pain subsides between spasms.

Gastric – Caused by the stomach becoming distended due to ingestion of foods that swell (i.e., unsoaked beet pulp) or a buildup of gas from ingesting fermented matter (i.e., grass clippings or moldy hay).

Tympanitic – This, too, is caused by fermenting feed matter or excessive quantities of apples or clover. Gas builds up in the intestines and the abdomen swells. This is acutely painful and can lead to a twisted gut.

Surgical colic – When a portion of the intestine loses its blood supply, due to a twist, a tumor wrapping around the intestine or redworm damage, the tissue dies, and without immediate surgery, the products of digestion in the tract pass through the damaged tissue and cause toxicity and death.

Signs of Colic

- Sweating and kicking at the belly, or kicking out behind.
- Rolling repeatedly.
- Increased respiration, temperature and pulse.
- Off feed and dehydrated.
- Passing no droppings, or less than normal. Those that are passed might be either very hard, or liquid.
- Lethargic.
- Swollen abdomen.

First Aid and Tests

Call your vet immediately. While waiting for him or her to arrive:

- Keep your horse as comfortable as possible.
- If in a stable, make sure there is lots of bedding on the floor and banked around the walls.
- Allow the horse to lie down if it wants to.
- Keep the stable door open to give you an exit. Make sure your horse has on a headcollar or halter with a long rope attached; keep a loose hold on the rope and use it to try to prevent the horse from hitting its head against the walls, and to steady it as it tries to get up.

- Alternatively, if your horse is thrashing around, try to lead it to an arena or field where there is less chance of it becoming cast.
- If your horse stands up, lead it around the box or on grass for a couple of minutes.
- If your horse does not want to move, don't force it to.

The vet will want to know whether your horse has passed anything; is eating or drinking and if its diet has recently changed, has recently been wormed (and what product was used); if it has had access to anything potentially toxic; how long the symptoms have persisted, and whether the pain appears intermittent or continual. The vet will then:

- Check the temperature, pulse and respiration.
- Check for dehydration and capillary refill time.
- Check the color of the mucous membranes.
- Listen for gut sounds on both sides of the horse.
- Perform a rectal examination to check the intestine for impactions or twists.

Maybe insert a tube up through the nose and down the esophagus into the stomach. This can show if there is gas or fluid in the stomach. The stomach tube also is used to administer some treatments.

In severe cases, the vet might perform a peritoneal tap to diagnose complications such as a ruptured intestine. A small square on the lowest part of the abdominal cavity is clipped and surgically prepared. A needle is inserted and a sample of fluid drawn off.

Blood tests also may be done.

Treatment

- Pain management with strong analgesics such as phenylbutazone or Banamine.
- Liquid paraffin or mineral oil administered via a stomach tube.
- Sedatives may be given to calm and relax the horse.
- In severe cases, surgery may be an option. The cost of surgery is high and the outcome not guaranteed. In these instances you have to make a difficult decision based on the vet's

prediction for the chance of recovery, the health and age of your horse, and finances.

DIARRHEA

Cases can range from mild to severe, and common sense must determine whether there is cause for concern. Many horses will pass loose stools in times of high excitement – when hunting for example, or at a show. Often, changing pastures can affect the stool for several days, but in these cases, the diarrhea should right itself quickly and the horse should exhibit no further symptoms. Sometimes a horse will develop diarrhea when it is on a course of antibiotics; antibiotics upset the microbial culture of the gut, causing loose stools. It is advisable to administer probiotics in cases like this, on the advice of your vet.

More serious causes of diarrhea can be caused by worm overload in the gut, ingesting either toxic or very rich matter, a bacterial or viral infection, tumors, changes to the gut wall or as a result of ulceration in the digestive tract.

Treatment

- Remove the cause, if obvious (i.e., take the horse off lush pasture).
- Make sure the horse is drinking and has access to good, clean water. If it is reluctant to drink, try adding powdered drink mix (Kool-Aid or similar) to the water.
- Give the horse electrolytes.
- Give the horse probiotics on the advice of the vet.
- In severe cases the vet will treat the diagnosed cause.

WHEN TO CALL THE VET
- If a foal has diarrhea.
- If your horse has diarrhea that persists for more than two days or is severe.
- If it is showing other symptoms such as an elevated temperature, is not eating or drinking, is listless, dehydrated, etc.
- If it is exhibiting signs of colic, including no gut sounds, distress, sweating, rolling, kicking at its stomach and not passing feces.
- If it has rapid weight loss or gain.
- If it has eyes that are sunken, dull or have discharge.

CHOKE

A blockage in the esophagus can prevent food that is eaten from traveling down and into the stomach. Feeds that are most likely to cause a blockage are those that swell in water (i.e., unsoaked beet pulp pellets and some pellet feeds, and straw or dry hay cubes). Once a blockage occurs, a horse will show signs of distress, green fluid with particles of feed will come down its nose, it might cough repeatedly, carry its head and neck rigidly extended and drool.

Choke is very alarming to witness, but don't panic if it occurs in your horse.

Remove all feed and water from the horse – if it continues to try and eat, the esophagus will fill with food and there is a danger of feed matter spilling over and into the trachea (windpipe).

Some cases of choke will right themselves, and the horse will manage to clear the blockage. If, however, this has not happened within 15 minutes, call your vet. In order to clear the blockage, the vet might sedate the horse to relax the muscles and may insert a stomach tube and flush water through.

Generally, the greatest complications with choke are those caused by damage to the esophagus wall inflicted by the stomach tube during the process of trying to dislodge the blockage. After a horse has choked, it should be fed sloppy feeds for several days, soaked hay, and taken off straw bedding.

GRASS SICKNESS

This is a devastating disease that occurs in Scotland, the eastern side of England, and Ireland; it is rare in North America but a similar disease occurs in Chile. The exact cause is not known, although it is associated with certain pastures and is

> Always moisten feeds before feeding; concentrates can be moistened with water or soaked beet pulp.

thought to be toxin related. Fields that have been grazed by horses that have contracted the disease should be avoided, and the grass should not be cut and fed as hay.

Most cases of grass sickness occur between the months of April and July, and statistically there are outbreaks of the disease after periods of eight to 10 days of cool, dry weather with temperatures ranging from 45–52°F (7–11°C). Horses between the age of 2 and 7 are most at risk; horses that have been stressed recently or are in good-to-fat condition also appear to be more prone to the disease.

The disease attacks the nervous system causing paralysis of the horse's entire gut, from the pharynx to the rectum.

There are three types of grass sickness — acute, subacute or chronic — and all three types show similar symptoms.

There is no cure for acute and subacute cases — acute cases die within four days, subacute within three weeks. Recently, progress has been made in treating chronic cases. Not all chronic cases are suitable for treatment, and should be humanely destroyed. However those that are deemed candidates for treatment have responded well.

QUICK REFERENCE – DIGESTIVE DISORDERS

- Horses rarely vomit due to the strong muscular sphincter between the top of the stomach and the bottom of the esophagus.
- Colic is an umbrella heading for abdominal pain, which can be caused by a number of things. It takes several different forms and ranges from mild to extreme.
- Don't force a colicky horse to walk; try to keep it as comfortable as possible.
- Diarrhea ranges from mild to severe. If it persists for more than two days, call the vet.
- Choke is caused by a blockage in the esophagus. Remove all feed and water from the horse and if after 15 minutes it has not resolved itself, call your vet.
- Grass sickness is associated with certain pastures and weather conditions – it is thought to be connected to a toxin.

Symptoms

- Similar to those for colic including sweating; rolling; abdominal pain; rise in temperature, pulse and respiration.
- Difficulty in swallowing.
- Drooling.
- Foul-smelling fluid may come down the nose.
- Dehydration due to inability to drink (swallow).
- The abdomen becomes distended.
- Muscle tremors.
- Rapid and severe weight loss leading to emaciation.

The symptoms in chronic cases come on more slowly than those in acute or subacute cases.

Treatment

- In acute and subacute cases, the horse should be humanely destroyed to prevent unnecessary suffering.
- Treatable chronic cases need to be kept clean, warm and dry.
- Affected horses benefit from human contact and stimulation.
- The appetite needs to be stimulated and the horse should be hand-fed frequently throughout the day.
- The drug Cisapride is given orally to help the gut work.

Respiratory Problems

Many horses suffer from respiratory problems, and many of these problems can be prevented, if not greatly aided, by good stable management. Dust and mold spores are two of the main culprits, so if your horse is kept stabled, make sure that the stable is thoroughly cleaned regularly, use good-quality dust-free bedding and always soak hay.

COUGHING

There are three main types of cough: an allergic cough, one caused by a virus such as equine influenza (flu) and one associated with an upper respiratory tract infection. A horse should not be worked if it is coughing, and the cause of the cough must be immediately investigated.

Help allergic coughs by soaking hay, providing the horse with a dust-free environment, avoid working it in a dusty arena and keep it away from fields of any strong-smelling plants such as canola, which can cause allergic reactions. If a cough persists, the horse should be seen by your vet.

EQUINE INFLUENZA

This is a highly contagious viral infection that will spread quickly through a yard of horses. Once your horse has been diagnosed with it, you must isolate it using full isolation procedures. You can vaccinate your horse against flu, and all horses should be vaccinated, especially those that travel to shows and events.

The incubation for flu is one to four days; once it has developed, the virus will persist for up to three weeks, and after the symptoms cease, the horse will need a further two weeks of recovery time before returning to work.

Symptoms

- Your horse will have a temperature and appear to be "off color."
- It will develop a hard cough.
- It will have nasal discharge that will turn thick and yellow.

Treatment

Call your vet; the following treatment may be advised:

- Isolate horse and equipment.
- Rest your horse initially in the stable, but once its temperature has gone down, your horse will benefit from being turned out during the day.
- Keep your horse warm.
- Medications may be prescribed including a bronchodilator to help alleviate muscle spasms of the bronchioles; a mucolytic drug to help break down the buildup of mucus and antibiotics if there is a secondary infection.

STRANGLES

This is another highly contagious disease; it is caused by the bacteria *Streptococcus equi*. Again, isolation procedures must be carried out immediately – strangles is passed from horse to horse through direct contact and through sharing equipment. Young horses are most commonly affected, although all horses are at risk. The bacteria will survive in the environment for up to a month, so isolation procedures should remain in place for this length of time. Any yard that has a case of strangles should not allow new horses in, and no horse should leave to prevent spreading the disease. A vaccination is available against strangles.

Symptoms

- Rise in temperature and the horse appears "off color."
- Nasal discharge that turns thick and yellow.
- Mucus-filled cough.
- Swollen lymph glands, especially those under the jaw. They will form hard, painful abscesses.
- Loss of appetite (due to pain when swallowing).
- Roughly 10 days after the first symptoms the abscesses burst releasing large amounts of purulent pus. The horse should then start to recover.

Treatment

At the first sign of strangles, you must call your vet.

- Feed soft feeds that are easy to swallow.
- Apply hot fomentations to the abscesses.
- Once ruptured, flush the abscesses with antiseptic solution or PSS/Bet.
- Keep your horse clean, warm and dry.
- Antibiotics, normally penicillin, may be prescribed by the vet.
- Your horse will need a long period of recovery before going back to work.

QUICK REFERENCE – RESPIRATORY DISORDERS

- **Dust and mold spores are prime causes of coughs.**
- **A horse that is coughing should not be worked.**
- **Equine influenza is a highly contagious viral infection, and affected horses must be isolated.**
- **There is a vaccination for equine influenza and it is highly recommended that it is given — especially to horses that travel to shows.**
- **Strangles is also highly contagious, and is caused by the bacteria *Streptococcus equi*.**
- **There is a vaccination available for strangles.**
- **Bastard strangles can be very serious — if a lymph node abscesses in the abdomen and ruptures the horse will get peritonitis and die.**
- **Purpura hemorrhagica can occur three weeks after the horse has recovered from strangles. Only 50% of horses that contract it survive.**
- **COPD is related to dust, mold spores and sometimes pollens. Always feed the horse soaked hay or haylage and moisten concentrates.**

Complications

When the infection spreads to other lymph nodes in the body it is called "bastard strangles." Providing these nodes are near the surface of the skin, they will abscess and drain. Occasionally, the nodes surrounding the trachea will be infected and swell so extensively that the horse is in danger of suffocating. In this case, an emergency tracheotomy must be performed, or the nodes will burst and emit pus into the airways causing pneumonia. If lymph nodes in the abdomen are infected and burst into the abdominal cavity, the horse will get peritonitis and die.

Occasionally, horses develop purpura hemorrhagica after recovering from strangles. Purpura is an allergic reaction to the byproducts of the breakdown of the bacteria in the circulation. Symptoms develop approximately three weeks after the horse has recovered from strangles, and are seen as severe swelling in the limbs, eyes, nose and lips; bloody diarrhea, colic and difficulty swallowing. There is a 50 percent fatality in horses with purpura.

CHRONIC OBSTRUCTIVE PULMONARY DISEASE (COPD)

Also known as recurrent airway obstruction or heaves, COPD is a common allergic condition, and can become serious if the cause is not addressed. Horses affected can be allergic to a number of different things, including and primarily dust, but also mold spores and some grass and tree pollens.

Symptoms

- Asthma-like symptoms; breathing becomes increasingly labored, and as this happens over time, a "heave" line appears on each side of the barrel, along the lower edge of the abdomen. This is caused by the muscle working overly hard in an effort to force air out of the lungs.

- The horse will cough with exercise and, in severe cases, at rest.
- There can be thick nasal discharge.

Treatment

Call your vet for a diagnosis and advice.

- If possible, keep your horse at grass (unless it suffers from pollen allergies) and out of a dusty environment.
- If the horse has to be stabled, use paper bedding over rubber mats.
- Completely muck out every day and do not deep litter.
- Feed haylage or good-quality, well-soaked hay.
- Feed dampened concentrates.
- If your horse has mild symptoms it can be lightly worked, otherwise it must be off work.
- The vet might prescribe bronchodilators, mucolitics and antibiotics if a secondary infection is suspected.

WHEN TO CALL THE VET

- **If your horse has a thick yellow or greenish discharge coming down its nose and appears depressed.**

Nursing a Sick Horse

It is helpful for one handler to assume responsibility for a sick horse; there will be continuation in nursing, and the smallest change will be noted. The primary objective when dealing with a sick horse is to keep the animal as comfortable as possible. As it will be restricted to box rest, or mostly box rest, it will have to contend with frustration and boredom on top of its symptoms. Be aware of this, and also that any animal in distress will invariably behave abnormally i.e., be bad tempered, excitable or depressed.

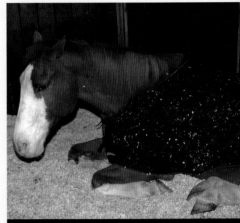

It is essential to keep a sick horse as warm and comfortable as possible

- Keep your horse warm, but make sure it has good ventilation.
- Manage its feed and medications according to your vet's directions, and unless otherwise instructed, provide ad lib soaked hay.
- Keep a daily record of your horse's temperature, pulse and respiration, note any changes (improvements and deteriorations). Note what the horse is passing and whether or not it is eating and drinking. By keeping a full account it can greatly aid your vet in monitoring the horse's continued therapy.
- Make sure the horse has a friend in sight at all times.
- Stimulate the horse by daily grooming and interaction, without harassing it.
- Keep the stable and water clean. Pick up droppings as frequently as possible and change water twice daily.
- Provide the horse with a radio playing quietly.

- Try to keep the stable yard quiet and calm.
- With contagious illness, keep the horse in isolation, but try to keep another horse in eyeshot, either in the field or in a separate stable block.
- Follow full isolation procedures keeping all equipment including buckets, brushes and rugs separate. Wear overalls, boots and gloves when handling the horse, and remove these before handling other horses. Use separate mucking out utensils. Do not allow any other horses anywhere near the isolation stable. After isolation thoroughly disinfect the entire stable and all equipment.

Vaccinations, Worming and Records

Vaccinations

In order to establish maximum immunity, a vaccination program needs to start with a series of shots. The number of shots, and the time lapse between them will vary dependent on the vaccine as will the number and timing of boosters. The following information is only a guide, and you should consult with your vet to set up a vaccination and worming program for your horse.

In general, to start off a course of vaccinations the horse will need:
- First shot.
- Second shot 4–6 weeks later.
- Third shot 6 months later.

- Fourth shot 12 months later.
- Following this, shots given annually, bi-annually, quarterly or every two years depending on the vaccination.

All vaccinations must be given by a veterinarian, who will advise a suitable program for each individual horse based on its age and usage.

Many vaccinations now come in "combination" shots, which cuts down on the number of times the horse has to be stuck.

Tetanus – Should be given either every two years, or annually, and should be boostered when your horse is injured.

Equine influenza – Should be given two to four times a year to competition horses for best immunity. (Annually to pleasure horses.)

Equine herpes virus (Rhinopneumonitis or EHV-1, EHV-4) – Should be given two to four times a year to competition horses.

Equine herpes virus, EHV-1 – Can cause abortion so vaccination with Pneumabort K should be carried out on pregnant mares at five, seven, and nine months of pregnancy to protect against abortion.

Strangles – Should be given four times a year.

Equine viral arteritis – Annual but check with your vet. After vaccination the horse will appear to be "seropositive" in a blood test, so must therefore have a blood test showing "seronegative" taken before vaccination.

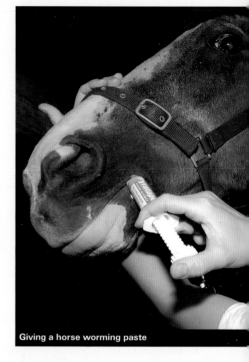
Giving a horse worming paste

Worming

All horses need to be wormed regularly. If many horses are kept on the same pasture, they need to be wormed more frequently.

Certain wormers need to be given at certain times of the year to target different worms (see chart). For the rest of the year, and while

Trainer's Tip
Using a year planner like the example here, mark out your worming and vaccination program for the year and keep in a prominent place so you don't forget.

Trainer's Tip

To help horses that are really hard to worm get them used to being given oral medication by giving them a molasses solution out of a 60 cc catheter tip syringe. Most horses enjoy the flavor of molasses, and if given the solution regularly will learn to tolerate having substances administered orally – the molasses is then swapped for the worm paste at worming time!

doing periodic worming, rotate different wormers each year to prevent the risk of a resistance to the wormer building up; i.e., ivermectin (Equell, EquiMax, Equimectrin, Zimecterin) with moxidectin (Equest) and fenbendazole (Panacur). On top of this the horse will need to be wormed with pyrantel embonate (Strongid, Strongylecare, Rotectin, Equi-cide) every 6–12 months to kill tapeworms. Horses fed a daily wormer in their feed will not be provided with sufficient protection against bots and tapeworms.

Some wormers need to be given more frequently; moxidectin (Equest), for example, protects for up to 13 weeks, while fenbendazole (Panacur) protects for 6 weeks. Overworming is a danger due to certain worms developing serious resistance to some of the drugs available, so it pays to have a fecal egg count done prior to worming to determine the necessity for worming drugs. There is also a tapeworm antibody test available to check tapeworm levels. Wormers are constantly being improved, so always check with your vet as to the frequency that they need to be given.

Good stable management and removing droppings from the field is one of the best ways to cut down on worm infestation, and this should be routine alongside a sensible deworming program.

Keeping Records

Each horse should be allotted a file with its name clearly on the front and all its details inside. Similarly, in a yard situation, each horse should have a stable card outside its stable detailing its name, feed and any pertinent information. If charts are made up in advance then each entry only requires a couple of minutes, and in the long run having comprehensive records can be very helpful.

SAMPLE STABLE CARD		
NAME	Horse: Sugar Daddy	Owner: Lilly Sweet Contact: 555-4511 Vet: G. Better 555-9800
FEED - CONC.	7 am and pm*: 2 lbs (900 gm) Country Cubes 8 oz (250 g) Scoop Chaff 8 oz (250 g) Scoop Beet Pulp 1 Measure Multi Vit * without vitamins	Noon: 3 lbs (1.4 kg) Country Cubes ½ Scoop Chaff ½ Scoop Pulp Beet
FEED - FORAGE	5 lbs (2 kg) Hay Post Work	15 lbs (6 kg) Hay
TURNOUT INSTRUCTIONS	4 hours turnout daily, use boots, turn out with Archie	
TEMPERAMENT	Good to handle, doesn't like dogs	
ALLERGIES	Barley	
COMMENTS	Always work in boots all around and overreach boots	

SAMPLE FARRIER RECORD

NAME		Horse: Sugar Daddy	Owner: Lilly Sweet
DATE		**FARRIER**	**COMMENTS**
07/02/08		Mark Riddle	Full set 2 road nails each shoe
14/03/08		Mark Riddle	Reset
19/04/08		Sam (Apprentice)	Full set, stud holes all around + road nails
24/05/08		Mark Riddle	Slight bruise at toe but no pain/pus
			Full set, stud holes all around + road nails

SAMPLE VACCINATION RECORD

NAME		Horse: Sugar Daddy		Owner: Lilly Sweet	
DATE	**VACCINATION**	**GIVEN BY**	**LOCATION**	**NEXT DUE**	**REACTION/COMMENT**
10/03/08	Flu/Tet combo	G.Better MRCVS	L Side neck	10/09/08	No
10/03/08	Equine herpes	G.Better MRCVS	R Side neck	10/09/08	Stiff/lethargic next day — Fine 48 hrs later

SAMPLE WORMING RECORD

NAME		Horse: Sugar Daddy	Owner: Lilly Sweet
DATE	**WORMER**	**GIVEN BY**	**COMMENTS**
06/02/08	Equest	Lilly	No
28/02/08	5 Days Panacur	Lilly	No
02/04/08	Double Dose Strongid P	Lilly	No

SAMPLE MEDICAL RECORD

NAME		Horse: Sugar Daddy	Owner: Lilly Sweet
DATE	**SYMPTOMS**	**VET**	**TREATMENT/COMMENTS**
10/03/08	Stiff/lethargic slight swelling over injection site (equine herpes)	No	Temp, resp and pulse normal. Replaced breakfast and lunch with bran mash, supper 1 lb (450 g) of mix, 1 lb (450 g) bran. Turned out all day for gentle exercise. Swelling gone by following day. Normal food rations, gentle hack. Back to normal by third day.
24/06/08	Very Lame L Fore	Yes G.Better	Removed a nail from foot before vet arrived — kept nail and showed him angle it was in foot. Removed shoe, scrubbed foot, soaked then flushed hole. Prescribed poultice and tubbing for one week, flush hole twice daily, then dry dressing for further week. Analgesics 3 days antibiotics 7 days. Don't think internal structures were damaged. Healed well, no further vet visits, back in work 3 weeks later.

	JAN	FEB	MARCH	APRIL	MAY	JUNE	JULY	AUG	SEPT	OCT	NOV	DEC
WORMING	Beginning January Routine Wormer i.e. either ivermectin, moxidectin or fenbendazole. Rotate these yearly to prevent worm resistance	5 days fenbendazole (Panacur)	Beginning March Routine Wormer	Double dose pyrantel (Strongid, Rotectin, Strongylecare, Equi-cide or something similar)	Fecal exam Routine Wormer 2 wks another fecal		Beginning July Routine Wormer		Beginning September Double dose pyrantel (Strongid, Rotectin, Strongylecare, Equi-cide or something similar)	Beginning October Routine Wormer	Beginning November 5 days fenbendazole (Panacur)	After 1st frost Eqvalan
VACCINATIONS U.S./CANADA			Equine Influenza; Equine Herpes EHV-1, EHV-4; Tetanus; Rabies; Eastern, Western, Venezuelan Encephalomyelitis; Equine Viral Arteritis (breeding stock)	West Nile; Potomac Horse Fever; Strangles		Boosters for competition animals; Equine Influenza; Equine Herpes EHV-1,4			Boosters for competition animals; Equine Influenza; Equine Herpes EHV-1,4	Strangles; West Nile; Potomac Horse Fever; Strangles		Boosters for competition animals; Equine Influenza; Equine Herpes EHV-1,4
TEETH			Equine dentist to check teeth – seniors & youngsters						Equine dentist to rasp teeth			

Index

Acknowledgments

I should like to express my very grateful thanks to everyone who contributed to, and participated in this publication including, Chrissie Lloyd, Louise Dixon, Amy Carroll and the rest of the staff at Carroll & Brown who made this project work.

Jules Selmes for his fantastic photography, patience and sense of humor.

Redwings Horse Sanctuary, Hapton, Norwich, NR15 1SP, U.K., to the horses and wonderful staff who were so helpful, in particular Nicola Markwell and the team of veterinary surgeons and nurses – this project could not have happened without them.

Paul and Sarah Holdsworth for their time and the use of their horses, in particular Alaska.

Rochelle Read for her time and the use of Joe.

Terry Read, Hempnall, Suffolk, for his valuable farriery time.

Rachel Burton, equine dental technician, of Ilketshall St. Andrew, Suffolk, U.K. for her valuable dentistry time and the use of Bailey.

The staff at Ride N Drive, Henstead, Suffolk, U.K., for the use of their tack and equipment.

Rachel Hillier for her equestrian training, friendship and advice.

Cindy Webster, of CW Western Training, Ockley, Dorking, Surrey, U.K., for her valuable time, patience, the use of her horses and her modeling. A big thank you to all the staff at CW Western Training for their time and help, and in particular thanks to Ashleigh Gossage and her lovely horse Troy.

Debbie Symes for the use of her horses.

Emily Rozkalns for her time and modeling.

Dr. Kim Taylor DVM and Dr. Tom Berry DVM of the Big Horn Veterinary Hospital, Buffalo, Wyoming, U.S. for their advice, help and friendship over the years.

Sylvia Fairbairns, sorely missed, whose training, advice and friendship over the years was invaluable.

Finally, heartfelt thanks to my parents, for everything.

Picture Credits
p8–9, p38 TL,TR, p39 BL, BR, p52, p142, p186, p188, p197, p200, p206 Kit Houghton/Houghtonshorses Photolibrary. p221 Redwings Horse Sanctuary.